The Object of Jewish Literature

The Object of Jewish Literature

A Material History

Barbara E. Mann

Yale UNIVERSITY PRESS/NEW HAVEN & LONDON

Published with assistance from the foundation established in memory of Calvin Chapin of the Class of 1788, Yale College.

Set in Adobe Garamond Pro and The Sans types by Westchester Publishing Services.
Printed in the United States of America.

Library of Congress Control Number: 2021945795
ISBN 978-0-300-23411-4 (hardcover : alk. paper)

A catalogue record for this book is available from the British Library.

This paper meets the requirements of
ANSI/NISO Z39.48-1992 (Permanence of Paper).

10 9 8 7 6 5 4 3 2 1

For Bertha Mann z"l (1929–2021),
in loving memory

Contents

Acknowledgments

This book's idea was planted during my graduate studies at the University of California, Berkeley, where I was fortunate to have mentors in Robert Alter and Chana Kronfeld. Years later, the idea became a full-fledged intellectual project in a summer writing group with my neighbors and colleagues Rebecca Kobrin, Rachel Mesch, and Gillian Steinberg, whose interest pushed me to expand the project's scope. Those conversations affirmed a truth of my work—that smart, kind colleagues make academic life worthwhile. Early exchanges with Vanessa Ochs reminded me of the difference between objects and texts. Jack Kugelmass encouraged my *yizker* book explorations over lunch in Tel Aviv. Yoni Brafman gamely endured my pestering about secularism. Laura Levitt helped me appreciate the affective power of objects. Ronit Eisenbach nudged me to get the images right. Leora Auslander, Laura Liebman, Anita Norich, Tahneer Oksman, Naomi Seidman, and Vered Karti Shemtov provided critical feedback on drafts of individual chapters and grant proposals. Nancy Sinkoff has been my yardstick for scholarly integrity, and so much more. Two candid anonymous readers of the entire manuscript challenged me; their thoughtful, generous comments helped shape the book's final form. If any missteps remain in spite of all this excellent counsel, they are my own.

Books are physical companions. My comrades at the Salt Lake Community College NEH Summer Institute "The Book: Material Histories and Digital Futures" in 2018 nurtured my own bookmaking practices, as did workshops with Roni Gross at the Center for Book Arts, New York. Arik Kilemnik and the staff and artists at the Jerusalem Print Workshop welcomed me into their beautiful space. Learning about early modern Jewish books with Elisheva Carlebach and Michelle Chesner in the Rare Books Room at Columbia University confirmed my sense of how modernity has altered the material presence of books. Students in my spring 2020 seminar at the Jewish Theological Seminary in the middle of the COVID-19 pandemic affirmed the essential role material objects play in our lives, even—or especially—in the most virtual of settings. Their resilience and creativity are an inspiration.

A special thank-you to all the librarians and archivists who have aided and encouraged me, without whom this book would not have been possible. The staff of the Library of the Jewish Theological Seminary supported my research and made *yizker* volumes available to me during a period of tremendous transition. Agnieszka Reszka at the archives of the Emanuel Ringelblum Jewish Historical Institute provided easy access to important artifacts. Amanda Siegel at the Dorot Division, New York Public Library, graciously offered assistance at every stage, including some last-minute requests during the pandemic. I am especially indebted to Stefanie Halpern, who—as always—went above and beyond. The expertise of her colleagues at the YIVO Institute for Jewish Research also supported my teaching of a class, "Jewish Stuff: Objects from the YIVO Archives," an especially memorable haptic experience.

Research funds and sabbatical leaves from the Jewish Theological Seminary supported the writing of this book, as did summer grants and an annual award from the National Endowment for the Humanities. Sarah Eligberg's indefatigable, levelheaded work on securing permissions and Jennifer Brynes's attention to the images were crucial to this book's final laps. I also benefited from presenting portions to audiences at conferences of the Modern Language Association and the Association of Jewish Studies and in lectures at Johns Hopkins University, the University of Chicago, the Katz Center for Advanced Judaic Studies at the University of Pennsylvania, Bar-Ilan University, Bard Graduate Center, and the POLIN Museum of the History of Polish Jews.

Sarah Miller at Yale University Press believed in my proposal and trusted I could write the book. I am also appreciative of the professionalism-under-pressure of Heather Gold and Eva Skewes, who shepherded the book to publication.

Finally, I am abundantly grateful to family and friends who have unfailingly humored my ongoing fascination with "stuff."

The Object of Jewish Literature

Introduction The Object Matter of Modern Jewish Literature

How can a pile of books be a work of art? In Jack Jano's *Say Little, Do Much* (1995), books are stacked against the wall in a thin pile rising a little over five feet, and topped with a small house-shaped object made of wood and paper. Jano's work directs our attention to the aura of books and their constituent parts, from the shapes of their individual letters and the physical qualities of their pages, bindings, and covers to their ubiquity as symbols of cultural transmission. The stack bears some resemblance to a biblical *gal-ed,* a memorial heap of stones left in the desert to "witness" the presence of the sacred, the dead, or some moment of consequence—an encounter with God or a divine promise. On the peeled, fraying spines facing outward, only a few titles are visible in traces of gold letters; they are, however, unmistakably *sifrey kodesh,* sacred texts of study—folio editions of rabbinic texts such as the Talmud or other esoteric, liturgical, or legal collections. Wide at the base, narrowing toward the top, the books provide a sturdy platform for the house. This house-like structure repeats in Jano's work: sometimes constructed from paper, covered with Hebrew and Arabic script, sometimes more firmly wrought from wood and glass, the structure recalls a house as well as a tomb or sacred space.[1]

Jack Jano, *Say Little, Do Much* (1995). Courtesy of the artist.

Somewhere between ready-made and assemblage, Jano's work juxtaposes found objects such as books and other ritual items with dirt, stone, glass, string, canvas, and wrought iron to create totemic works that toggle between religious and aesthetic experience. Within the limits of Israeli art historical discourse, where art is viewed in terms strongly distinguishing between secular and religious forms of expression, Jano's work—at once mildly irreverent and deeply spiritual—occupies a special position.[2] Having grown up surrounded by iconic images of the Sephardic sages and miracle-making saints of his native Morocco origins, Jano resists the ostensible divide between the religious and the secular, insisting instead on the sacred potential of the mundane. Some readers may wonder why these particular books were not deposited in the *geniza*, the traditional location for the proper disposal of sacred texts no longer in use. Clearly, for Jano and the contemporary observer, "the book" has become something else, something more than itself. And it achieves this additional meaning through attention to its material contours.

My own fascination with the materiality of literature dates from a discovery in the basement stacks at the Bancroft Library, University of California, Berkeley, in the early 1990s: while looking for research materials, I came across a copy of one of the earliest modern Hebrew journals in Palestine, a 1908 issue of *Ha-omer*, published in Jaffa. The journal's crumbling pages were browned with age, and its binding was split open, revealing threads and packing material. As I gingerly examined the damaged, peeling spine, I could see that the journal had been bound using pieces of Russian newspaper. Perhaps the pages of Cyrillic print had been the lining of a trunk, or a coat, of a recently arrived immigrant; or maybe the newspaper had arrived in the port city in a shipping container, wrapped around items in a commercial delivery, or in the possession of a crew member on board. This repurposing of newspaper as part of the printing process also indicated a contemporaneous scarcity of paper and the need to work with the materials at hand for a new secular Hebrew-language press. I appreciated this feature as somehow alluding to the relatively precarious conditions of Hebrew literature in Palestine at the turn of the century—making do with what the Russian Hebrew author Y. Ch. Brenner memorably, and somewhat myopically, referred to as the "impoverished" state of the landscape.[3] The fact that Russian constituted the spine of the book—the physical feature most essential to the codex form—also neatly referenced Russia as a key cultural context and site of origin for modern Hebrew literature, within the Pale of Settlement that was home to millions of Jews.

However, beyond the material features of the book itself, this small allegory seemed to point to something more. After all, the long twentieth century that saw the emergence of a broad, multilingual canon of writing by Jewish authors was a period of tremendous physical upheaval and geographic movement; what if a sense of literature's materiality—its qualities as an itinerant object that was vulnerable, yet endured—resided within the text in some other fashion as well? *The Object of Jewish Literature: A Material History* reads twentieth-century Jewish literature through the lens of material culture, analyzing the material qualities of texts, the literary depiction of objects, and discourse about materiality during a period shaped by migration, war, and social and political change.[4] The primary contours of this study's field of investigation are literary expression in Hebrew, Yiddish, and English, mostly relating to the experience and culture of eastern European Jewish communities. Within these boundaries, my approach is comparative; furthermore, like recent scholarship on the relation between language and Jewish identity in the modern period, I use the term *Jewish* "provisionally, as a formulation of a continuum, one worth questioning and contextualizing, rather than as a self-evident category."[5] That said, the category of Jewishness mattered to many of these writers, and was often an express part of their method. Examining how transition and rupture have refashioned Jewish textuality in relation to material culture will bring Jewish studies into conversation with the study of material forms, enrich our sense of literature's complex relation to its environment, and provide a model for other transnational studies of Jewish literatures across different linguistic and temporal contexts.

My investigation of literature and materiality across genres is linked through the idea of "affordances," a term originating in the fields of architecture and design, where it indicates how specific properties inherent in materials lend them to different uses. A certain kind of metal or glass, for example, one that could withstand high temperature or was especially durable, would be appropriate for particular uses in construction or manufacturing. The idea of affordances plays a role in the history of the book, in which "the story of the book's changing form is bound up with that of its changing content."[6] Historians of the early modern world like Robert Darnton have described the elaborate circuit through which books are produced, circulated, and consumed. The French cultural historian Roger Chartier highlights the importance of "communities of readers" and insists on the centrality of material form and embodiment to the reading process.[7] According to Chartier, "Authors do not write books. Rather they write texts which become objects copied, handwritten, etched, printed, and today computerized. This gap, which is rightly the space in which meaning is constructed, has too often been forgotten."[8] While my study describes some physical features of books, I take the idea of materiality as residing in some other fashion within the linguistic or formal attributes of the text under discussion.

In this, I adopt Caroline Levine's use of affordances in *Forms: Whole, Rhythm, Hierarchy, Network* (2015). Affordances allow Levine to consider literary forms such as the novel in relation to other kinds of forms, especially networks of social and political power. In her view, affordances help us "grasp the constraints on form that are imposed by materiality itself."[9] Levine also offers this valuable caveat, describing what is at stake in a material reading of literary form: "Literature is not made of the material worlds it describes or invokes but of language, which lays claims to its own forms—syntactical, narrative, rhythmic, rhetorical—and its own materiality—the spoken word, the printed page. And indeed, each of these forms and materials lays claim to its own affordances—its own range of capabilities. Every literary form thus generates its own, separate logic."[10]

Genre is a particular instance of form, for example—prose works such as the novel or poetic works such as the lyric. I am interested in what kinds of material affordances inhere in the varied features of these genres. I understand genre here not as a static taxonomy of conventions but as a dynamic performance whose evolving form is embedded in, and shaped by, the historical circumstances of its production.[11] Therefore, this study will traverse paradigmatic corpora of writing by Jewish authors with attention to each genre's distinct material affordances, that "range of capabilities" generated by the genre's own mobile boundaries. Furthermore, an attention to materiality in literary genres potentially expands our sense of the canon, allowing for the inclusion of new, contemporary forms of literary expression.

The methods of this study also align with the current intellectual exploration of "things" as a critical method for understanding literary history. Indeed, writing that emerges from Jewish culture, whose theological tradition has had a charged relation to embodied forms such as idols, is an ideal forum for exploring how literature deploys physical objects as emblems of ideas, emotions, and psychological dramas about the self, and how books themselves function as "things."[12] Drawing on models of commodification and exchange from Marx, ideas about the symbolic value of the fetish from Freud and Claude Lévi-Strauss, and Bruno Latour's influential concept of the "hybrid," my project engages recent work on things in canonical American literature by Bill Brown, W. J. T. Mitchell, and Sherry Turkle regarding the power of "evocative objects."[13] Like Jahan Ramazani, I recognize the affinity multilingual forms necessarily have for transnational networks of production and exchange, a set of conditions that allows books (and ideas) to move between different geographic, linguistic, and cultural settings.[14] This study is also in conversation with the work of Leora Auslander and Ken Kulton Fromm, both of whom describe the specific challenges of Jewish studies scholarship about materiality, given the field's privileging of the text as a normative basis for historical claims.[15] I argue that attention to the book as an object brings intellectual history (the study of texts) and cultural history (the study of artifacts) into productive conversation. Auslander has suggested a similar kind of "detente" between text and artifact for historians, and argues that the emergence of visual culture—a broad range of media including maps, photographs, and film—offers scholars an opportunity at last to engage the three-dimensional quality of textual artifacts *as* material culture.

Classical Jewish texts have always possessed a material dimension, deriving from both their tendency to serve as markers for lost spaces and their connection to a sacred tradition. Texts such as the Torah scroll or prayer book were handled with respect and sensitivity, as befitting holy objects. One might expect this sacred, material dimension to fade, or disappear entirely, with the advent of literary genres such as the novel, lyric poetry, and other "formations of the secular," to use Talal Asad's term. However, some sense of materiality continued to animate Jewish writing and was refigured within modern literary genres; this is especially true for those texts written in Hebrew or Yiddish, whose orthographic connection to "Holy Writ" is more overt than writing in other languages. This book explores various instances of what could be called a kind of material translation—that is, how the material core of the (sacred) Book is translated into secular forms. Those cataclysmic changes embedded within modern Jewish literatures point to a wider phenomenon wherein modern literary expression stubbornly retains a sacred trace of traditional textuality, recalibrating it for secular forms.

In discussing these secular forms—the literary genres that are the heart of my study—I loosely engage Charles Taylor's analysis of the "secular age." In his massive volume *The Secular Age* and in many critical essays, Taylor takes issue with what he calls the "subtraction theory" of secularism.[16] He critiques the sociological writings of Max Weber, according to which a modern "disenchantment" with religion produced an adherence to the material qualities of the world in-and-of-itself, a rejection of both theology and transcendence; for Weber, and the theories of modernity that came in his wake, what remains after removing the presence of a divine mover is "merely" those features of the world that we can access with our senses, or measure with our rational intellect, through a scientific method of inquiry. However, according to Taylor's revision of the term, this new secular condition should be understood not as the loss or "subtraction" of faith, but rather as a dialectical engagement with it, in settings that may actually create new conditions for belief. Moreover, Taylor takes issue with a purely doctrinal understanding of religious belief, noting that ideas about God are also woven into social space and "given expression on the symbolic level."[17] God-talk resides in what he calls, adopting a French term, "the social imaginary." Taylor seems to be referencing here work such as Henri Lefebvre's *The Production of Space,* whose capacious sense of how space shapes and supports social relationships expressly includes the domain of aesthetic production. This "imagined space" consists of those cultural and artistic forms particular to any given society, including that of literary expression.[18]

Adopting Taylor's model for a discussion of secular literary genres, I argue that the presence of materiality within these forms constitutes a trace marker of the sacred, the residue of that dialectical engagement with belief and transcendence. Furthermore, in my view, the binary distinction produced by Weber's influential account of secularism—between intellect and matter, in which the world is reduced or diminished precisely due to its materiality—fails to account for the meaningful affective qualities of haptic or sensory experience. For the purposes of this study, this experience would include not only the physical handling of a book but also the increasingly creative ways in which materiality itself becomes a conceptual and pragmatic ground for aesthetic production.

Due to the specific historical conditions in which modern Jewish literature emerged in the late nineteenth and early twentieth centuries, we can more clearly identify the rise of secularism and the consequent pressure upon cultural forms to retain some evidence of what Walter Benjamin has called "aura." My book suggests how the particulars of twentieth-century Jewish experience—its mass migrations as well as physical and psychological traumas—have shaped materiality's emergent role in literary forms by Jewish authors. Moreover, this process is not unique to modern Jewish culture; rather, it is simply a more visible instance of a broader condition: the residue of theological or religious concerns in ostensibly secular cultural formations.[19] My project thus critiques the already weak distinction between religion and secularism, analyzing examples from Jewish literature to shed light on this wider phenomenon. To the degree that my project is a history of modern Jewish literature, it is also a history of modernism and modernity's ongoing engagement with premodern modes of representation, specifically those embedded in religious and theological belief systems. The fate of the Jewish book is therefore a heightened, more easily discernible version of the fate of the book everywhere, a set of conditions in which, as Edmond Jabès lamented, "any book is but a dim likeness of the lost book."[20]

FROM APOLLO'S STATUE TO THE BOOKCASE

We find an appreciation for the text's material qualities—its existence and value as a physical artifact—from the very start, as an inescapable feature of modern Hebrew literature's canonical core. "Facing a Statue of Apollo" (1899) by Saul Tchernichovsky (1875–1943) and "Before the Bookcase" (1910) by Ch. N. Bialik (1873–1934), both central figures from the fin-de-siècle Hebrew "Revival" in eastern Europe, might serve as the foundational moments of "the object matter" of modern Jewish literature. The emergence of Hebrew as a literary vernacular—a language for secular literary, political, and cultural discourse—was shaped by an engagement with the world of the visual arts, a domain that during this period was newly available for Jewish artists and audiences.[21] Poetry, with its long history in both liturgical and prophetic texts, became a central and authoritative genre within early modern Hebrew culture; writers were appreciated, for better and for worse, as architects of new modes of personal and collective identities, a process that leaned on both older, more traditional models of society and more newly available, post-Enlightenment structures.

Tchernichovsky's lyric "Le-nokhaḥ pesel Apollo"—"Facing a Statue of Apollo"—is considered modern Hebrew's first ekphrastic poem. Ekphrasis, in which a poem takes as its central theme a work of art—a painting or a sculpture—usually includes some degree of detail and description of the work itself; the practice is understood as a test of language's visual powers: can poetry deliver the intensity achieved through the visual, three-dimensional experience of the fine arts? An ekphrastic poem is therefore ambivalent from the get-go: on the one hand a kind of homage, an expression of admiration for the artistic work described therein; on the other hand a robust declaration of poetry's own special talents, calling on the power of language to conjure and affect the reader. The ekphrastic poem draws on the material object's allure and appeal, and—in some sense—seeks to replace it.

Tchernichovsky, a central figure of the European Hebrew revival in the late nineteenth and early twentieth centuries, was renowned as a poet of nature, classical themes, and elaborate meditations on history and world culture. A translator of Homer, he mastered and imported demanding poetic forms such as the corona or crown of sonnets from Russian and German into Hebrew. With these thematic and formal preoccupations, Tchernichovsky perhaps contributed more than any of his contemporaries to the secularization of Hebrew as a modern literary vernacular. Here the poetic speaker describes himself as a representative of his people; he greets a statue of Apollo, overflowing with adoration and praise, and then reminds the Greek god of their acrimonious past:

> I come to you, forgotten god of the ages,
> God of ancient times and other days,
> Ruling the tempests of vigorous men,
> The breakers of their strength in youth's plenty.
> God of a generation of mighty ones and giants.
>
> . . . .
>
> I have come unto you—do you know me?
> Here I am, the Jew: we have an eternal quarrel![22]

Scholars have traced the putative inspiration for the poem to a reproduction of this famous statue, apparently on display in a gallery at the University of Heidelberg while Tchernichovsky was a student there.[23] Yaakov Shavit offers a vivid imagined portrait of the young poet walking the streets of Heidelberg, reveling in its public spaces.[24]

What does it mean to write a poem in modern Hebrew about a statue of a Greek god? We might begin by noting that the first ekphrastic poem in modern Hebrew dwells less on the object itself and more on the encounter with it. As an example of ekphrasis, then, the poem is pretty much a failure—it doesn't really give readers a strong visual sense of the object. This failure is implicit in the use of the term *le-nokhaḥ* in the title, which alerts readers that the poem is more interested in the experience of being in the presence of the statue than in the statue itself. The encounter provokes the recitation of normative arguments, setting a Hellenism of beauty and the body against a Judaic attention to ethics and the text; Apollo's youth, vitality, strength, and light contrast with the Jewish god's decay and weakness: "The people is old—and its gods have grown old." The speaker declares his allegiance to the statue and the god it represents, an oath of loyalty in which he declares: "Here I am, the first to return to you," assuming a pose of devotional obedience:

> I come to you, before your statue kneeling,
> Your images—symbol of life's brightness;
> I kneel, I bow to the good and the sublime,
> to that which is exalted throughout the world.
>
> . . . .
>
> I bow to life, to valor and to beauty,
>
> . . . .
>
> I bow to all precious things—robbed now
> By human corpses and the rotten seed of man,

Who rebel against the life bestowed by God, the Almighty—
The God of the mysterious wildernesses,
The God of men who conquered Canaan in a whirlwind—
Then bound Him with the straps of their phylacteries. . . .

The poem's surprising concluding turn somewhat collapses the divide between the Judaic and the Greek, with its claim that devotion to Apollo is actually a "return" to primal, long dormant currents within ancient Judaic culture. Indeed, the poem ultimately suggests that Apollo's virtuous qualities may well find their source in biblical Canaan, where this vital life force was first bound in leather prayer straps. Therefore, when the poet asks if Apollo "knows" him, he is asking if he "recognizes" him—that is, remembers him from a time when they were not of seemingly hostile worlds. The poem deploys the language of ritual—the prostration of prayer, the straps of the phylacteries—to suggest that the fetters of rabbinic practice have ruined the dynamism and strength of biblical desert culture. To write a modern Hebrew poem about a statue of a Greek god is thus both to engage an ostensibly antithetical sphere and to appropriate that sphere as one's own. As a bid to gain entry for Hebrew writing into modern European letters, Tchernichovsky's poem amounts to a neat trick: adopting an ekphrastic tradition that is already a bit anxious about boundaries between literature and the fine arts and using it to announce modern Hebrew's arrival as the true source of Apollo's vitality and beauty.

The poem's turn to the desert as a source of vitality represents a typically Orientalist gaze toward the Levant and the Zionist reliance on its own version of the East to cure the perceived ills of the Jewish diaspora—the phylactery ties that bind.[25] As the same time, given the relative dearth of sculpture by Jewish artists in this period, a poem about a statue was, de facto, usually a turn to something non-Jewish. Tchernichovsky returned to the ekphrastic mode at least twice after "Apollo:" a poem titled simply "Pesel" (Statue, 1924), marks what Avner Holtzman notes as the relative "normalization" of the genre within Hebrew writing as Judaic prohibitions recede.[26] One of Tchernichovsky's very last poems, written in 1937 in Tel Aviv, describes an entire set of statues on his desk—including Moses, Homer, Isaiah, Shakespeare, and Goethe. The world of the fine arts, interpolated through the ekphrastic register, thus had tremendous significance for Tchernichovsky. In part through his work, an engagement with the visual arts became a marker of modernity for modern Hebrew literature, an essential part of Hebrew's claims as a *world* literature, not as an ancient tongue or the language of religious observance; this commitment to the plastic arts helped drive the production of a literary idiom liberated from its roots in the domain of religious texts, devoted to a more sensual, material sensibility.[27]

We can observe a different iteration of this process in a poem by the period's most influential figure, Chaim Nachman Bialik; Bialik's generic inventiveness led to the creation of an oeuvre that included epic, historical long poems, lyric love poems, natural odes, and what became known as *shirey za'am* (poems of wrath), wherein the poet castigated everyone—Jews, gentiles, and God—for the disastrous and often brutal state of Jewish life in eastern Europe. Many readers have understood Bialik's poem "Lifney aron hasfrarim" ("Before the Bookcase")—another scene of doomed apostrophe and failed recognition—as a kind of response to Tchernichovsky's poem. In unpublished fragments of what has been considered a first draft of "Before the Bookcase," Bialik even writes in the dactylic hexameter that Tchernichovsky preferred.[28] The poem was written shortly after Bialik had completed work on *Sefer Ha-agada* (The Book of Legends), a massive anthology of classical Judaic texts to which he had devoted several years of work—and it is an engagement with these texts, represented metonymically through the bookcase, that takes center stage in the poem. Opening with a typically Bialikian scene, the speaker views religious tradition from an estranged position; Bialik's well-known image of standing on the doorstep of the study house—*al saf beyt hamidrash*—captures the ambivalence of a character caught between two worlds, with literally one foot in the world of secular enlightenment and the other attached to traditional Jewish learning. Here, the speaker greets the bookcase of his youth after returning from "foreign lands," a metaphorical reference to secular learning:

> Bear up under my greetings, ancient scrolls,
> Accept the kisses of my mouth, old dusty ones.
> From journeying to foreign isles my soul has returned.
> . . . .
> Do you still know me? I'm John Doe!
> . . . .
> Only you alone know my youth,
> You were like a garden to me on a warm summer day
> And a pillow for my head on cold winter nights,
> I learned to bundle in your scrolls the deposit of my soul
> And bind within your columns dreams of holiness.
> Do you remember me? I did not forget—
> In the attic, in the deserted study house,
> I was the last of the last,
> The prayers of our fathers fluttered their last breath upon on my lips.
> And in hidden corner there, next to your bookcase,
> The memorial candle flickered out entirely before my eyes.[29]

The connection to Tchernichovsky's poem is most immediately apparent in the line that parodically rephrases the speaker's address to the statue: "Do you still know me? I'm John Doe!" In this case, however, the object of address is a bookcase. These two poems have become central emblems within modern Hebrew literature for the ostensibly distinct, even oppositional, paths they seem to present: the statue versus the bookcase. The conventional reading sets them, and their authors, against one another, and organizes modern Hebrew literary history around them: Tchernichovsky, the Dionysian poet of nature, translator of Homer, who introduced hexameter forms into modern Hebrew versus Bialik, prototypical yeshiva student tempted by the Enlightenment, whose work nonetheless remains indebted to the bookcase, the classics of the Jewish sages. Even while noting their similarities, the consensus seems to be that "the resemblance [between them] emphasizes of course the deep and essential differences between them."[30] However, reading Bialik's poem with an eye toward its appreciation of the bookcase and its contents as material objects makes the similarity between the two poems more apparent.

Indeed, the speaker in Bialik's poem encounters the bookcase in much the same way that the speaker in Tchernichovsky's poem encounters the statue of Apollo, at a remove; in almost totemic fashion, the presence of the bookcase provokes a series of meditations on the part of the speaker and revives memories of his youth and childhood. The image of a sputtering memorial candle suggests how the bookcase has fallen into disuse and prefigures the poet's desperate turn toward the end of the poem to digging their graves (a reference to their burial in the *geniza*). Also toward the poem's conclusion, the speaker looks to the natural world, a potential source of vitality and rejuvenation throughout Bialik's oeuvre. The poem's main drama, however, consisting of slightly over one hundred lines, is largely a retrospective, interior narrative of the speaker's relationship with the contents of the bookcase:

> And now, after the passage of time,
> and I am already wrinkled-of-forehead and wrinkled-of-soul,
> behold the wheel of my life has returned me
> and stood me once again before you, hidden ones of the bookcase,
> descendents of Lvov, Slavuta, Amsterdam and Frankfurt,
> and again my hand leafs through your scrolls
> and my eye gropes, weary, between the lines
> searching silently between the letters' coronets

The three centers of Hebrew printing—Slavuta, Amsterdam, and Frankfurt—mark a cultural and mercantile sphere produced through the circulation of books, including the Talmud, across Europe and the Levant beginning in the late fifteenth century.[31] Despite its title, the actual items in the poem are named almost exclusively as *gvilim,* the Hebrew word for "scrolls." However, the term *gvilim* can also mean "corpses," which brings readers even closer to those hand-lettered works prepared by a scribe on parchment or vellum, animal skin specially treated and prepared for this purpose. The fact that the Hebrew word for bookcase—*aron*—can also mean "coffin" further amplifies this connection. The volumes are described as *atikey gvilim, tsrur be-gvilim,* and *karua gvilim*—ancient scrolls, bundled in scrolls, torn scrolls. That the speaker insistently touches and strokes them with his mouth, eyes, and hands further amplifies their material connotations: their tactility is also suggested through the dust on his fingers, and associatively through his "wrinkled forehead and wrinkled soul." These texts eventually become completely inscrutable, physically collapsing into their constituent elements—columns, pages, "every single letter orphaned unto itself."[32]

> Let me look, let me see—and I do not recognize you, old ones,
> from within your letters,
> open eyes will no longer gaze
> into the depths of my soul,
> sad eyes of ancestral ones,
> and I no longer hear from there the whisper of their lips,
> murmuring in a forgotten grave, untouched by human foot.
> Like a strand of black pearls, their string cut,
> Are your columns to me; your pages widowed
> and every single letter orphaned unto itself—

The image of the scrolls as a broken string of pearls includes objects that doubly refer to writing: *Ḥaruz,* "bead," also means "rhyme," and *pninim,* "pearls," recalls the phrase *ktav pninim* (pearl writing), meaning very small letters or calligraphy. The poem thus embeds this image of the broken string of pearls in poetic language that specifically reminds the reader of the text's status as a made object—its formal qualities (rhyme) as well as its material origins (calligraphy on parchment). Finally, for a mostly meditative poem written in iambic pentameter, without much express play with rhyme, two of these lines conclude with a nice bit of consonant inversion—*ḥutam* (their string) sort of rhymes with *ytsuma* (orphaned)—with the rhyme again calling our attention to the poem as a made object.

The special significance of the premodern scroll, as opposed to the book, lies in its singularity as a handmade object—its aura, in a Benjaminian sense. Yet there is something more. While Bialik's work has been read as negotiating the ostensible divide between the natural world and the world of textual study, the repeated image of the *gvilim,* the scrolls—whose material origins in the animal world are implicit—seems to represent a third option; in Bruno Latour's terms, the presence of the nonhuman that inevitably shapes the subject world of human production.[33] It's not just that the poem engages the world of objects; other poems do that. The poem's innovation lies in its treatment of the text *as an object.* For the purposes of the poem, which depicts the speaker's anxious distance from the solace of both textual discourse and the natural world, *scrolls are better to think with than books.*[34] Their uniqueness, their objecthood, and especially their hybrid status as a kind of fetish, containing traces of the human hand as well as the natural world (animal remains): all these qualities make them an ideal symbol through which the poem thinks a different kind of language—something beyond both book and nature—a newly conceived material relation to text.

Bialik's speaker stations himself as the *aḥaron le-aḥronim* (last of the last), an echo of Tchernichovsky's *harishon le-shavim* (first to return). Both speakers therefore occupy liminal positions, perhaps on opposite sides of the same threshold. Together, these two foundational texts in Hebrew literary history chart an entanglement with the material world, whether through a potentially sacrilegious domain of sculpture and the visual arts, or an insistent, almost morbid, adherence to the scroll as a physical object. This entanglement shapes, and even enables, the emergence of Hebrew as a language of modern literary discourse. Indeed, the interpenetration of textual and visual registers emergent in Bialik and Tchernichovsky becomes symptomatic of a transnational, multilingual creativity that played out in different locales. Furthermore, the book in particular was the object of aesthetic mediation focused on its symbolic value as an emblem of cultural and social affiliation, especially when the books in question were treasured personal possessions. As Benjamin notes in "Unpacking My Library," "ownership is the most intimate relationship that one can have to objects. Not that they come alive in [the owner]; it is he who lives in them."[35]

MODERNISM AND THE JEWISH BOOKCASE

This dynamic relation to books is also evident in the Russian Jewish poet Osip Mandelstam's writing about his family and childhood. Like his Anglo-American imagist contemporaries such as Ezra Pound, Mandelstam's early volumes *Stone* (1913) and *Tristia* (1922) drew extensively on materials from the visual and plastic arts. Mandelstam's poems that evoke Jewish themes often do so in opposition to a preferred "Hellenic" worldview, similar to the tension described in Tchernichovsky's address to Apollo. Jewishness in his early work operated either "in disguise" or as the device through which the poet will "enter the portals of Christian culture."[36] However, his prose of the middle to late 1920s, collected under the title *The Noise of Time,* demonstrates "a concerted effort to reconcile his Jewish heritage with his quest for world culture, on the one hand, and his struggle to place both himself and his culture in relation to the new Soviet state, on the other."[37]

The essays of *The Noise of Time* describe the poet's early exposure to language within what he calls "the Judaic chaos"—"the unknown womb world whence I had issued, which I feared. . . . The chaos of Judaism showed through all the chinks of the stone-clad Petersburg apartment: in the threat of ruin, in the cap hanging in the room of the guest from the provinces, in the spiky script of the unread books of Genesis, thrown into the dust one shelf lower than Goethe and Schiller, in the shreds of the yellow ritual."[38] In the spirit of the Acmeist commitment to "the word as such" and the simplicity of "A = A," the Jewish world of Mandelstam's childhood is rendered primarily through objects and fragments. Books are simply another kind of object, to be feared for their biblical "spiky script" or forgotten under the dust.[39] Whereas for Bialik the fact that tradition has ceased to signify—that books no longer recognize him—precipitates an existential trauma, for Mandelstam this same situation simply provides another opportunity to revel in the material world. This idea is elegantly conveyed in Mandelstam's vivid memory of the family bookcase. The description is worth citing at length for its uncanny similitude to the scene in Bialik's poem:

> The bookcase of early childhood is a man's companion for life. . . . There was nothing haphazard in the way that strange little library had been deposited, like a geological bed, over several decades. The paternal and maternal elements in it were not mixed, but existed separately, and a cross section of the strata showed the spiritual efforts of the entire family, as well as the inoculation of it with alien blood.
>
> I always remember the lower shelf as chaotic: the books were not standing upright side by side but lay like ruins: reddish five-volume works with ragged covers, a Russian history of the Jews written in the clumsy, shy language of a Russian-speaking Talmudist. This was the Judaic chaos thrown in the dust. . . . This was the level to which my Hebrew primer, which I never mastered, quickly fell. . . . The Hebrew primer as illustrated with pictures which showed one and the same little boy, wearing a visored cap and with a melancholy adult face, in all sorts of situations—with a cat, a book, a pail, a watering can. I saw nothing of myself in that boy and with all my being revolted against the book and the subject. . . .

> Above these Jewish ruins there began the orderly arrangement of books; those were the Germans . . . the old Leipzig and Tübingen editions, chubby little butterballs stamped in claret-colored bindings. . . . All this was my father fighting his way as an autodidact into the German world out of the Talmudic wilds. . . .
>
> Still higher were my mother's Russian books—Pushkin in Isakov's 1876 edition. . . . The color of Pushkin? Every color is accidental—what color could one choose for the purl of speech. Oh, that idiotic alphabet of colors by Rimbaud![40]

Mandelstam's elaborate description underscores the variety of cultural alternatives available to eastern European Jewish intelligentsia. The bookcase—a metonymy for the canon—is the site of a stratified intellectual hybridity, shot through with "alien blood." Knowledge is understood in gendered terms, either maternal or paternal in origin. In contrast to Bialik's religious "scrolls," the specifics of Mandelstam's "Judaic chaos" are examples of secular genres—a history book and a Hebrew schoolbook. His estrangement, however, from the "Jewish ruins" is absolute and articulated in relation to his parents, central European immigrants who had adopted Russian language and culture. The poet's embrace of his mother's culture is specifically related to language—her "sonorous Russian:" she was "the first of her whole family to achieve pure and clear Russian sounds." "Her vocabulary was poor and restricted, the locutions were trite, but it was a language, it had roots and confidence." His father, in contrast, "had absolutely no language; his speech was tongue-tie[d] and languagelessness. . . . A completely abstract, counterfeit language, the ornate and twisted speech of an autodidact, where normal words are intertwined with the ancient philosophical terms of Herder, Leibniz, and Spinoza, the capricious syntax of a Talmudist, the artificial, not always finished sentence: it was anything in the world, but not a language, neither Russian nor German."[41]

Mandelstam's ars poetical leanings are evident in the preference for a simple, rooted language, and in the free-floating importance of color throughout the bookcase description. The beginnings of Mandelstam's own penchant for German and Russian classics are also evident here, while the Acmeist insistence on language's visual, material qualities—the "color of speech," the "alphabet of colors"—acquires a domestic setting, at once both Russian and Jewish. His description of this primal scene is informed by an essential bond between Jewish culture and textuality. Yet Mandelstam renders the bookcase in visual, sensual terms—through color, texture, even taste and scent, and through the arrangement of books on shelves, whose spatial rendering repeats the conventional opposition between Semitic chaos and classical order.

The bookcase is also at the center of a painting by Moses Soyer, *The Lover of Books* (1934). Soyer and his twin brother Raphael (also a painter) were born in

Moses Soyer, *The Lover of Books* (1934).

Russia in 1899 and emigrated to the United States in 1912. Both studied art in New York, and both were involved in left-wing political activity during the 1930s. Moses, a member of the art committee of the World Congress of Jewish Culture (YKUF), was associated with Yiddish cultural and political circles.[42]

In *The Lover of Books,* an aging figure stands before shelves of crumbling folios and a collection of painted and sculpted forms; he grasps both a large book and a picture frame. The book seems the size of an art folio, but it could just as well be a volume of the Talmud. The painting's depiction contains more than a hint of Rembrandt's depictions of Dutch Jews and biblical scenes. The works behind the central figure span the entirety of Western art: a classical bust on the left, a photograph of a dancing woman and a robed figure on the far right that recalls a Pietà. The old man stands among them like another art object, particularly in the placement of his head and torso, which rise above the shelf like a bust. It appears that the Jewish lover of books, like the objects behind him, is fit only for museum display, an object of purely historical interest; the powerful example of the book has been challenged, and perhaps even superseded, by that of the visual, material object. For Soyer, as for Bialik, Tchernichovsky, and Mandelstam, the bookcase symbolized a complex vision of the modern Jewish self.

We have seen how Hebrew writing engaged the objecthood of the material world; this entanglement with visual objects shaped its emergence as a literary vernacular. What was rhetorically expressed in Tchernichovsky's poem about Apollo and implicit in Bialik's attention to scrolls as things became the stuff of modernist poetic manifestos, and laid the groundwork for the emergence of a truly vernacular literary discourse. Lyric poetry—with its relatively compact form—is perhaps an ideal genre through which to examine the affinity between the textual and the material. As we will see in the following chapters, poetry's paradigmatic status can help us frame questions about how materiality matters for other genres as well—how individual books and copies of journals circulate and become part of private collections and public archives; how the rich social world of the novel is studded with possessions, furnishings, the detritus of daily life; how text and image still present as potential rivals in contemporary graphic narratives.

Chapter 1 Jewish Imagism

Virginia Woolf's famous observation that "on or about December 1910 human nature changed" has by now served as the point of departure for numerous explorations of modernist culture, mostly centered in and around the environs of Bloomsbury.[1] I cannot say for sure what date would be similarly productive for modernist Jewish writing: perhaps the Kishinev pogrom of 1903? The 1909 establishment of a neighborhood north of Jaffa that eventually became Tel Aviv? The Triangle Shirtwaist Factory fire of 1911? This trio of events, both traumatic and triumphant, well illustrates the enormous range of experiences that shaped and informed modern Jewish writing across geography and language. In this chapter, we explore the transnational flowering of one such genre—"Jewish imagism"—my term for poetry in an imagist vein that also engages some kind of expressly Jewish theme or situation. By "imagism" I refer to the broad set of poetic trends emerging in the early twentieth century in mostly urban, cosmopolitan settings; this poetry aspired to a visual or material quality and sought to recast poetry's stylistic, formal properties to fit the tempo and contours of the modern age. As described in one typical manifesto, published in 1919 by a group of poets in New York: "In our age of the big metropolis and enormous variety in all domains, this life becomes a thousandfold more complicated and entangled. We Introspectivists feel the need to convey and express it. . . . Just as contemporary life created new clothing, new dwellings, new color combinations, and new sound combinations, so one needs to create a new art and different rhythms."[2] This ubiquitous call for a poetry to fit the age was written in Yiddish, the native tongue of its authors, all eastern European Jewish immigrants; they situated their claims for Yiddish in relation to contemporaneous trends of American imagism: "We believe in Yiddish. We love Yiddish. . . . We think that our language is now beautiful and rich enough for the most profound poetry."[3]

Adopting the prescriptive tone common in manifestos of the period, "Introspectivism" details what poetry should, and should not, look like: "Each poem must have its *individual rhythm.* By this we mean that the rhythm of the poem must fit entirely this particular poem. One poem cannot have the same rhythm as any other poem. Every poem is, in fact, unique."[4] While the list of requirements is not quite as punitively rendered as Ezra Pound's "A Few Don'ts for the Imagiste" (see below), its assessment is no less polemical and may serve as an introduction to the poetry discussed in this chapter. Though modernist Hebrew poetry in both Europe and Palestine drew more directly on the legacy of Bialik and Tchernichovsky, we can nonetheless locate significant parallels in the contemporaneous work of Yiddish modernists like the Introspectivists in New York; furthermore, poetry in English by young American Jewish authors was also shaped by a desire for writing that is new, precise, and object-driven.

According to their 1919 manifesto, the work of the *Inzikhistn*—the Introspectivists—signaled a firm break with an earlier, no less influential generation of American Yiddish poets, *Di Yunge*—the Young Ones. Poets such as Mani Leyb may have "led Yiddish poetry out onto a broader road"—that is, the path of secular, European literary form—but as a group the Introspectivists "belong only to their own time," constituting "a bridge to a new poetry."[5] This "new poetry" rejected symbolism's "well-rounded mood" as a kind of "embellishment" or "ornament." Instead, poetry should be characterized by introspection and individuality, principles shaping both form and content. Formally, "free verse" is more suited to the "rise of the big city with its machines, turmoil, and its accelerated, irregular tempo." Rhyme, as we shall see later in this chapter's discussion of Anna Margolin's work, should be used judiciously, not automatically, and only when it is "woven naturally into the verse."[6] In terms of subject matter, poetry can be *about* anything, yet the poem itself must be a unique occurrence, the product of an interaction between the poet's own individual "internal panorama" and the world around her or him:

> We Introspectivists want first of all to present life—the true, the sincere, and the precise—as it is mirrored in *ourselves*, as it merges with us.
>
> The human psyche is an awesome labyrinth. Thousands of beings dwell there. The inhabitants are the various facets of the individual's present self on the one hand and fragments of his inherited self on the other.[7]

We find in these lines a general principle of radical newness common to modernist poetry in other languages: within the rallying cry to "make it new," we may also note the presence of "it"; in other words, the call is not for a rejection of history but rather a refashioning of it—a process that treats the past as a collection of material artifacts, not "well-rounded" but in fragments. The poetic process involves an intuitive, deductive encounter with the world; its "major tools" are "association and suggestion," an adherence to "spoken language in [a poem's] structure and flow," and an avoidance of "superfluous adjectives": only these will lead to the creation of an "authentic, individual image."[8]

This drive for precision and clarity, together with a desire for an "authentic, individual image," found expression in the work of a paradigmatic group of poets: David Fogel [Vogel] (1891–1943), working mostly in Hebrew in European settings; the Hebrew poet Esther Raab (1894–1981), writing in Palestine; the Yiddish poet Anna Margolin (1887–1952) in New York; and Charles Reznikoff (1894–1976), writing in English, whose "Objectivism"—a central trend within American modernism—is also considered a point of origin for American Jewish literature. The work of these poets is linked by a materialist concern for language as such; a devotion to minimalist form, precise descriptive terms, and the sparest of syntax; an interest in made objects and visual forms, especially the plastic arts of painting and sculpture; and a reverence for the essential "itness" of the material world. For each poet, I will consider exemplary poems from his or her debut volume in relation to contemporaneous manifestos and other documents that specifically address questions of poetic form in "Jewish" languages. For example, for David Fogel, Hebrew was a box to be creatively chafed against; for Charles Reznikoff, it was a haunting presence, an ideal form to aspire to. For both poets, Hebrew mattered as a "Jewish language." To explore how these ideas shaped their poetic practice is not to go down the path of Jewish essentialism; on the contrary, it is an attempt to recover the diverse particulars of poetic meaning and to appreciate these details against the broader grain of historical context.

The title pages and front covers of the poets' volumes hint at their particular aesthetic allegiances. The title page of David Fogel's *Lifney hashar haafel* (Hebrew, 1923; *Before the Dark Gate*) displays an affinity for geometric form; its

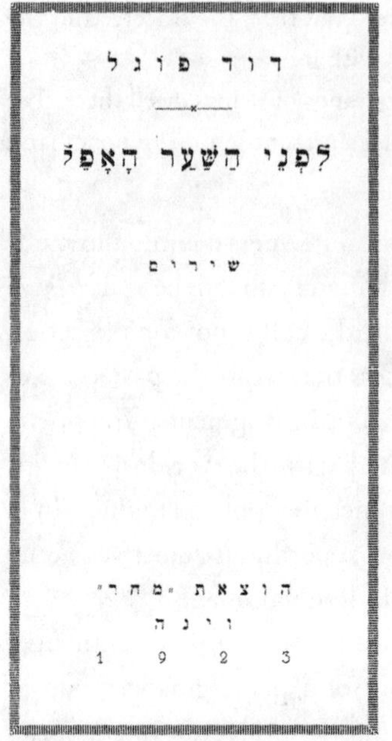

דוד פוגל

לִפְנֵי הַשַּׁעַר הָאָפֵל

שירים

הוצאת "מחר"
וינה
1923

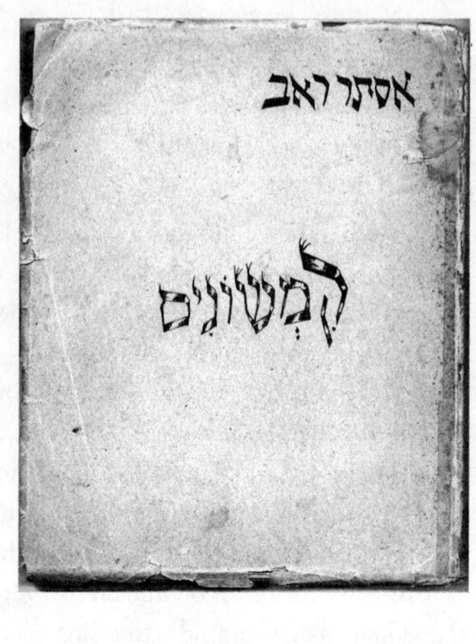

אסתר ראב

קמשונים

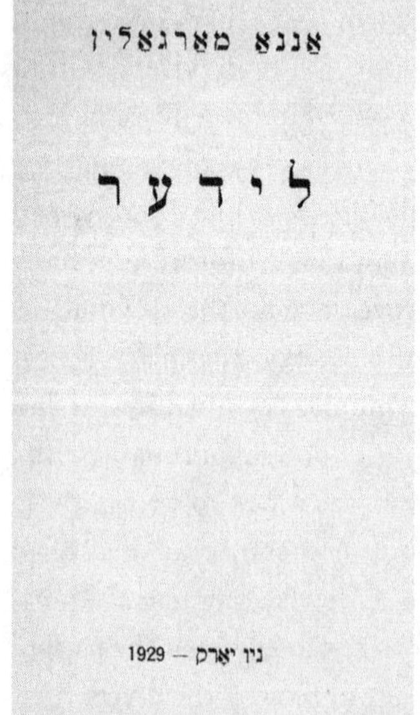

אננא מארגאלין

לידער

1929 — ניו יארק

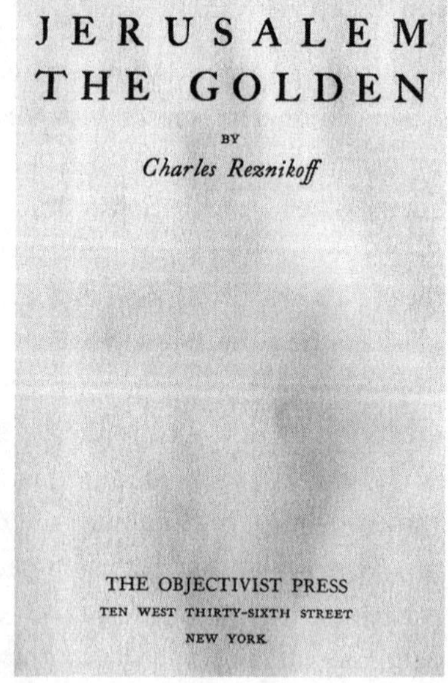

JERUSALEM THE GOLDEN

BY

Charles Reznikoff

THE OBJECTIVIST PRESS
TEN WEST THIRTY-SIXTH STREET
NEW YORK

(*top left*) David Fogel, *Before the Dark Gate* (1923). (*top right*) Esther Raab, *Thistles* (1929). Courtesy of the New York Public Library, Dorot Division. (*bottom left*) Anna Margolin, *Poems* (1929). (*bottom right*) Charles Reznikoff, *Jerusalem the Golden* (1934).

tightly etched border shimmers due to the carefully staggered spacing of its tiny lines, and the art deco font of the numbers 1-9-2-3 are perhaps a nod to the Viennese surroundings. On the cover of Esther Raab's *Kimshonim* (Hebrew, 1929; *Thistles*), the hand-lettered name of the author is fragmented and bold, like the poetics within; the crowns on the title's lettering are a well-known feature of Hebrew calligraphy, especially in biblical scrolls. Here, however, the three-pronged crowns trail raggedly upward like weeds, a key feature in the poet's pastoral vocabulary and a neat allusion to the relation between text and landscape in her work. In contrast, note the relatively austere character of the volumes printed in New York by Anna Margolin and Charles Reznikoff, reflecting perhaps a commitment to the ascendent spartan imagist practices of the day. The cover of Margolin's *Lider* (Yiddish, 1929; *Poems*) seems particularly frugal, and the name of the publisher—Oriom Press—is hidden in small print on the very last of the volume's 144 pages (Margolin's is the largest of these poetry collections by far). Reznikoff's elegant title page *Jerusalem the Golden* (1934) references the two modes of allegiance—Jewish and Objectivist—that his work sought to merge.

What, specifically, might modernist poetry "afford" in terms of materiality? As observed in the introductory discussion of Bialik, a preoccupation with language's material aspect developed into an abiding concern as modern Hebrew writing became an increasingly secularized endeavor.[9] For this later generation of modernist poets, the development of both Hebrew and Yiddish as literary vernaculars coincided with the rise of modernist conceptions of language, ideas that expressly privileged the creation of poems meant to resemble objects. Central among these was the notion of *Dinggedichte* (thing-poems), a form associated with Rainer Maria Rilke's work, especially poems such as "Archaischer Torso Apollos" (1908). Like Tchernichovky's "Facing a Statue of Apollo," Rilke's poem uses both the mythical figure of Apollo and his modern material incarnation to formulate an aesthetic statement. Rilke's *Neue Gedichte* (New Poems) featured a supple syntax coupled with an attention to the inner animating essence of things, "in which the focus was thrown off the lyrical speaker of the poem and onto the thing seen."[10] Inspired in large part by the poet's admiration for the sculptor Auguste Rodin, Rilke sought to produce poetry that would "belong to the world of things," demonstrating a commitment to craft and a serious work ethic in which "syntax, especially, becomes a *tensile material*" (emphasis added).[11] A devotion to objects—encapsulated in William Carlos Williams's well-known "no ideas but in things" (1926)—appears in other texts from the period, including the manifestos of Russian Acmeism and Anglo-American imagism, which called for a replacement of subjective, mood-oriented dreaminess with a commitment to craft, precision, and the symbolic value of "small, dry things."[12]

In one of the era's definitive statements, Ezra Pound delivers a short prescriptive list followed by a longer, no less regulatory text, "A Few Don'ts for the Imagiste":

> 1. Direct treatment of the "thing" whether subjective or objective.
> 2. To use absolutely no word that does not contribute to the presentation.
> 3. As regarding rhythm: to compose in the sequence of the musical phrase, not in sequence of the metronome. . . .
>
> The immediate necessity is to tabulate A LIST OF DON'TS for those beginning to write verses. I can not put all of them into Mosaic negative.[13]

Pound's admonitions here and his notion of the image—"that which presents an intellectual and emotional complex in time"—resonate with the tenets of the Introspectivist manifesto, with its economy of form and language.[14] Furthermore, Pound's assertions skirt remarkably close to our concerns here, his notorious antisemitism notwithstanding. It may seem odd to revert to the language of biblical prohibition within a modernist poetic manifesto; I would argue that Pound's tethering of materialist poetic principles to the "Mosaic negative" highlights the lingering pervasiveness of religious taboos within "secular" forms, taboos exemplified for Pound by the "Mosaic negative," including the Second Commandment prohibition on graven images. In fact, my examination of Hebrew and Yiddish poetry will demonstrate the degree to which writing in Jewish languages constituted a more visible instance of the general presence of the sacred in modern secular forms.

Beyond the challenge of creating poems whose materiality and objecthood exceed the limitation of ink figures on a page, these poetic practices posed a particular dilemma for Jewish imagism: the perceived "sacredness" of Hebrew and Yiddish by virtue of their iconic connection to the alphabet of ancient texts and liturgical forms.[15] Though orthography is only one element of language, and it has developed different functions over time, it should be appreciated as an essential material strand within the matrix of traits and features that shape literary expression. Treating language as a material substance and writing poems that may be perceived, even revered, as objects—perfectly fine goals for a modernist poet—could be construed as idol worship in Hebrew and Yiddish. In a sense, Jewish imagism presents the limit case for an alphabet of sacred texts being deployed within a secular literary form—the maximal stress created between the language's normative historical usage and an attempt to "make it new." This materialized version of "the Word" skirted close to idolatry regard-

אורי צבי
פארן צלם
I N R I

Uri Tsvi Greenberg, "Uri Tsvi before the Cross" (1922).

ing both the inner animism implied in the materiality of language and the object-poem forged, as well as in its casting of the poet in the role of creator.

Modernist writers in Hebrew and Yiddish took note of Judaism's potential ambivalence toward the visual and how it might stymie poetry in an imagist vein. Avraham Shlonsky and Reuven Ayzland [Iceland], two key figures in the period, explicitly addressed this issue in a pair of short essays. Shlonsky's "Tselem" (Icon) appeared in the journal *Hedim* in Tel Aviv in 1924 and Ayzland's "Art un profanatsiye" (Art and Profanity) appeared in *Der Inzel* in New York in 1925. Both manifestos respond to the perceived strictures of the Second Commandment; their "solution" however, is not more art but an embodied material language.

"Tselem" demands a specific kind of poetic expression: a kind of three-dimensional plasticity for language deriving from a rejection of the Second Commandment prohibition. *Tselem* comes from the biblical phrase "in God's image" (*tselem elohim*); I translate it as "icon" to convey the three-dimensional poetic expression that Shlonsky privileges. Proposing the term *tselem* as an emblem of a new Hebrew poetic style was itself a provocation, given the meaning of the Yiddish word *tseylem:* the Christian cross. Shlonsky's "Icon" exemplifies modern Jewish artists' fascination with Christian iconography.[16] Uri Tsvi Greenberg's "concrete" poem, the 1922 "Uri Tsvi farn tseleym" (Uri Tsvi before the Cross), which grew out of the poet's experience in the trenches during the First World War, represents an extreme example of this engagement.[17] Greenberg (1896–1981) was a central figure in Hebrew and Yiddish modernism. Like other treatments of Jesus, Greenberg's poem distinguishes between the historical image of Jesus, a Jew from Nazareth, and theological iterations of Jesus as a figure within Christian doctrinal belief. Thus for Greenberg, "Jesus remains fixed on the border between 'brother' and 'other.'"[18] The poem, published in the Warsaw Yiddish-expressionist journal *Albatros,* appeared typographically in the shape of a cross; it was censored by the authorities.

Shlonsky's manifesto of two years later seems to share some of the same spirit. His blend of hyperbole and expressionism was an attempt to secularize the sacred, a break framed in the language of tradition itself.[19] Dismissing both the lyric's "wordiness" and ethical expectations for poetry (that it must have a moral [*nimshal*]), Shlonsky calls for an embodied, visual poetics:

> I want to see the voices.
> For this wordy lyric is abstract, spiritist, neurasthenic; she has no flesh.
> . . . .
> Even moods should be sculpted from the marble of words, for poetry is—
> "dynamic sculpture": statues shake here, make sounds.[20]

How can language become material? Through a symbolic register that rejects the allegory's interpretive depths and peers, instead, at the surface, elevating the image's cohesive vitality over other kinds of figuration: "We must distinguish between the image (*d'mut*) and the simili (*d'mui*), between icon (*tselem*) and comparison: between the mythic picture and the literary, rhetorical 'like.'"

Instead of the "simile"—derided as "simple analogy" (*gzeyra shava*)—Shlonsky proposes a more intimate, immediate kind of "vision": "an idolatrous sensibility which elevates metaphor to the level of an icon, a symbol, a mythological creation." Thus the manifesto rejects any rhetorical device announcing the imagination's comparative work; instead, the symbol should efface the gap between language and the represented world, creating a poetic object that is at once embodied and iconic. Shlonsky frames this relatively garden-variety preference for the image, and a more material poetic language, as a reiteration of the people's historical desire for the golden calf over the ethical mandate of the tablets. The manifesto is in part a bold revision of Exodus 20, in which the children of Israel receive the Ten Commandments, described in the Bible as a multisensory experience: hearing the thunder, shaken by the smoke and the sound of the shofar. Shlonsky's manifesto concludes with a "pagan" rereading of the revelation at Sinai:

> I exalt the "[golden] calf" more than I exalt the "tablets," and even Moses wasn't at peace until he *saw* God. Even if it was only his back.
> For man wants the body. And the *tselem*.

In March 1925, using language remarkably similar to Avraham Shlonsky's "Icon," the Yiddish poet and critic Reuven Ayzland published "Art and Profanity," a manifesto analyzing the problems facing modern Yiddish literature. Like Shlonsky in his critical distinction between image and simile, Ayzland privileges "the sense of the living word" and "true beauty" over "swollen *melitsa*" (poesy) and "conventional beauty." He begins, however, by outlining the debilitating effects of the Second Commandment on the development of Jewish culture:

> When the Jewish people became monotheistic, it became hostile to all art. "Thou shalt not make an idol . . ." is the most important of all the commandments. . . . Hatred of the image has remained in the blood until the present day. We are therefore so unartlike, even when we speak about art. . . .
>
> Like all unaesthetic people, we cannot understand that every phenomenon has its own right to exist, and we have to give it some sort of function. It must serve some sort of purpose for us. . . . A large part of our contemporary literature is no more than a freak of our old-time allegory.[21]

The thematic and rhetorical similarities between "Icon" and "Art and Profanity" are breathtaking; their near-simultaneous publication affords insight into the degree to which Hebrew and Yiddish writers in different social, cultural, and geographic situations struggled with what they considered to be the problem of the Second Commandment for literary expression. Note again how neither poet counters the perceived prohibitions of the Second Commandment with a call for more "Jewish art." Both instead insist on the supremacy of "the word itself," unburdened by what Ayzland calls "that old-time allegory," and what Shlonsky refers to as "the ethical idea."[22] The context of Jewish culture, for both the Hebrew and the Yiddish poet, situates what is an otherwise fairly commonplace modernist proclamation vis-à-vis "the word" as a defense—a defense framed in terms of the traditional Jewish taboo on visual representation.[23] Thus, the rhetoric of the image-making ban informs Hebrew and Yiddish modernist appraisals of "the word itself."

Neither Shlonsky nor Ayzland, as influential as each was in his own time, succeeded in implementing his own poetic mandate. However, the poems of Fogel, Raab, Margolin, and Reznikoff all share a sense of language as a malleable substance that may be formally manipulated through techniques such as enjambment, abbreviated syntax, and attention to rhyme. This attention to "the word as such" manifested somewhat differently for each: Fogel addressed the problem of Hebrew's sacred authority for modernist poets directly in a short lecture, and in his poetry through manipulation of color and verb tense; Raab's grammatically dense "miniatures" of the Palestinian landscape subverted dominant poetic treatments of the land's ancient legacy; Margolin's poems used rhyme to draw attention to their status as made objects; Reznikoff's "Objectivist" verse (what he retrospectively tagged as "chiefly Jewish, American, urban") plumbed the meaning of traditional Judaic forms in a cosmopolitan setting. These diverse explorations of poetry's material potential exemplify a transnational phenomenon: the emergence of a tangled relation between sacred traditions and secular literary forms.

DAVID FOGEL AND THE COLOR OF POETRY

David Fogel's relatively slim poetic output during his lifetime and somewhat larger body of posthumously published work have drawn an outsized amount of critical and scholarly attention.[24] A single volume of Hebrew verse published in Vienna in 1923 and a series of luminous, erotically charged prose works served as belated inspiration for a later generation of Israeli poets who delighted in the poetry's spare minimalism and strange interior landscapes.[25] A collection of prose published in 1990, including evocative selections from Fogel's early diaries, the translation of a sprawling Yiddish novel based on his wartime experiences in France, and the more recent discovery and publication of a previously unknown novella set in Vienna further deepened critical appreciation of this unique writer.[26]

Fogel's poems demand from the reader an intense participatory visualization. Indeed, contemporaneous reviews of his volume *Before the Dark Gate* (1923) characterized the distinctiveness of Fogel's poetic achievement in terms of the visual arts: Bialik is said to have claimed that they reminded him of abstract painting, while Asher Barash noted their resemblance to metallurgy: "There is something in them not found in Hebrew poetry until now: a thin, silvered style, almost filigree."[27] Both observations underline the material aspect of Fogel's poetic language—the propensity for formal, spatial relations implied in the reference to abstract painting or the metaphorical comparison with filagree, a technique that preserves some of silver's molten dynamism within the finished object. Even harsh critiques of Fogel's poetry—and there were quite a few—mentioned some visual aspect. Shlonsky's assessment notes the monotony of the lyrics with a focus on color: "Its outside: a black cover. And its inside: 'black closets,' 'black birds,' 'black ship,' . . . and night-night-night. Also father has a 'black coat' and 'his beard is black' etc."[28] Or Avigdor Hameiri's somewhat less scathing remembrance of his initial response to Fogel: instead of telling a story about a landscape, he merely gives pictures of it.[29] These evaluations all suggest that the poems of *Before the Dark Gate* are meant to be looked at, even touched, as much as read.

Key components of this "touchability" of Fogel's poetry was its treatment of language as a material substance, and a tendency to minimize the significance of Hebrew's referential qualities. Modern Hebrew poetry often relied on the language's historical depth and sacred authority; stripping words of those very qualities that created poetic meaning was potentially an act of creative suicide. Yet we find a call for just such an iconoclastic treatment of Hebrew in Fogel's "Language and Style in Our Young Literature" (1931), a public lecture that remains his most explicit statement concerning the creation of a modern Hebrew literary idiom.[30] In Fogel's view, at the root of Hebrew literature's "complete anarchy" was an overly deferential view of the Hebrew language—"that attraction to the holy tongue whose origins lie in the days of the *Haskalah*":

> This attraction unconsciously distorts our judgment when we come to discuss a piece of Hebrew writing. Although our language has since then turned into a spoken language for thousands of Jews, and is already used in secular expression for vital everyday needs, we still treat Hebrew as a holy thing. . . . Our special attachment to the Assyrian script [*ktav ashuri*] is the root of this trouble. We tend to judge leniently everything written in Hebrew, especially a work written in the ornate holy tongue that is full of lexical and expressive innovation.[31]

In Fogel's view, Hebrew's linguistic "material"—its abundant classical authority—thwarted the modern writer's ability to shape it according to his own individual style. Yet is it precisely these deeply referential qualities that made Hebrew so valued a tool in national identity construction. How does what Fogel elsewhere called his "malnourished" Hebrew find expression in his work?[32]

"Assyrian script" refers to the calligraphic form of the Hebrew alphabet used in texts of traditional Jewish learning such as the Mishnah. Language's most overtly visual facet—its orthography—is the material difference that sets Hebrew and Yiddish writing apart. As mentioned above, this visual aspect was central to early critical assessments of Fogel's poetry, and critics have noted the abundance of color in his work.[33] Indeed, the relation between color and language fascinated modernist poets and critics alike; it is at the core of Rilke's passionate reaction to Cézanne's work in 1907, recorded in his *Letters on Cézanne.*[34] The collection remains one of modernism's quintessential statements on the complex relation between poetry and painting. In Rilke's view, Cézanne's "painting is something that takes place among the colors, and how one has to leave them alone completely, so that they can settle the matter among themselves. Their intercourse: this is the whole of painting."[35] For Cézanne, paint could be both color and object—the signifying medium itself, revealed in thick, patchy brushstrokes, as well as the fruit in all its unnerving, quivering realness on the canvas. This duality was most acutely felt in Cézanne's attention to surface, where the plane of the canvas carried the scene's full depth through the use of *passage. Passage* manipulates surface/depth relations through an elision of contour and boundary, privileging surface and elevating color at the expense of form, making color the primary device through which painted objects coalesce before the viewing eye.[36] The viewer of a Cézannian landscape is called upon to perceive the scene from the painter's idiosyncratic point of view, to participate in its composition, compiling its elements in comprehensible fashion.[37] The reader of Fogel's work is similarly engaged, through the deliberately "malnourished" Hebrew, in the process of poetic *passage.* Specifically, poetry that strips language of its referential qualities—in the case of Hebrew, of its historical depth and authority—may be understood as a linguistic equivalent of Cézannian passage.[38] Instead of relying on their deep, allusive meaning—for example, their reference to biblical tropes and figures—the poems insist upon the flat surface of the words themselves.

Reading *Before the Dark Gate* therefore entails intense visualization on the part of the reader. The poems resist reading, if by "reading" we mean a traditional, word-bound, temporally driven activity. Instead, they ask to be *seen* and comprehended through their material presence and visual cues. The Fogelian stanza is typically compact and self-contained, often consisting of a single sentence, with little enjambment. Enjambment would force the eye to read along the poem more strongly. Instead, the individual strophes pile up against one another, their concise, vivid images interacting along the axis of the poem as it unfolds down the page. The entire volume works in a similar fashion. When reading the numbered poems in sequence, a fluidity of image seeps from poem to poem, creating not simply repetition but a cumulative effect, akin to what Joseph Frank called modernism's "spatial form."[39] Reading poems 25 and 26 in sequence provides an excellent illustration of how this spatial form and poetic passage function.[40]

The poems render complementary versions of the same situation: a woman longing for her lover. In poem 25, the speaker is outdoors and mobile, in

Poem 25

From night's edge here I stray
and my wild hair
sweeps black the blue of my nightshirt.

At the foot of a hill
a hidden eye/spring
whispers darkly to the night.

—Strange eye/spring,
has not my beloved drunk
from your waters?—

Like a dark stain
mute crouches a wood
upon the horizon.

Perhaps his weary soul
is resting
upon the carpets of her shadow?

Like a noonday sun
my flesh blazes
through the night.

And my sparks fall
like stars
into the darkness.

Poem 26

Upon the paleness of my bed
glows silent naked my torso
like a white flame.

The night of my hair
like a dark cascade descends,
onto the rug's design.

Come, my beloved!
My modest beauty blazes eternal
to your eyes' blue.

Come———

The redness of my walls will deepen.

A lone evening
approaches my couch
and spreads a black dress
upon me.

The two streams of my legs
the bright ones
I [will] no longer see.

I cry in the dark.

poem 26, inside and stationary. For the Hebrew reader, this nocturnal scene of desire recalls the Song of Songs, a biblical text that occupied a privileged position in modern Hebrew poetry. With its semantic specificity and plentitude of terms relating to the human body and the natural world as well as its densely textured allegory, the Song's linguistic and thematic arsenal was an important part of any modern Hebrew poet's tool kit. However, in keeping with his general disdain for Hebrew's classical cache, Fogel strips the biblical setting of this exemplary specificity, granting it generalized, surreal, almost gothic overtones.[41]

The poems should be "seen" as a series of clusters of colors and spatial relationships that are reconfigured and reemerge throughout. Binary distinctions—surface/depth, light/dark/, night/day, wet/dry—are manipulated in such a way as to suggest the gradations of a palette, rather than firmly oppositional categories. For example, poem 25 opens with an ambiguous location—"night's edge"—a phrase that spatializes night by giving it a physical marker. The description of the speaker and her hair sweeping across her nightshirt is picked up in poem 26 as "the night of my hair / like a dark cascade" and the evening's "spread[ing] a black dress"—a kind of visual scramble of the colors and their motion in poem 25. Imagery is formed through relations among solid objects and planes, and the confusion of subject and object. In perhaps the most delicately wrought cluster of images, Fogel's poems confound both physics and natural biology—turning solids into streams of light or air, and rendering light what is normally dark. In poem 25, the speaker's power is so great her flesh blazes like a sun at night. In poem 26, the sound of the word *blaze* ("LoHET") is echoed in the description of the speaker's torso as a gleaming flame ("LaHEvET").[42] In another series of surface-dependent imagery, water falls like light onto dark backgrounds: in poem 25, the spring's waters murmur in the darkness, while in poem 26, the speaker's legs are described as bright "streams" in the dark, and the final image is of tears. Elements of these clusters of spatial relations and color intertwine and overlap, just as *passage* operates in a painting.

With this appreciation for Fogel's densely wrought imagery, we can return to the meaning of color in his work, keeping in mind that color symbolizes painting's nonreferential qualities, those very features that support the creation of modernist poetry unburdened by Hebrew's historical baggage. Poem 26 is remarkable for having a color-related word in every stanza, except the single-word stanza, line 10: *bo'ah* ("Come").[43] These patches of color unfold in a series of progressive actions: "Come" (twice), "deepen" (in its imperfect progressive form), "approaches," and the hypothetical future of the line "I [will] no longer see."[44] The tension between the poem's shifting sequencing and its patches of color illustrates a general principle regarding the use of color in *Before the Dark Gate:* these instances slow down the flow of the verse. The unusual forms of blue and black in poem 25's first stanza jammed up against one another provide a concise example of this principle: "my wild hair / sweeps black the blue of my nightshirt." Grammatically adjectives, they function syntactically as adverb and object. Their proximity on the line briefly reduces their syntactic function, the line's flow or sequence. Color acts almost spatially, mitigating the poem's narrative progression.

Thus color, which enabled the move from impressionism to expressionism in Fogel's poetry, also promotes the treatment of language as a material substance.[45] Fogelian passage, with its attention to the surface matter of things, binds various moments in the poems together in order to "thicken" time. The furthest extreme of this reification of time, and the "culmination" of passage in art historical terms, was cubism, whose view of history Wendy Steiner has astutely characterized: "Cubism . . . tells us to think of history in a new way, not as a plotted narrative moving toward a resolution, but as a cubist painting whose elements maintain their heterogeneity—objects, people; things, signs."[46] We may intuit from this observation one plausible context for critical resistance to Fogel's style, despite its later influence: the erasure of Hebrew's referentiality, its historical authority, moved against the grain of the period's predominant poetics, a maximalist form tied to progressive, redemptive narratives of nation-building.[47] Instead, Fogel's poetics built directly upon the protomodernist engagement with visual, material registers in Bialik and Tchernichovsky. In embracing such a poetics, Fogel's work forced Hebrew to participate in that revolution of human consciousness that Virginia Woolf claimed occurred in or around December 1910. For a truly cubist poetics, we must look to the setting of Hebrew modernism in Palestine, where an encounter with the immediate particulars of landscape shaped the emergence of a new set of poetic practices.

THE PLAIN MEANING OF BRAMBLES: HEBREW IMAGIST POETRY IN PALESTINE

In spite of their critical differences, Fogel and Shlonsky seemed to share a desire for a more material form of language; furthermore, both acknowledge the particular challenges facing Hebrew, given its historical baggage (for Shlonsky, the perceived prohibition on visual forms; for Fogel, an attachment to "Assyrian script"). The problem of Hebrew's materiality took on different dimensions within the context of Hebrew literature written in Palestine, where the burden of textual, biblical reference to the land was compounded by the presence of the land itself. Hebrew literature in Palestine during the interwar period privileged landscape depiction that referenced the land's Jewish provenance and openness to the Zionist gaze. Shlonsky's landscape poems are replete with the idea of the land as a text that should be read expressly in relation to traditional Judaic sources. For example, "Gilboa" (1927) begins: "Behold my land a wild corpse. / her skin like parchment, / parchment for the Torah."[48] The experience of the Palestinian landscape is utterly mediated here not simply by textual reference but by textual experience itself. The problems involved in "reading" this landscape are thematized in the same series:

> Gilboa—it sounds like *remez-drash-sod* [symbolic, homiletic, esoteric].
> And like the dove of the sages, the divine presence is cooing here.
> It is the scent-of-scrolls, or the name of god pronounced,
> from Mapu's vineyard of *melitsot* [poesy].
> But it is also a living clod. And the *p'shat* [literal] of brambles.
> Of the mountain's rust. Of the jackal-howl at night.
> It is the vision's interpretation, in the skittering of herds,
> that a boy from the *akeda* [binding of Isaac] sees the horns of the ram.[49]

The name Gilboa evokes a series of learned connotations: the midrash, the Bible and maskilic literature all unfold in support of the poet's secular sanctification of the mountainous terrain. The poem specifically mentions three of the four stages of traditional hermeneutic interpretation—*p'shat-remez-drash-sod,* meaning "literal, symbolic, homiletic, esoteric." Thus the landscape must be fathomed, interpreted in all these stages. Indeed, its very fertility lies in its ability to be productively read as part of a national allegory. The poem implicitly distinguishes between three forms of exegesis—*remez-drash-sod*—and the *p'shat,* or plain meaning of a text, embodied in the "living clod" and the "brambles." This unadorned version of "the landscape itself" lasts but briefly, two lines split into four neat clauses, piled associatively one on top of the other. Then the poem swerves back into its long interpretative gaze: the landscape is the allegorical rendering of a historical process begun with the biblical binding of Isaac. The landscape is worthy as a poetic object only if it may be understood in relation to a broad historical pattern of Jewish textual discourse.

I read Shlonsky's lines as an ars poetical statement of principles, commensurate to the call for a visual, material poetics described in this chapter's opening discussion of "Tselem." Specifically, the notion of *p'shat shel dardarim*—"the plain meaning of brambles"—proposes a relationship between landscape and language that circumvents the land's figurative, symbolic value and privileges the land itself (and not—as Wallace Stevens would parse it—an idea about the land), elevating the humble bramble as a poetic model. From our vantage point today, it feels like Shlonsky-the-poet never quite succeeded in implementing his own stated tenets and principles. Despite his considerable impact on his contemporaries, his linguistic and formal innovations as a poet, and his tremendous influence as an editor and translator, we need to look to another figure entirely for the truly idolatrous sensibility described in such vivid terms in "Tselem."

Esther Raab's first book, *Kimshonim* (Thistles, 1930), was remarkable on a number of accounts. Born in Palestine, Raab spoke Hungarian and Yiddish at home and studied in both French- and Hebrew-language schools during a period in which Hebrew was emerging as a spoken vernacular. Her relationship to Hebrew differed from that of contemporaries like Shlonsky, for whom Hebrew was originally a language of religious discourse associated with traditional Judaic learning.[50] The qualities of her early work—the lyric's immediate visual brevity on the page; direct treatment of the object, in this case the landscape; the use of convoluted or truncated syntax; the synasthaesic treatment of space, depicted through color and sound—all mark the presence of a unique voice in Hebrew letters, a true imagist poet. A sensitive early review identified these visual qualities in Raab's work: "The picture is not meant to explain or clarify, but to serve as a symbol, a beautiful symbol alone . . . one feels not only the power of sight, but also the power of looking."[51] Raab's poems are not merely visually evocative, they are committed to the "power of looking"—with an emphasis on the progressive quality of the word as well as its implicit self-reflexivity, the interdependence of human subject and the object viewed. Though the poems seek to emulate the world's "thing-like" quality, they in fact also give form to its imperceptible processes. They reveal the space of nature as defined by swarming, noisy change, and disrupt or "jam" the temporal flux of language. While this kind of "jamming" of language may be characteristic of poetry generally, and of the lyric in particular, Roland Barthes identifies its extreme use as essential to the haiku form: a kind of "*flat* language . . . what we might call the 'lamination' of symbols. . . . What is posited is *matte*, and all that one can do with it is scrutinize it."[52] The chief attraction of a matte surface is its opaqueness, its refusal to reflect; it calls attention to itself as an object. This self-reference is at the center of Raab's treatment of the land as modernist icon—not symbolic of some historical narrative, but in and of itself imbued with power.

A pair of landscape poems from *Thistles* will help illustrate these general principles in Raab's work. "Tel Aviv" addresses the building of the city with great ambivalence and in the form of a frustrated lament:

How can I weep when there is no tear,
walking mincing on rebellious feet
upon the sand of your earth—you.
Neither threshing floor nor olive,
spoiled rows
you wring out here,
and cement-stones
on your skinny chest.

Your evenings will still spray a bit
of star-juice or sea-moisture;
I will cling to the edges of your hills at evening
like a parched wailing weed.[53]

The poem features the syntactic, linguistic, and figurative opacity typical of Raab's early work. The poem's first word recalls the beginning of Lamentations, a biblical text driven by the metaphor of Jerusalem as a profligate, impure woman whose "unfaithfulness" leads to her own ruin (Lamentations 1:8). The poem signals a fidelity to the original text, and then proceeds to distort it at every turn. The first line appears to be winnowed from the biblical text: "How [*eykha*] does the city sit solitary, that was full of people, how is she become like a widow, she that was great among the nations" (Lamentations 1:1). The poem's first line shrinks the biblical form *bachu* ("weep," plural) to *eyvkh*—a monosyllabic construction that mimics the inability to weep, the sob caught in the throat; the negative *eyn* becomes *ayin* (same letters with different vocalization). The compacting effect continues, first as grammatical compression—human action relayed passively, in adjectival form—*haloch ve-tafof* (walking mincing)—and then figurative compression, as the city/woman is related synecdochically through her feet. The poem's mid-portion consists of a collage-like interaction of tangible materials, the spoiled threshing floor indicating a failed cultivation of the land. The land's pavement-covered chest provides scant nourishment: only "spoiled rows" of crops survive upon its "skinny chest."[54] The poem embraces the city's rebelliousness as well as its physical meagerness. Though the city is not the "land of milk and honey," the speaker finds solace in the evening's brief spray of moisture—the fantastical "star-juice"—and the dampness of a sea breeze.

After all this opaque difficulty, the poem's concluding couplet does feel like a refreshing breeze, a bracingly clear, straightforward statement of an emergent poetic voice: "I will cling [*edbak*] to the edges of your hills at evening / like a parched wailing weed [*ḥilfa*]." *Edbak* and *ḥilfa* both contain multivalent qualities: the *ḥilfa,* distinguished by its deep, tough roots, usually occurs in the masculine form, whereas Raab has grammatically gendered it feminine.[55] This wild plant representing the poet's voice is also part of the domestic realm, being used to weave floor mats. It "clings" to the city as in Genesis 2:24 a man cleaves to his wife, effectively transferring the intimacy of sexual partnership onto a relation with the land. The three-letter root D-B-K is etymologically related both to the abstract noun *dvekut,* "devotion," and the concrete noun *devek,* "glue." This richness of meaning occurs within the context of the poem's only explicitly metaphorical statement (indicated by the use of the comparative "like") and in lines composed in standard word order, with neither linguistic compression nor syntactic contortion. Is there a correlation between the syntactic transparency of these last two lines and its explicitly figurative language? Conversely, can the syntactic opaqueness of the rest of the poem—and Raab's early verse in general—be linked to a refusal of metaphor, of equivalence, of a one-to-one relationship between symbol and object or, ultimately, of nature representing culture as culture effaces it? Significantly, this figurative and syntactic transparency describes the culmination of the poetic speaker's encounter with the land. Voice, stymied in the first line, is transposed onto the natural world—the weed wails in her stead. "Tel Aviv" does not simply personify the land (others certainly did this); it merges the poet's voice into it. Though other of Raab's poems stress the physical viewpoint of the land itself, "Tel Aviv" traces a transition that blurs the relation between speaking/observing subject and "the land before her."[56] Landscape seems to speak in Raab's work through this compressed erasure of the human subject.

Like "Tel Aviv," the following poem opens with a biblical echo, in this case the "land of milk and honey"; however, the milk of this land is neither produced by, nor for the benefit of, anything but the land itself.

A thistle breached the loam
and spilled out like milk
onto the face of the earth;
and nights the moon laps
saucers of milk swaying
on slender stalks,
and clouds trail their white wake,
dip into the thistle-foam
torrential blossoming,
and masses of green bee-eaters
gargle and go wild
and gorge themselves
upon swarming insects
at the white thistle-saucers.
Screwbeans enveloped thistle
lest the sand be conquered too;
soft, dripping screwbean scent,
and sharp, prickly thistle scent—
embrace one another with devotion
and the expanses of loam filled up
flat with its clods.[57]

The poem seems to allow nature to speak through an associative rendering of color and sound: for example, the color green (*yaROK*) is transmuted into sound as the syllables echo in the bee-eaters (*shRAKRAKim*) and in the insects (*chaRAKim*). (My translation tries to convey this by alliteration with the letter G.) This noisy effect is amplified by a compact grouping of words with tetrameter roots (*shRAKRAKim* [bee-eaters], *yeGARGERu* [gargle], *yeLAHELU* [go wild]), which are alliterative by virtue of their grammatical structure. The poem's difficult syntax and use of multiple verb tenses works to jam the temporal effects of language. This mix of tenses creates a thick density of action, as each incomplete motion is layered upon the next. Though a good deal of motion is described, there is no clear temporal progression to events. Nature is conceived as essentially impervious to narrative design or order—that is, in Shlonsky's terms, the poem rejects the simile, the simple analogy, the *nimshal,* the moral, the "like."

The poem's autoerotic ending, if read in historical context, challenges contemporaneous dictates within Zionist discourse regarding literary depiction of the land—that it be "fertile" and that it allow for national allegory or interpretation. Instead, the weeds turn over the loam, leaving them flat and sated—almost self-composting in today's terms, erotic but not especially productive. And while Raab's work certainly engaged the specifics of her native landscape, her poems were also part of global literary trends, the transnational circulation of modernist tropes—Hebrew imagist "thing-poems" about a bunch of local weeds.

I have used the terms *transparency* and *opaqueness* to describe two kinds of syntax: easy and difficult, or normative and distorted. As suggested earlier, this feature of Raab's work may be compared to cubism's multiperspectival canvas and use of collage. This connection has been noted regarding Anglo-American imagism: "The tension created by . . . syntactic ambiguity can be directly related to the cubist technique of including the ambiguous or contradictory overlapping of planes, or of fusing, or metonymically displacing, the material qualities of objects."[58] For Raab and modern Hebrew poetry, the implications of Jewish imagism within the realm of Hebrew culture in Palestine, during a period when nature was treated as an arena for national allegory, are profound and political: a poetics that works against narration implies a particular attitude toward the landscape and a refusal to recognize nature as subject to human intervention.

As we observed in the discussion of Moses Soyer's painting *The Lover of Books* and in relation to Bialik's and Mandelstam's primal "bookcase" scenes, Jewish writers and artists across the globe were reevaluating and refashioning the status of the book and materiality. Hebrew poetry "afforded" an attention to the image's figurative powers, exploiting an allusive practice that worked against historical reference, and a syntactic structure that thwarted narrative movement. What might Yiddish poetry afford in terms of material form?

YIDDISH *DINGGEDICHTE*: THE POEM AS IDOL AND THE VISIBILITY OF RHYME

The work of Anna Margolin, a loose affiliate of the New York modernist Introspectivist group, exemplifies their call for precision and clarity and their fervent belief in Yiddish "as a poetic instrument." Margolin's first and only volume, *Lider,* feels more expansive than the brief lyrical form characteristic of both Fogel's and Raab's early work; its emotional directness, variety of cosmopolitan scenes, rhythmic inventiveness, and the poignant, robust assertion of a personal voice all exploit the full register of Yiddish's history as a vernacular and its status as what Max Weinreich called a "fusion language"—a language that melds together aspects of several different language systems.[59] This sense of Yiddish as an amalgam, a kind of ready-made object, is at the heart of Margolin's poetic language.[60] Margolin's work is filled with focused descriptions of creation—shaping, sculpting, engraving, and, ultimately, writing itself; this creative impulse is often imagined in spiritual or religious terms. For example, the ars poetical lyric "I didn't know, my love" describes the creation of poems which are at once objects and idolatrous, revelatory renderings of her lover:

> I didn't know, my love [*lIbEr*],
> that with slow, yearning fingers [*fIngEr*]
> I engrave [*kritz*] you into [*ayn*] my poems [*lIdEr*].
> Now they have the hard gloss [*glANTs*]
> of your eyes, the sharp lines
> of your mouth, of your
> stubborn hand [*hANT*].
> The wonder,
> when my own word
> touches me with your hand.[61]

Godlike, Margolin creates her poems in her lover's image. The end product possesses such revelatory power it shocks even its creator, a sentiment perhaps common in ekphrastic depictions. Yet the object provoking this reaction is neither a painting nor a sculpted figure. Rather, the engraved object's seductive power is explicitly located in something fashioned by the poet—her poems.[62] The line endings—*lIbEr, fIngEr, lIdEr, glANTs, hANT*—are fine examples of

Margolin's fractured, assonant rhyme, key to Margolin's material treatment of language. The poem takes advantage of Yiddish's grammatical separation of verb stem and prefix—*kritz* and *ayn* in line 3—treating language as material to be chiseled and crafted; the resultant shape, *kritz,* is an especially "forbidden" object—the Christian cross.

A devotion to a certain kind of poetic language is directly addressed in Margolin's "Beautiful Words of Marble and Gold." The poem's aesthetic preference is clear: a rejection of a conventionally beautiful symbolist lyric that preserves, eternalizes, and "conspires against material reality" in favor of a distinctly modernist version of the self, one that may be understood only as a collage of transparent fragments.[63]

Beautiful words of marble and gold [*gOLD*]
Not you, not you did I want. [*gevOLT*]

In fact, I didn't want these poems.
But others—like fire and an ecstatic storm [*shtURM*]
that suddenly shreds transparent form. [*fURM*]

Too late . . .
I often hear unearthly steps. [*trIT*]
I often think about the last "exit"
and I swear [*shvER*]
by Lasker-Schüler, Rilke, and Baudelaire, [*BodlER*]
I will be mute, not lament.[64]

Rhyme is the ground against which two antithetical poetics are figured, through ironically mismatched rhymes: the neosymbolist couplet describing "beauty" contains an "imperfect" slant rhyme (*gOLD-gevOLT*), while the modernist call for a radical, "ecstatic" form uses a banal version of rich rhyme (*shtURM-fURM*). The poetic triumvirate of Else Lasker-Schüler, Rilke, and Charles Baudelaire is raised to witness an oath of muteness; this deliberate silence is also a declaration of poetic allegiance, a practice flagged, again through rhyme, below the semantic level of the poem. Note the expert interlinguistic end-stopped rhymes: *trIT* with the English "exit" (in English in the original poem) and *shvER* with the proper name "Baudelaire" (*BodlER*), which "nativize" the non-Yiddish words. The Roman orthography of "exit" forces the reader's eye to the end of the line and back in order to read it properly. In both instances, the word pairs—*trIT*/exIT and *shvER*/*BodlER*—have a similar sound but divergent appearances; this gap leads to a dissonance for the reader. Elsewhere subtle differences in sound—as minute as that between a voiced and unvoiced consonant (*gOLD-gevOLT*)—create a kind of visual stutter in which the temporal, linear progression of the poem is obstructed, held in a sort of stasis. Rhyme, conventionally understood as an auditory device, in fact functions in Margolin's poems to bolster their spatial and visual qualities. The fact that *shtUm* (mute) is just a vowel away from *shtIm* (voice) probably did not go unnoticed by Margolin.

Indeed, Margolin's creation of a material language is most visible in her fine handling of rhyme. Rhyme—whether heard as the poem is read or viewed upon the page—focuses attention on poetic language as such, drawing our attention to the poem as a made object. Rhyme was especially a matter of contention for modernist Yiddish poets and a marker of modern Yiddish poetry's rapid stylistic development in the early twentieth century.[65] The Introspectivist poet A. Leyeles addressed his distance from an older generation of poets specifically in terms of rhyme: "In the old, rhymed poetry, rhyme came as something that must come, that the reader was *expecting*. . . . For us—who have adopted free verse as the main mold of poetic creation—rhyme comes not as an expectation but as a surprise. It comes suddenly. A halt in mid-leap."[66] Written in a fusion language, modern Yiddish poetry had a relatively high tolerance for rhyme and drew on vocabulary from different linguistic strata to dramatic effect.

Margolin's correspondence with her lover and literary mentor, Reuben Ayzland, an epistolary debate of cultural and literary matters that was also a courtship of sorts, details her specific stance toward rhyme.[67] A letter dated January 17, 1921 contains a lengthy argument between the two over matters of form, in the guise of what Margolin calls, in English, an "Imaginary Conversation." The substance of the disagreement centers on Margolin's use of "bad rhyme." The remarks may have been provoked by a comment reported to her by Ayzland just a week earlier, when he describes the New York café reception of Margolin's poetic debut, "To Be a Beggarwoman," in the *Fraye arbeter shtime*.[68] Ayzland makes specific mention of Mani Leyb's reaction; he appreciated her "delicate handling and fine language" but not, significantly, the "half rhymes," an issue Margolin then expands upon in her letter of January 17. Delineating the gap between herself-the-reader and Ayzland-the-poet, she notes the latter's admiration of what she calls Mani Leyb's "parve verses," wonderfully punning on the aural and orthographic proximity between *parve* and *fraye* (free).[69] Margolin defends herself against Ayzland's critique of her use of rhyme, and in the process creates a document of tremendous self-awareness and prosodical insight regarding modernist verse. Rhyme is the ground upon which Margolin will stake her aesthetic claims, modeling herself in these letters as a modernist poet who just happens to write in Yiddish.

Here is an excerpt from Margolin and Ayzland's imaginary conversation:

> Reuben: Why do you need rhyme at all? I: You should say as follows: it must be because my material demands it of me. Not to rhyme [*rhymen*]—but to clang together. I need bad rhymes, because good ones I do not want. Don't think I'm making my own shortcomings into a strength. I know: "*shvayg*" goes with "*tsvayg*," "*shtayg*"; "*lebn*" with "*shvebn*" and "*shtrebn*"; "*himl*" with "*driml*." I myself have used them all many times in my own poems.[70]

Yet Margolin prefers a more fragmented kind of rhyme: "Let the third or fourth line only weakly point to the first with the color of a word, with a sound, that is just a shadow, a pale echo . . . *flight-zayd-toyt* is for me a thousand times better than *royt-noyt-broyt*." Likewise, *redn, fekher; laydn, rayfer; shtarbn-leopard.* She concludes her multilingual list of examples with a droll observation: "The *goyim* call it assonance."[71]

Margolin dismisses two kinds of "good" rhyme—rhymes like *rOYT-nOYT-brOYT* (red-need-bread), associated with the socially oriented verse of an earlier generation of Yiddish poets—as well as rhymes characteristic of Di Yunge symbolist moods, for example *hIML-drIML* (heaven-slumber). Instead of this auditory and semantic congruence—what she rejects as "beautiful words of marble and gold"—Margolin prefers a dissonant, momentary, almost accidental "clanging together"—*tsuzAMENklANGEN.* For Margolin, effects of this heightened assonance are simultaneously aural and visual—the "shadow" or "color" of a word, the "echo" created by the repetition of vowels surrounded by what she calls "hostile" consonants. Her almost physical conception of rhyme—where rhyme foregrounds or upsets the passage of the poetic line—is quintessentially modernist. As the final rejoinder about gentile poets suggests, Margolin viewed her own work's assonant rhyme, and its potentially visual or material qualities, as a marker of this international affiliation, a step outside Yiddish's rich but admittedly small corner of modernism.

Margolin's formulation of rhyme in terms of color was actually a common metaphorical usage for modern poetry. In Baudelaire's words: "The only really surprising thing would be that sound could not suggest color."[72] The Futurists also spoke of the "living coloration" of the word created by phonetic combinations, while Potebnja construed "rich" and "poor" rhymes in terms of color. In his seminal article on Hebrew prosody, Benjamin Harshav addresses this idea of "colorful" (or rich) rhyme, in which most of a word's smallest rhyming units ("rhymemes") contribute to the rhyme.[73] The "colorfulness" of rhyme—a kind of overdetermined hyper-rhyme—focuses attention on poetic language as such. This frequent description of rhyme in terms of color also points to another distinction that Harshav draws, between the *retsef* (sequence) and *makom* (place) of the rhymeme.[74] The reader thus experiences rhyme both temporally and spatially.[75]

Margolin's shattered rhyme should be equally understood as a kind of hypersensitivity to Yiddish's own polyphonic lexical resources, its historically rich sound repositories, and the interlinguistic rhyme enabled by Yiddish's status as a fusion language composed of Germanic, Slavic, Hebrew, and Aramaic elements. It is these very qualities that made Yiddish an ideal linguistic medium for expressing a hybrid cultural affiliation. Margolin's letter to Ayzland demonstrates an impatience with his incomprehension or resistance to modernist experimentation with rhyme as well as a kind of envy—gentile poets even have a name for it: assonance. In upsetting rhyme's aural and semantic harmony, Margolin treats the poem as a made object, in the spirit of Rilke's *Dinggedichte* or "thing-poems."

Rhyme animates normally mute items in Margolin's "Today All the Mute Things Speak." The word for "mute" (*shtum*) contains a sense of stillness as well as silence. Like its equivalent in Hebrew, *domem,* it may also allude to a painted still life, conventionally a domestic genre, one "constructed as the lowest category of picture-making."[76] The granting of agency to normally silent objects is characteristic of the still life's power as a genre: "Iin that effacement of human attention, objects reveal their own autonomy: it is as though it is the objects that make the world, and the unconscious force stored in their outwardly humble forms—not their human users."[77] Margolin's "still life" is also a landscape of sorts, and its expressly visual frame is not mute—it "speaks." The poem records the sudden dynamism of objects in a contemplative tone that builds steadily until collapsing in the poem's closing lines:

Today all the mute things speak
Like dew flows
the blue current of slender cloud.
High clever words rustle in the crowns of trees,
of the old, mighty dreamers,
and fall in my heart with each leaf and each star.
And can you hear,
how the sand trembles
under the slow lonely tread of the night?
And fiery and grand,
an ample song
rolls out
from the gray, shadow-ringed stone.
And you, my love, my love,
you are silent.[78]

Mute things speak using a variety of sounds, through slow, continuous actions that appeal synesthetically to several senses at once. Poetry already exists in almost fossilized form within the natural world; it simply seeks the appropriate form of expression. The poem applauds those voices that speak the language of *Dinggedichte* through Margolin's fractured "bad rhyme"—a heightened, internal chain of assonance slinking through the poem, binding it together tightly and lending it a kind of sculptural density. This intense crafting of rhyme also reminds readers that the poem is a made object. Nearly every sound in the poem repeats in some fashion: the vowel sound *OY* occurs seven times in the first five lines, surrounded by varying consonant patterns, creating a noisy, rhythmic effect. Assonance's greatest achievement may be felt in the poem's clusters of internal rhyme, a kind of "halt in mid-leap."[79] Even the more predictable end-stopped rhymes—*aROYS-gROYS* and *shtERN-hERN*—do not close or fix the syntactic unit, but work against the syntactic sense of the poem. Actual processes of aural comprehension ("hearing," "song") are dragged out or manipulated orthographically on the line: the phonemes of *SHTERN* ("star") are broken down visually in the next line: *kenSTu HERN* ("can you hear"). In lines 8–9, the sand trembles and is broken apart by the night's steps, wavering from *ZAMd* ("sand") to *eynZAMe lanG-ZAMe* ("lonely, slow") before being transformed into a *geZANG* ("song"). This "song" actually rolls out at the end of three short lines. After the dizzying amount of internal rhyme in the poem as a whole, the dominant rhyme of these last two lines (the repetition of *MAYN LIBER*) comes as a kind of prosodic full stop.

The image of a song rolling out from a gray stone in the face of her lover's silence resembles the bitter soliloquy delivered in Margolin's "Epitaph," in which the poet continues to speak after death, instructing graveside visitor and reader alike in the ways of memory: "Tell that until death / she faithfully guarded with pure hands / the fire that was entrusted to her, and in the selfsame fire she burned."[80] The gravestone's textual inscription represents a radically material version of language, one that shatters any easy distinction between text and its physical form. The elegiac tone pervades the work of Margolin's poetic contemporaries, who mourn homes left behind in eastern Europe and sense the imminent decline of Yiddish's centrality as a language of Jewish cultural expression.

CHARLES REZNIKOFF'S OBJECTIVISM: "CHIEFLY JEWISH, AMERICAN, URBAN"

Rooted among roofs, their smoke among the clouds, factory
chimneys—our cedars of Lebanon.
—Charles Reznikoff, *Jerusalem the Golden* (1934)

Materials of the world at hand, as found: *words* as materials.
—Charles Bernstein, "Reznikoff's Nearness" (1999)

Charles Reznikoff's English-language "Objectivist" poetics were shaped, in part, by a view of Hebrew as a material artifact. While my claims thus far regarding the materiality of language in Hebrew and Yiddish poetry's have relied on their iconic tie to sacred texts, Reznikoff's work—especially *Jerusalem the Golden*—provides an instructive counterpoint: without the direct iconic reference, how is the materiality of language experienced? Ruth Wisse begins *A Little Love in Big Manhattan,* her study of American Yiddish modernist poetry, by referencing a scene from Reznikoff's fictional autobiography in which the poet's mother berates his father for reading a Yiddish newspaper.[81] In Reznikoff's telling, an English-language newspaper gradually replaces the Yiddish, the exchange alluding to the eventual ascendance of English as the language of choice for American Jewish writers. In another retrospective account, Ruth Whitman, a poet and translator of Yiddish poetry, remembers an evening in the early 1970s, a public reading of Jewish poets in New York City: "The place was crowded with poets—Cynthia Ozick, Harvey Shapiro, Kadya Molodovsky, and many more. . . . Charles Reznikoff came up to me . . . and asked me if I would like to exchange books."[82] In both of these accounts, Reznikoff appears to occupy the edges of a history of American Jewish writing whose complicated origins story concerns the demise of Yiddish and the eventual triumph of English as the lingua franca of American Jewish cultural expression. Reznikoff defined, belatedly, his own poetic project as "chiefly Jewish, American, urban."[83] His critical elevation as an "Objectivist"—by both his contemporary Louis Zukofsky and later generations of American poet-scholars—represents a significant station in modernist Jewish writing and an important presence for this study's transnational claims. How does Reznikoff's English-language "Objectivism" relate to my claims for material form in Hebrew and Yiddish?

A number of scholars have sought to locate Reznikoff's oeuvre in relation to both Yiddish *and* Hebrew—not in a pragmatic sense, as functional literary vernaculars, but as exemplary models for poetic practice. Most notably, Stephen Fredman's work has persuasively articulated the meaning of Hebrew in Reznikoff's work; according to Fredman, Hebrew, which Reznikoff apparently learned only in his thirties, informs his work as a kind of exemplary "road not taken."[84] This view is expressly announced in the opening poem from *Jerusalem the Golden*:

The Hebrew of your poets, Zion
is like oil upon a burn,
cool as oil;

after work,
the smell in the street at night
of the hedge in flower.
Like Solomon,
I have married and married the speech of strangers;
none are like you, Shulamite.[85]

The poetic speaker revels in his command of a new mother tongue—"the speech of strangers"—while noting the affective and spiritual qualities of Hebrew: a sensual balm that soothes, itself embedded in the landscape of antiquity, alluded to in the figure of Shulamite from the Song of Songs.

Reznikoff's poems contain other moments of ambivalent recognition of Hebrew's classical cache. Note the resemblance of his poem "Hellenist" to Saul Tchernichovsky's primal encounter with Apollo's statue:

As I, barbarian, at last, although slowly, could read Greek,
at "blue-eyed Athena"
I greeted her picture that had long been on the wall:
the head slightly bent forward under the heavy helmet,
as if to listen; the beautiful lips slightly scornful.[86]

The speaker's self-ascribed status as a "barbarian" stems from his Jewish identity, specifically the perceived cultural opposition between Greek civilization and the rabbinic culture of late antiquity, which Reznikoff would have understood as "Hebrew." Louis Zukofsky's reading of "Hellenist" is the pretext for his influential "Sincerity and Objectification: With Special Reference to the Work of Charles Reznikoff" (1931) a short, notably unprogrammatic document that has nonetheless been viewed as a statement of principles, a manifesto of sorts, in which he remarks upon the poem's halting syntax, the "purposeful crudity of the first line."[87]

This description of the poem's "objectness" resembles the deliberately awkward syntax we have observed in Raab and Fogel. Reznikoff's own retrospective definition of the term is only marginally more helpful: "'Objectivist'; images clear but the meaning not stated but suggested by the objective details and the music of the verse; words pithy and plain; without the artifice of regular meters; themes, chiefly Jewish, American, urban."[88] This elevation of plainspoken precision explains why some have suggested considering Reznikoff a "Yiddish poet writing in the American language."[89] Here is an example that partakes of the urban pastoral vein so richly mined by his Yiddish contemporaries:

In steel clouds
to the sound of thunder
like the ancient gods:

our sky, cement;
the earth, cement;
our trees, steel;
instead of sunshine,
a light that has no twilight,
neither morning nor evening,
only noon.
Coming up the subway stairs, I thought the moon
only another street-light—
a little crooked.[90]

The sardonic point of view, with its mix of sacred and profane, calls to mind the voice of the Yiddish poet Moshe Leyb Halpern; in Halpern's book-length poem series *In New York* (1919), the speaker is an anguished new immigrant, far from home and on foreign soil, who also revels in Manhattan's modernity and takes pride in the relative sparseness of his surroundings, sarcastically referred to as "our garden," with its lone tree, "bare but for seven leaves."

Alternatively, Fredman notes the resemblance between Reznikoff's elevation of precise diction and biblical Hebrew's "condensation and terseness."[91] Indeed, while we may note the dominant presence of Jewish figures within the loosely defined cohort of Objectivists—Zukofsky, Reznikoff, George Oppen (and—perhaps—even the tentative affiliation of Gertrude Stein)—the express connection between their Jewishness and their poetics remains elusive, at best, as do their particular ars poetical tenets.[92] The vagueness of it all is summed up in an authoritative critical anthology on the subject: "Although 'Objectivist' as a term has some clear meanings, it is nevertheless unstable. . . . There may be a shared vocabulary, but its applications and gloss differ from writer to writer. In short, the term 'Objectivist' has situated meanings, not an absolute one."[93]

One such "situated meaning" was surely the lingering effects of childhood in a multilingual setting. While Reznikoff himself acknowledges the example of contemporaneous developments in American verse, he also clearly rebuts the notion of "influence" per se, offering a more expansive sense of how a poetic sensibility emerges from a particular milieu: "I do not believe writers are *merely* influenced by others. . . . There must be a fertile soil to begin with for ideas to grow and flourish."[94] What was the soil that fertilized his English-language lyrics, biblically infused, imagist, Objectivist? An attention to language as something malleable and fungible, intuitively drawn from his multilingual childhood, shaped by contemporary currents in American writing and his own increasingly sensitive ear to the importance of concrete "testimony" in legal discourse, a genre that began to preoccupy him in the interwar period.[95] The poet's own sense of his fraught relation to Hebrew is conveyed in the following short lyrics:

> How difficult for me is Hebrew:
> even the Hebrew for *mother,* for *bread,* for *sun*
> is foreign. How far have I been exiled, Zion.
>
> I have learnt the Hebrew blessing before eating bread;
> is there no blessing before reading Hebrew?[96]

In Fredman's reading of these lines, "Hebrew is portrayed . . . by Reznikoff as so material that it requires a blessing before being employed. . . . [He] presents Hebrew as the language in which the material world is said to be sacred."[97] The "materiality" of Hebrew in Reznikoff's work both resembles and is distinct from the treatment of poetic language by Hebrew and Yiddish poets discussed in this chapter. Unlike Fogel's attempts to desacralize Hebrew, Reznikoff's distance from the language is profound and productive; Hebrew exists as a kind of ideal language, something to pine for and aspire to: its absence is felt as a kind of formative shadow, much like the source language in Walter Benjamin's evocative meditations in "The Task of the Translator." For Benjamin, the translation necessarily contains an "echo of the original": "A real translation is transparent; it does not cover the original, does not block its light, but allows the pure language, as though reinforced by its own medium, to shine upon the original all the more fully."[98]

In formal terms, Reznikoff's short lyrics approximate the distinctive features of Fogel's and Raab's work, particularly that of sequencing and juxtaposition. The poems of *Jerusalem the Golden* resemble Fogel's use of compact imagery, seriality, sequence, adjacency, and the preference for detail or fragment over the whole. Charles Bernstein describes the meaning of these features in his beautiful and delicate exploration, "Reznikoff's Nearness." Bernstein's essay itself is a series of increasingly complex propositions about Reznikoff's poetics, especially his signature sequencing of short, fragment-like poems, which Bernstein calls "cubo-serialism."[99] Other affinities with Fogel's work abound: like Fogel's poems in *Before the Dark Gate,* the poems of *Jerusalem the Golden* work adjacently, in paratactic fashion—side by side, like "chiefly Jewish, American, urban"—what Bernstein calls a poetics of "adjacency" or "nearness." The poems "share thematic connections, with subject clusters connected by family resemblances."[100] Finally, Bernstein describes Reznikoff's work in terms similar to those I used to underscore the visual, material features of Hebrew imagist poetry: the description of "cubo-serialism" resembles Raab's cubist syntax. In addition, the emphasis on surface at the expense of allegorical depth, observed in relation to Fogel's poetry, also characterizes Reznikoff's work: according to Bernstein,

"Reznikoff rejected the 'depth' of field. . . . By constantly intercutting, or jump cutting, between and among and within material, the poem's surface of local particularities gains primacy, in contrast to the rhetorical depth of narrative closure that is aimed for in such 'epic' montage formats as 'The Waste Land.'"[101] These materialist features common to imagist poetry globally are filtered here through the presence, though not the actual use, of Hebrew. Charles Hatlen argues that this "collage poetics" allowed Reznikoff, and perhaps other of his Objectivist peers, to explore "what it means to be simultaneously a Jew, the child of immigrant parents, and an American."[102]

Paramount in Reznikoff's mythology of self as a poet is an event that Fredman refers to as his "primal scene of poetry": the burning of his grandfather Ezekiel's manuscript of Hebrew poetry.[103] Reznikoff's grandmother destroyed the poems because she believed they could be viewed with suspicion by the tsarist authorities and thus endanger the family. The scene is recounted in fictionalized form in *By the Waters of Manhattan* (1930), in verse in "Early History of a Writer" (1969), and as a kind of talisman throughout Reznikoff's work:

> My grandfather, dead long before I was born,
> died among strangers; and all the verse he wrote
> was lost—
> except for what
> still speaks through me
> as mine.[104]

Mutlilingualism, and the possibility of translation, is implicit in this poetic ventriloquy; some spectral remnant of the grandfather's verse "still speaks through me / as mine."

Another "situated meaning" for Reznikoff consists of his sensitivity to print and the book as a made object. Reznikoff often printed first editions of his books; in a March 1927 letter to a friend and colleague, Albert Lewin, he reports: "I bought a press (worked by a treadle) in January and had it set up in our basement. I have printed (the blackest ink on glaring white paper) almost 32 pages of [my collected works,] a book of verse and plays (to run about 200 pages). I just blunder along."[105] For the young poet, this process circumvented conventional avenues of publication; the limited editions were an attempt to resist commodification of his art, and demanded an intense, almost meditative encounter with the physical processes of production.[106]

> Later, when I was to have much time and little money,
> I learnt how to print;
> indeed, setting type by hand and running a platen-press by foot

is not too hard:
the great wheel turning, the rollers moving down over the sticky black platen,
shining arms sliding smoothly into their grooves
and the type closing on the blank paper—
to leave a printed sheet.
I would stop the wheel at each revolution,
unable to feed the press as a printer could
but, slow as I was, I would print four hundred sheets in a couple of hours—
more than enough.[107]

The production of poetry is presented here as a physical process in which the poet's body (hand and foot) becomes enmeshed in the body of the machine press (its "shining arms"), a demanding and exacting set of activities that is nonetheless satisfying. This "more than enough" was an express rebuke to those magazine editors who had rebuffed the poet, asking him to revise his work: "Publication in a magazine, pleasant as it would be, / seemed less important than perfection."[108]

These "little" magazines are the subject of the following chapter: indeed, they did not strive for "perfection," but they were devoted to literature's material presence, exploring the potential of newly emergent secular genres and offering creative variations on the text-image relationship.

Chapter 2 The Little Magazine: From Font to Network

> Every synagogue always had a small library. The cases hold some of the oldest editions of the Talmud and other religious texts, each with front-pieces, decorative devices, and tailpieces. These few pages fulfilled the same function in their time as illustrated journals do in our own day: they familiarized everyone with the art trends of the period.
> —El Lissitzky, "The Mohilev Synagogue: Reminiscences," *Milgroym-Rimon* (1923)

> A bridge, four walls, and a rafter for the lone and homeless poets as they roam through foreign lands to the many centers of the Jewish people's extraterritoriality. Literary diffusion.
> —Uri Tsvi Greenberg, "Proclamation," *Albatros* (1922)

In the years following the impromptu ethnographic field trip that was the subject of El Lissitzky's above-quoted "reminiscences," his companion, Issachar Ber Ryback, published *Aleph Beit* (1917) in *Albatros,* an oversized Yiddish journal published first in Warsaw, then in Berlin, and notable for its avant-garde aesthetics and the exhortatory manifestos of its colorful, erstwhile editor, the young Uri Tsvi Greenberg.[1] All three would become central figures in a transnational

Issachar Ber Ryback, *Aleph Beit*, 1917, Oil on Canvas. The Ryback Collection, Courtesy of The Bat Yam Museum for Contemporary Art, Reproduction: Elad Sarig.

explosion of Jewish cultural creativity: El Lazar [Eleazar]) Markovitch (1890–1941), born in Smolensk, Russia, began as a printmaker and designer of Yiddish children's books and went on to create some of modernism's enduring designs; Ryback (1897–1935), a painter and sculptor from Ukraine, meshed iconic Jewish forms with Jugendstil and cubist motifs; and Greenberg (1896–1981), a Galician-born poet and provocateur, went on to become a member of the Israeli Knesset.[2] The tromp-l'oeil collage of geometric shapes and ritual objects treats the Hebrew alphabet as a set of iconic forms, thereby exemplifying El Lissitzky's provocative comparison between the material features of the Talmud and contemporaneous art journals: here, the painting insists, is a particularly Jewish style in an assertively modern idiom. This, it announces to readers, is what's happening in our own day.

Indeed, these journals, often referred to as "little magazines," were a staple of modernist culture—an arena in which artists and writers exchanged new work and debated ideas across national borders and international time zones. The condition of Yiddish writing within this not-entirely-utopian flow of ideas and images is exemplified in an anecdote about the editors—Yankev Glatshteyn, Aaron Leyeles, and Nachum Minkov—of the New York–based journal *Inzikh;* compared to other journals of the day, *Inzikh* was relatively long-lived, publishing in the same city, albeit not always regularly, from 1919 to 1939. Harriet Monroe, the editor of the renowned journal *Poetry* in Chicago, received a copy of the young Yiddish literary entrepreneurs' inaugural issue: she replied thanking them for their journal and asking if it was in Chinese.[3] This exchange reveals a few things about the little magazine's meaning as a genre: its reliance on circulation and audience; the necessity of a cosmopolitan, urban setting for production; the existence of an editorial cabal signaling the collaborative nature of the endeavor; and—in the particular instance of Hebrew and Yiddish little magazines—the iconic, material quality of the Hebrew alphabet as a formative building block that, as evidenced by Monroe's reaction, variously shaped the experience of readers. Moreover, the very materiality that stymied non-Yiddish readers—typography—others heralded as a marker of avant-garde expression. Finally, the meaning of Yiddish as a language of literary expression extended beyond the pragmatics of readership, especially when readers were themselves often multilingual. As suggested in this chapter's second epigraph, the little magazine was a protective yet mobile abode, signaling an attachment, even devotion, to a particular form of secular culture stretching across physical borders and landscapes.

The contemporary reader's encounter with the little magazine of the interwar period is more often than not a virtual experience, mediated by the screen and various archival and digital technologies (known, or derided, by some as "booksquashing"). Within the broad arena of Yiddish little magazines of the interwar period, I have limited my discussion to volumes that I have been able to access and handle, often in restricted library settings.[4] Given their relatively brief publication spans and peripatetic nature—editorial centers were often moved between cities—very little detail remains regarding the material conditions of their production. Most seem to have been printed in relatively small print runs—between five hundred and two thousand copies at most. The quality of production is also uneven: some are lavishly printed on fine paper, while others are more crudely produced on thin cardboard stock that today crumbles at a touch. The journals' material and visual distinctiveness cohered in an amalgam of features, including their signature manifestos, cover design, typography, and other visual components such as woodcuts and linocuts, tables of contents, and advertisements.

Like other genres, the little magazine's hybrid nature emerged from specific historical conditions. Yiddish interwar émigré culture was part of the transnational explosion of artistic production in this period, following and largely spurred by the utopian promise of the 1917 Russian Revolution.[5] After World War I, émigré writers and artists moved frequently, if not always easily, within Europe, and from Europe to the United States, Asia, and Latin America. Little magazines—their production, circulation and consumption—are symptomatic of the mobility and the crossing of national borders of this period, especially for Yiddish journals; Yiddish was the lingua franca of clusters of young Jewish avant-garde artists and writers, themselves part of the orbit of emergent ethnic and national configurations in eastern Europe. The journals were in some sense symbols of their peripatetic movements; at the same time, they may also be understood as a temporary refuge of sorts—a "bridge, four walls, and a beam"—within the broader condition of Jewish "extraterritoriality"—the condition of living between different geographic settings.

Scholarship on modernist magazines notes how specific historical pressures on clusters of individuals promoted the little magazine's discursive uniqueness.[6] Cultural historian Raymond Williams describes what he calls "formations," groups offering a platform for collective cultural production that resembled early modern guilds, movements, and schools. In Williams's terms, "Among the relatively or wholly informal groups and associations, the rapidity of formation and dissolution, the complexity of internal breaks and of fusions, can seem quite bewildering."[7] These groups formed (and re-formed) around personal relationships and a common ideological or aesthetic program and—in the case of the cosmopolitan avant-garde—were especially characterized by what Williams calls "paranational" features: "a high proportion of contributors to avant-garde movements were immigrants to . . . a metropolis, not only from outlying national regions but from other and smaller national cultures, now often seen as culturally provincial in relation to the metropolis." Indeed, metropolitan settings, with their "concentration of wealth and the internal pluralism of

Archival remainders. *Khalyastre* 1 (Warsaw, 1922). Courtesy of the Library of the YIVO Institute for Jewish Research.

Khalyastre 2 (Paris, 1924), cover by Marc Chagall. © 2020 Artists Rights Society (ARS), New York / ADAGP, Paris. Courtesy of the Library of the YIVO Institute for Jewish Research.

metropolitan-immigrant functions," increasingly created conditions supportive of avant-garde, even "dissident" groups.[8]

Williams's description aptly describes the conditions surrounding the creation of the numerous Yiddish little magazines in the interwar period published in cities like Kiev, Lodz, Warsaw, and Berlin.[9] These journals were usually short-lived affairs, lasting only a few issues, collaboratively produced and published in runs of a couple of thousand or fewer, whether due to financial restraints, the peripatetic nature of their émigré editors, arguments over content and ideology or, perhaps, differences in personal temperament.[10] While largely written in Yiddish, they also used other languages such as Polish, English, Russian, and German for their iconic features as well as in advertisements and basic information on the masthead (place and frequency of publication, price, address of editorial office, and so on); in such, they assumed a comfortably multilingual audience.

A significant number of these journals were conceptualized and produced by an evolving but relatively stable cast of characters. They were known as the Khalyastre (the Band or the Gang), a group of artists, editors, and writers who collaborated on a series of journals in eastern Europe, moving steadily west out of Lodz and Warsaw to Berlin and Paris: *Yung-Yiddish* in Lodz (1919–20), *Ringen* in Warsaw (1921–22), *Khalyastre* in Warsaw (1922) and in Paris (1924), and *Albatros* in Warsaw (1922) and in Berlin (1923).[11] The group was itinerant at its core; that is, even when centered in Poland, the Khalyastre group's main proponents were from elsewhere.[12] Like their Dadaist and surrealist peers, these Yiddish platforms operating in the wake of World War I expressed a kind of disgust for settled notions of culture and aesthetic form; they viewed themselves as the avant-garde of modern, more age-appropriate visual and literary expression, one that had little patience for the existing order of things and a great desire to provoke and antagonize. The little magazine, often cheaply and quickly produced, provided an ideal vehicle for Jewish culture's relatively homegrown, early twentieth-century version of *épater la bourgeoisie.*

As a group, the Yiddish journals set a high bar for design and typography, published leading writers of the day, and served as important platforms for the visual arts, featuring figures such as Henryk Berlewi (1894–1967) and Marc Chagall (1887–1985). Each journal also projected, or aspired to promulgate, a prescriptive worldview in the form of a manifesto, an ostensibly coherent set of principles formulated in a contemporary, often political, idiom.[13] Each individual issue existed within a series, however short-lived, and was thus a unique metonymic marker of an extended project. The word *magazine* itself suggests something of the genre's material affordances: from the late sixteenth-century

French *magasin* (warehouse, storage) and the Italian cognate *magazzino,* the word originally stems from the Arabic *makasin,* plural of *maksan* (storeroom); like the Hebrew *machsan,* the term indicates a space in which a collection of items is stored together. This sense of the magazine as a container foregrounds its status as a made object whose form coheres in the gathering of a series of related artifacts: poems, essays, illustrations, front and back covers, and so on. Something more than a "miscellany," however, the magazine's contents were carefully curated to reflect the principled tastes and preferences of the editors.

The magazine was also intended from the start as a traveling object, an item that could be sold and circulated, moving from the location of its publication to subscribers and other readers in libraries, shops, and the like. Its existence as a kind of synchronic node—marking a connection among a particular coterie with a shared sensibility—is complicated by this mobility, its diachronic stretch across space and time and across different modalities of production and ownership. While these conditions also hold for the relation between books and readers more generally, the little magazine's "power derives from the fact that the form could circulate better than any individual title."[14] The singularity of the little magazine as a genre is thus determined, in part, by its mobility. Information about distribution and audience would no doubt give us a more concrete sense of this mobility. However, recovery of these details is no easy task. Indeed, generally speaking, as noted by the editors of *The Oxford Critical and Cultural History of Modernist Magazines,* a massive collection of essays covering every nook and cranny of the field, "the question of who reads these publications—essentially niche products with, most frequently, low print runs and short life-spans of a year or so—hovers over the study of small magazines."[15] Distribution—whether through subscription or various settings (for example, newsstands, bookstores, and schools)—could offer an indication of readership, but it feels largely like guessing in the absence of actual financial or other records. Indeed, what holds for little magazines generally might especially pertain to the Yiddish little magazine: "Distribution seemed . . . to depend on the more conventional methods of booksellers or the post office, but information on the actual composition of readerships is very sparse."[16] Given the destruction of Jewish archives and other institutions of record during the Shoah, the odds of entirely retrieving these details are relatively remote.[17]

Social and political institutions that generally promoted cultural activities in schools and other public settings were among the key early supporters of Yiddish little magazines. For example, the Kultur-Lige (Culture League), the name for Yiddish institutions founded in eastern Europe beginning in Kiev in 1918, received support from the Ukrainian authorities and later was subsidized

Milgroym (Berlin, 1922). Courtesy of the Library of the YIVO Institute for Jewish Research.

by the Soviet state. The Kultur-Lige was responsible for the publication of numerous Yiddish books; however, by the mid-1920s, local branches had largely lost their independent focus and instead became "appendages of Soviet bureaucratic organs directed by Jewish communists."[18] The small pressruns typical of these journals also allowed for more idiosyncratic and personal forms of funding. For example, some little magazines depended on the relative largess of their editors; the artist Marcel Janco had enough money from his work as a graphic artist and architect to finance the Romanian constructivist magazine *Contimporanul.*[19] The Berlin magazine *Pomegranate*—published in oversized format in both Yiddish (*Milgroym*) and Hebrew (*Rimon*)—seems to have been financed by the personal fortunes of its editors, and benefited from the inflationary conditions of the German mark.[20] *Milgroym/Rimon* was part of the vibrant Hebrew print culture that flourished in Weimar Germany, where publishers such as Shlomo Saltzman, writers like Bialik and S. Y. Agnon, alongside artists such as Joseph Budko, and scholars including Mark Wischnitzer and Rachel Wischnitzer Bernstein, the editors of *Milgroym/Rimon,* produced books of aesthetic excellence and enduring design.[21]

More typical of the era's scale of publishing is the following anecdote about the New York journal *Shriftn:* "One volume of *Shriftn* was put out on the

Shriftn (New York, fall 1919). Courtesy of the Library of the YIVO Institute for Jewish Research.

strength of a $75 contribution from Joseph Opatoshu and a gold chain pawned by Mani Leyb. [David] Ignatoff [an editor] intended to send 200 of 500 copies overseas, to Poland. A local bookseller bought up the whole edition for $140, leaving the contributors with a debt of about the same amount they still owed the printer."[22] Further cryptic details regarding the material conditions of *Yung-Yiddish*'s production, financed by a wealthy Lodz businessman, are hinted at by Seth Wolitz and other scholars: Wolitz says *Yung-Yiddish* was printed on packing paper, and Marek Bartelik names the journal's patron (Max Szydlowski), noting that archival copies of *Yung-Yiddish* from Warsaw's Jewish Historical Institute "are printed on the back of pages from a book on Egyptian art."[23]

Part of the difficulty of *placing* these journals, of locating them in terra firma, a specific geographic location, has to do with their multi-authored nature and the movements of their artists and writers in and out of places, in and out of editorial configurations.[24] Indeed, they refuse to be placed; my method here—less an argument that limits, more a set of descriptions that reveals—is meant to place them through their material features. This lateral juxtaposition of its constituent parts, such as manifestos, cover art, and design, will make visible the Yiddish little magazine's uniqueness as a literary artifact.

MANIFESTOS AND THE LANGUAGE OF LITERARY DIFFUSION

The modernist manifesto is practically a genre unto itself. Like the Introspectivist and imagist manifestos, they can be prescriptive, even didactic, in tone. The rhetoric of manifestos from Yiddish interwar little magazines is declamatory and hyperbolic, in keeping with the volatile spirit of the age. Encountering these documents written a century ago is to enter a world that seems to be both at the end of an era and on the brink of a new one—at the end of something familiar and on the edge of something unknown. The devastating effects of the war and its aftermath shape the language and sentiment in these documents: the angst and the struggle, a felt need to flex some sense of agency after so many years of being the victims of violence and upheaval. The artistic desire to give form to chaos informs these manifestos, which display a sense of exhilaration and opportunity mixed with a little bit of fear: the old structures and ideals have been destroyed, blown to smithereens, and nothing has yet emerged to replace them. In the words of the famous concluding refrain of *The Waste Land*—"These fragments I shore against my ruins." In addition to their language of crisis, struggle, excess, and hyperbole, these manifestos share an attention to form, especially an awareness of traditional modes of expression and their withering or fading accompanied by an anticipatory sense of something new (a form, an expression, an era) that is yet to unfold, or is unfolding *right now.* Their authors imagine themselves as members of an expressionist avant-garde, the anticipatory ones who clearly see what of the past can be recycled, how it should be refashioned, and maybe even offer a glimpse of what will emerge.[25] For example, Jankel Adler's "Expressionism (Fragments from a Lecture)," opens with this plaintive yet robust lament:

> We are the children of the twentieth century. Our lullabies were drowned by the noise of the street. We spent our childhood in brick houses of [a] great city similar to army barracks. . . .
>
> We, the young, have quite lost the relationship to God of our fathers. . . . In our hearts we are weighed down with the burden of a great, great longing for God and eternity, for the power that made Creation happen, for Logos.
>
> The art of the twentieth century, Expressionist art, was born from this longing and it is the seventh day and the week of the commonplace is over.[26]

The expressionist drive may have supplanted the theological spirit, yet the manifesto retains the language of sacred and secular, describing the advent of a new "seventh day," a creative surge that will end the long "week of the commonplace."

Adler hailed from Lodz and together with Moyshe Broderzon (1890–1956) was a founding member of *Yung-Yiddish;* he was broadly involved in expressionist circles and his work was later included by the Nazis in "degenerate" art exhibits in 1933 and 1937. The paradoxical sense of both loss and possibility in Adler's manifesto marks the work of many of his contemporaries and fellow travelers, as does his blending of sacred and secular references. Religious or spiritual motifs were common in postwar expressionist circles as artists struggled to find new meaning in "age-old materials."[27] In his 1921 "The Struggle for a New Form," the prominent typographer and graphic artist Henryk Berlewi (1894–1967) uses the language of crisis as well as biblical tropes to describe the enormity of the creative task ahead: "We lack the ground under our feet; tradition has disappeared. We are left as if after an earthquake, or a violent storm, and we are forced to take up building anew. . . . We are as naked as Adam. . . . Thus we confront a great task: to create a new world, a world of forms." Notably, for Berlewi, the process is also potentially hampered by an attachment to tradition: "If only we would break off completely! We get entangled in the remains of the heritage of old forms." Ultimately, however, the artist needs to "approach the divine source of all forms," a claim that gives credence to my broader concern in this book regarding the presence of sacred traces in secular forms.[28]

Berlewi's influence came to define Yiddish modernism's visual profile, and he eventually became a major figure in constructivist art throughout Europe.[29] His views on form and contemporary art are an important frame for the distinctiveness of modern Jewish cultural expression—its sources as well as its future paths. In a review essay in 1922, Berlewi identifies two competing trends in contemporary Russian art—Western influences from France like cubism, Cézannism, and Futurism, on the one hand, and more local, "primitive," even mystical influences of the icon, *lubok* (a Russian print with scenes from literature or folklore), and hand-painted signs.[30] According to Berlewi, only Chagall, a Jewish artist, has effectively integrated the two:

> He is perhaps the only artist who has successfully brought together two entirely different artistic worlds. The formal elements that compose his works emerge clearly: Russian *luboks*, old Jewish murals and Cubism. But due to his transnationalism . . . he has succeeded in raising himself above formal particularism. In his own metaphysical universe, he has transformed two supposedly disparate worlds into a powerful, harmonious, ringing chorus—oriental exoticism with all its mystical content and strict European monumental Cubism. I reiterate: Chagall is unique in this respect.[31]

Regardless of the accuracy of this account of Chagall's uniqueness, Berlewi's synthetic description aptly assesses the visual character of these journals. He notes that this quality—due in part to what he calls Chagall's "transnationalism"—may also be related to the old canard about Jewish hostility to visual arts: "Their versatility—let's call it the 'encyclopedic nature' of their art—which probably draws as much from a specific Jewish spirit as from the lack of a well-established artistic tradition is immensely great."[32] Berlewi's view here of the field of Jewish art—an empty arena in which "versatility" may thus emerge—approaches the comments of his contemporary Franz Kafka; in an oft-quoted journal entry, Kafka lauded the potential achievements of "small literatures," linguistic traditions that, in his view, lacked a singular, overbearing presence—a Goethe or a Shakespeare—that might inhibit creativity. What appeared to be a deficit was actually an advantage of sorts, in that it allowed for greater diversity and, in Kafka's terms, more "liveliness."[33] In both settings—German Jewish writers in Prague, Polish Yiddish artists in Warsaw—Jews are an ethnic minority who are also part of a privileged cultural center, an "insider-outsider" status that allows for a unique view of social change.

These manifestos called for new art forms in language that was itself new. Two essays by Lissitzky and Perets Markish appeared in 1922 in the final issue of the landmark Warsaw little magazine *Ringen*—whose publication was, according to the critic and historian Yankev Shatzky, "a serious event in Jewish artistic life."[34] The fact that this dramatic assessment was formulated and delivered not from some position of historical hindsight but in the moment—published in the Polish-language Warsaw daily *Nasz Kurier*—only underlines the visibility of these little magazines. In "Overcoming Art," Lissitzky insisted that art must be both more pragmatic *and* more creative, and abide by the expressionist elevation of invention: "The engineer discovers, he creates the new in nature; the artist, by contrast, creates only that which already exists."[35] Lissitzky also includes here the concept of the "Proun," an acronym for the Russian "Project for the Affirmation of the New," which will inspire his eponymous series of abstract works beginning in 1919: "Proun does not compose; it constructs. This is a fundamental contrast to the image."[36] The claim that art should be both revolutionary and functional circulated in the halls of the Vitebsk Art Academy, founded by a short-lived collective including Lissitzky, Chagall, and Vladimir Malevich.[37] The distinction also hints at the eventual disavowal of folk motifs and natural forms (art nouveau) in favor of the more technologically inspired frames of constructivism and Futurism.

"The Aesthetics of Struggle in Modern Poetry" by Perets Markish (1895–1952) is a veritable avalanche of words, a juggernaut of opaque formulations hailing the tumultuous emergence of new artistic expression and the violent overthrow of old forms.[38] The stormy Markish was a central figure in eastern European Jewish literary expression, moving between Kiev, Berlin, and Warsaw and collaborating with other writers and artists in various journals and editions of his work.[39] As Seth Wolitz notes, "A profusion of Hebrew-derived words assaulted the reader, along with neologisms of yoked words and substantives made adjectives and vice versa."[40] The poet's equally dense opening statement from *Khalyastre* 1 (1922) draws on images of the biblical flood and the Tower of Babel; the text's overwrought language seems to mimic a violent, destructive flood. Karolina Szymaniak's reading deftly catalogues Markish's devotion to a new cataclysmic sense of language, an age-appropriate tool to describe the horrors of the postwar period.[41] The untitled text appears on *Khalyastre*'s first page, effectively making it a manifesto for what follows. It concludes thus:

> How crazy and insane is the horrific path of humanity itself.
> This is the language of dispersion in the shattered tower of our brain. This is our song.[42]

In addition to its biblical significance, the figure of the crumbling tower, especially in relation to the anatomical imagery of the text's opening images, seems also a specifically male expression of the postwar condition, part and parcel of the crisis of masculinity in Germany and Great Britain described by George Mosse and others.[43] Indeed, unlike their American counterparts, where women editors were often "midwives" of little magazines, Yiddish little magazines were largely the product of male editorial boards, a condition memorialized in photographs of the period that feature (mostly) male authors, mooning with pained expressions and their arms draped around one another in bored sympathy.[44] While scholarly critiques of the discursive uses of Jewish masculinity in this period have typically targeted Hebrew-Zionist culture, it appears that Yiddish writing too deployed images that call for a gendered reading of its language of catastrophe.

The appearance of Uri Tsvi Greenberg's concrete poem "Uri Tsvi farn tseylem" in the journal *Albatros* was both influential and, ultimately, controversial. Following publication of the cross-shaped poem, Greenberg—accused by the Polish authorities of "contempt of Christianity"—fled Warsaw for Berlin. These events no doubt also shaped the evolution of the poet's views on the future of Jewish life in Europe and his eventual rejection of the "extraterritorial" norms that shaped *Albatros*, a process that reached an apex of sorts in his movement away from Yiddish to Hebrew as well as his eventual move to Palestine.[45] In the inaugural issue's opening "Proclamation," Greenberg vividly depicts a bleak spiritual landscape: "a generation bleeding from the throat; puking from the mind. A lacerated age running or writing in convulsions." Greenberg refers to himself and his fellow poets as "Albatrosses of Young Yiddish Poetry," poets with "heavy heads ablaze." The figure references Esther Shumiatcher's poem of that title, itself a reference to Charles Baudelaire's famous lyrical ode to the bird. The final line of Baudelaire's poem is a backhanded compliment, hinging upon the bird's awkwardness: "His giant wings hinder him from walking"—that is, the proper domain of these "vast birds of the deep" is soaring high above the sea. This yearning for a more transcendent poetics is undercut in Shumiatcher's poem, which flatly describes the bird as a hungry, wandering creature that searches for a home between the winds, the earth, and the waves: "Wandering is your fate . . . Circling / your hunger groping / toward earthly refuse."[46] The peripatetic Shumiatcher (1899–1985) was born in Belarussia, grew up partly in Canada, and traveled the world with her husband Perets Hirshbein, arriving eventually in Warsaw, where the two were a part of that city's lively Yiddish scene.[47] Greenberg's "Proclamation" privileges this kind of wandering as a new poetics, one that finds its home in a literary genre—the little magazine—that approximates its own restless movement: "A bridge, four walls, and a rafter for the lone and homeless poets as they roam through foreign lands to the many centers of the Jewish people's extraterritoriality. Literary diffusion."[48] The poetic language of "literary diffusion" is the essential toolbox for depicting this postwar era of horror and grief, when poets "remain as we are—with gaping wounds, with veins exposed and bones undone after the howitzers and the Hurrahs."[49]

THE YIDDISH LITTLE MAGAZINE AS A VISUAL ARTIFACT

Beyond Greenberg's dramatic rhetoric, readers arguably encounter *Albatros* primarily as a unique visual artifact because of its striking illustrations, layout, and attention to typography. *Albatros*'s large-format issues remain arresting decades later, even in facsimile edition. The alphabet adorns one page along the bottom, almost like a printer's proof—a clear indication of the journal's promotion of the letter as such, and its typographic status as a visual fact; another page spells out the numbers of the year and issue in words. *Albatros*'s distinctive and visually compelling covers demonstrate sensitivity to the letter as a pliable iconic form, signaling "affiliation by design" with avant-garde trends in other languages. The mix of numbers and letters on the *Albatros* covers resembles the practice of the Dada movement, which Lissitzky apparently referred to as "crimes of typographic disobedience."[50] Tristan Tsara (born Samuel Rosenstock; his

אלבאטראס

זשורנאל פאר דעם נייעם דיכטער- און קינסטלער-אויסדרוק

רעדאקטאָר: אורי צבי גרינבערג

דאס ערשטע העפט

*

פראָקלאַמירונג * מאַניפעסט צו די קעננער פון דער
נייער דיכטונג * פרץ מארקיש: פון דער
פאָעמע „ווײלאַנד" * מארק שווארץ:
„אין שייער" (לינאָלעאום-שניט) *
פרץ הירשביין: „וואָרצלען"
* אסתר שומיאטשער:
„אפריקאַס ווייטן"
„קארו" „מאורי
פרינצעסין"
„אלבאטראָס"
„וואַנגאַנואי" *
אורי צבי גרינ-
בערג: פון דער פאָעמע
„וועלט באַרג אראָפּ" * מלך
ראַוויטש: „די נייע, די נאַקעטע
דיכטונג" * הענריק בערלעווי: וויקינג עגגע-
לינג און זיין אבסטראַקט-דינאמישער פילם *
זאב ווײנטרויב: „מיינע אויסבליקן אין דער קונסט"

הילע געצייכנט פון
זאב (וולאָדיסלאַוו) ווײנטרויב

ווארשע — סעפטעמבער

טויזנט-ניינהונדערט-צוויי-און-צוואנציק

Albatros 1 (Warsaw, September 1922). Courtesy of the Library of the YIVO Institute for Jewish Research.

Albatros 1 (Warsaw, September 1922). Courtesy of the Library of the YIVO Institute for Jewish Research.

pen name, loosely translated from the compound French and Yiddish, means “sad trouble”) articulates the principle thus: “To put out a manifesto you must want: ABC / to fulminate against 1, 2, 3.”[51]

In Ze’ev (Vladislaw) Weintraub’s design for *Albatros* 1 (1922), the title seems to be levitating off the page, the letters distorted to resemble the shape of the large clumsy bird flying above the waves. The title also appears in smaller white letters on the horizontal leg of one of the alephs, alongside a small cutout of a bird. *Albatros* 3–4 (1923) has a different aesthetic, abstract and chunky, like build-

Albatros 3–4 (Berlin, 1923). Courtesy of the Library of the YIVO Institute for Jewish Research.

ing blocks. The German and Yiddish words are punctuated with geometric shapes; even the diacriticals resemble graphic ornaments. The cover of this later issue of *Albatros* feels almost like a purging of Jewish whimsy, commensurate with the rising influence of the idea of the artist as an engineer and visual forms suggested by technology, photography, and modernist architecture.

Indeed, the visual material in these little magazines displays an evolving amalgam of art nouveau, expressionism, and "constructivist" abstraction, with a healthy

"A heart crosses the world westward." *Albatros* 3–4 (1923). Courtesy of the Library of the YIVO Institute for Jewish Research.

dose of Jewish folkloric whimsy.[52] This combination of styles resembles those elements alluded to in Berlewi's assessment—"Russian luboks, old Jewish murals and Cubism"—and suggested by Lissitzky's privileging of the engineer over the artist. The fact that many of these journals were produced in different locations by a rotating cast of the same figures underscores the mobility of this modernist style ("traveling style," in Edward Said's terms). An enigmatic graphic on the cover of *Albatros* 3–4 alludes to this very quality: the phrase "From the land to the world, by way of the West" encapsulates a telescope-like circle—effectively mimicking a postal print—but from where to where?!

The movement between these styles was not unique to the Yiddish publications; it was part and parcel of cultural developments in the interwar period: art historian Christian Weikop notes that a "clear shift away from the primitivizing woodcut craft forms of Expressionism to a 'new typography' and highly experimental layouts was also evidenced by two magazines published in Berlin in the early and mid-1920s."[53] The fact that Lissitzky was involved in the production of these very magazines (one in French, the other in German) only underscores his centrality in the wider frame of European modernism. Indeed, both Lissitzky and Berlewi are key figures in abstraction and typography; they began in Yiddish and eventually worked in other languages. At the very least, it seems that their origins as Jewish writers familiar with the world of Yiddish sensitized them to the iconic properties of the letter as such. Moreover, their growing preference for abstraction may have made them more "communicative," more universal. In this way, we can appreciate these Yiddish little magazines as not simply "a part" of something broader—European avant-garde modernism—but in fact among that movement's conceptual architects. What was understood as Judaism's "handicap" in relation to artistic forms—its resistance to figuration—precipitates an evolution away from it; abstraction was perceived as more sophisticated than figuration, a more worldly alternative to allowing Jewish identity or tradition to shape aesthetic production. (This very same condition was, ironically, later used to lambast Jewish artists as "degenerate" and not sufficiently national.) Wolitz traces the various twists and turns in this movement between expressionism and abstraction, concluding: "He [the "Jewish abstract artist"] was too far in advance of his national constituency, which was still struggling to even admit a Jewish figurative and national art."[54]

In addition to *Albatros,* numerous other covers capitalize on the alphabet's visual form. Today we may take for granted the appearance of Hebrew print in a variety of typographical forms; it's worth remembering that these journals were quite new for their time, appearing during an era of increasing experimentation with fonts and typefaces, notably in Berlin's publishing houses and artistic journals but also driven by Lissitzky and his peers. Together with iconic works such as Lissitzky's *Khad Gádye* (1919), these journals emblematize a growing sense that the material objects of Jewish literature—books and little magazines—can and should possess an aesthetic design, with typography as a key element therein.[55] For example, the letters announcing an issue of *Yung-Yiddish* appear scratched across the page, leaving visible some of the shade and details from their woodcut.[56]

Stylistically, the letters possess some of the fragmented and slanting quality of "Rashi script," a font typically used in traditional Jewish commentary surrounding a biblical source text on the printed page. The direct yet provocative relation here suggests a confident, selective appropriation of tradition; indeed, issues of *Yung-Yiddish* were all dated in relation to the Jewish calendar. The founders of *Yung-Yiddish,* including Jankel Adler, were inspired by ethnographic expeditions in eastern Europe in the 1910s that documented local Jewish material culture, and they viewed the visual detail and ornament of synagogues and tombstones as a resource for new Jewish artistic forms.[57] When Ber Ryback and Lissitzky traveled to the Ukraine in 1915, they sketched colorful wall paintings in old wooden synagogues, expansive and kaleidoscopic murals with natural motifs and ornamental patterns; an impression of these styles, which may be observed in their subsequent drawings and attention to typography, left a lingering influence over the genre's search for a visual style, the subject of Lissitzky's "reminiscences" about the experience.[58] The pair traveled to these

Yung-Yiddish 2–3 (Lodz, Passover 1919). Courtesy of the Department of Special Collections, Stanford University Libraries.

synagogues specifically to root themselves in the sources of Jewish folk art. The great vault of the Mohilev synagogue contains an enormous frieze with "all manner of living creatures," many painted with human faces; the signs of the Zodiac; and imaginative renderings of Jerusalem, Solomon's Temple, and the Trees of Life and Knowledge. Noting the quality of light in the main room and

Eygns 2 (Kiev, 1920). Courtesy of the Library of the YIVO Institute for Jewish Research.

that of the painting, Lissitzky wrote, "Despite its transparency the painting is quite dense. Ochre, lead white, vermillion, green give the impression of weight, though less noticeably in the cooler tones of blue and violet."[59]

Indeed, Mohilev motifs seem to be the generative force behind a gorgeous example of cover art from this period: Ber Ryback's cover for *Eygns* 2 (Kiev, 1920) wraps around front and back in one continuous piece. The flowing, interlocking pattern in black and off-white consists of the silhouette of a fox-like creature rendered in mid-leap, with head turned back and forelock or mane flowing forward—going in both directions at once, this central figure has dramatically

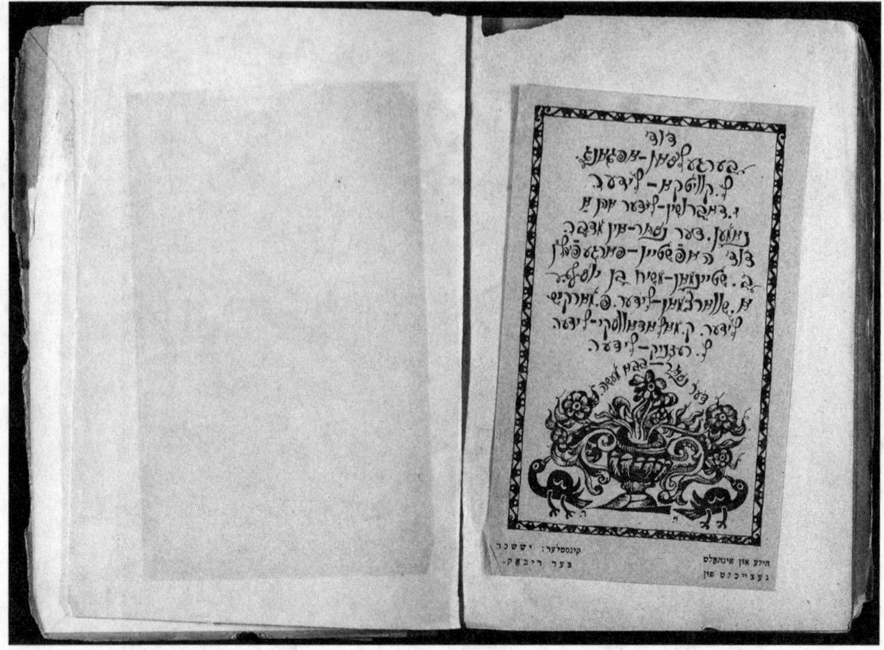

Table of contents, *Eygns* 2 (Kiev, 1920). Courtesy of the Library of the YIVO Institute for Jewish Research.

vital energy. It is surrounded by other natural elements, what look like a sunflower and tulip, all repeated in continual sequence, with no beginning and no end. Somewhere between folk art and an elegant art nouveau pattern, something you might even see on wallpaper, this vivid pattern serves as background for the title in slightly stylized orange Hebrew letters. The table of contents deploys similar motifs: listing stories by Dovid Bergelson and Der Nister and poetry by Dovid Hofshteyn, this stunning graphic contains some of the same natural elements, though in this case the guiding geometrical feature is symmetry, the flowers are potted, and the silhouetted creature is a bird. The hand-printed letters themselves resemble vegetation, sprouting tendrils like the flowers below. The entire list is treated to a decorative border, and the page itself is a work of art.

The title on *Ringen*'s large-format cover by Yitskhok Broyner (1887–1944) floats: stylized white letters set with some crosshatching relief to indicate depth in a cloud of ornamental colored, curling, interlocking embellishments (hence the title *Ringen,* "rings"). The cloud appears variously in pink, red, and green on different issues. A slim solid line border of the same color and another thinner, darker line frames the title, which sits alone on the cover. Resembling a

Ringen 2 (Warsaw, 1921). Courtesy of the Library of the YIVO Institute for Jewish Research.

kind of caricature of an ornamental plaque on a building, it's almost a playful rebuke to the geometric and constructivist abstraction called for by Lissitzky's essay in this very issue. The journal's name alludes to the collaborative, collective nature of the project, produced by editorial committee (*kolegiyum*).

Like many of the other remaining copies of little magazines from this era, the cover of *Szweln* (1923, Lodz and the Bronx; Threshholds) is intact and recognizable, but crumbing at the edges. A monochromatic print is pasted onto the cover along with the author's name, Marek Szwarc, and the technique

שוועלן

חודש-זשורנאַל פאַר ליטעראַטור און קונסט.

מאַרק שוואַרץ — בארעליעף.

באַנד I
לאָדזש

העפט I
נאָוועמבער 1923

Szweln (Lodz and the Bronx, 1923). Courtesy of the Library of the YIVO Institute for Jewish Research.

(bas-relief) underneath. The work is related to Szwarc's 1922 *The Seder* (*Passover*), part of a series of biblical scenes in hammered copper.[60] The figures are depicted in silhouette and styled in a primitivist fashion (this is more evident in the copper relief itself); you can pick out the letters for the word *Seder* in the background (again, more evident in the relief). Beards and head coverings indicate their piety. The title font is relatively plain and clear. Among the participants listed on the back cover are Moyshe Broderzon, another member of

Yung-Yiddish, and Rikuda Potash, whose earliest work was in Polish; the cover also indicates that the journal was printed in Lodz but had an editorial office in the Bronx. The simplicity of the Polish lettering on the back cover mirrors that of the Yiddish typography.

The creator of *Albatros*'s inaugural design, Warsaw artist and sometimes theater designer Ze'ev Weintraub (1891–1942), is also behind one of the most striking and original images in modern Jewish cultural expression: the orange bouquet of alphabet flames filling the cover of *Khalyastre* 1. The letters are treated first and foremost as iconic shapes, creating a sense of dynamism and movement. Is the image a torch of flames, a bouquet of flowers, a mask? Jagged orange letters spelling out the name of the journal funnel up and fill its cover, which contains no further identifying features about where or when the journal was published. The cover's absolute devotion to the alphabet's visual form exists in an avant-garde vacuum. Readers may decipher the vowels, diacritical bits floating under or between the dangling strands of letters. Even recognizing the white areas as background, the eye, slowing down to find the contours of each letter, still struggles to piece together the letters into a word. *Khalyastre*'s second issue was published in Paris and featured another sui generis cover by Chagall. The cover synthesizes important motifs for these journals: a cosmopolitan, urban setting; a playful, multilingual challenge to dominant cultural forms. The Dadaism-inspired, childlike sketch of Chagall and his friends storming Paris, planting flags atop the Eiffel Tower, suggest that Yiddish has indeed arrived in the metropole.

Alongside the elaborate cover art that constitutes a unique and essential form of creative expression, one particular technique deserves special mention for its role within these journals: the print, produced either from woodcut or linocut. This relatively inexpensive process of creation and reproduction retains something of the artist's "hand" through the appearance of individual knife cuts used for detail and background. The process is both physical and spiritual: "Every cut with the knife is a slice into the innermost self. This wood is truly flesh of thy flesh."[61] The woodcut was especially venerated among German expressionist artists for its historic pedigree of craftsmanship and what the critic Gustav Hartlaub called a kind of "racial predisposition."[62] In the evocative words of another contemporary, "It is as though the structure of the rough trunk . . . were especially suited to the . . . German character."[63] In his study *The New German Print* (1920), Hartlaub claims that the woodcut was "better adapted to the new expressive attention than any other technique" due to its "blocky, coarse, and yet spiritual and mysterious style" that also was "driven by . . . the inner demands of the times."[64]

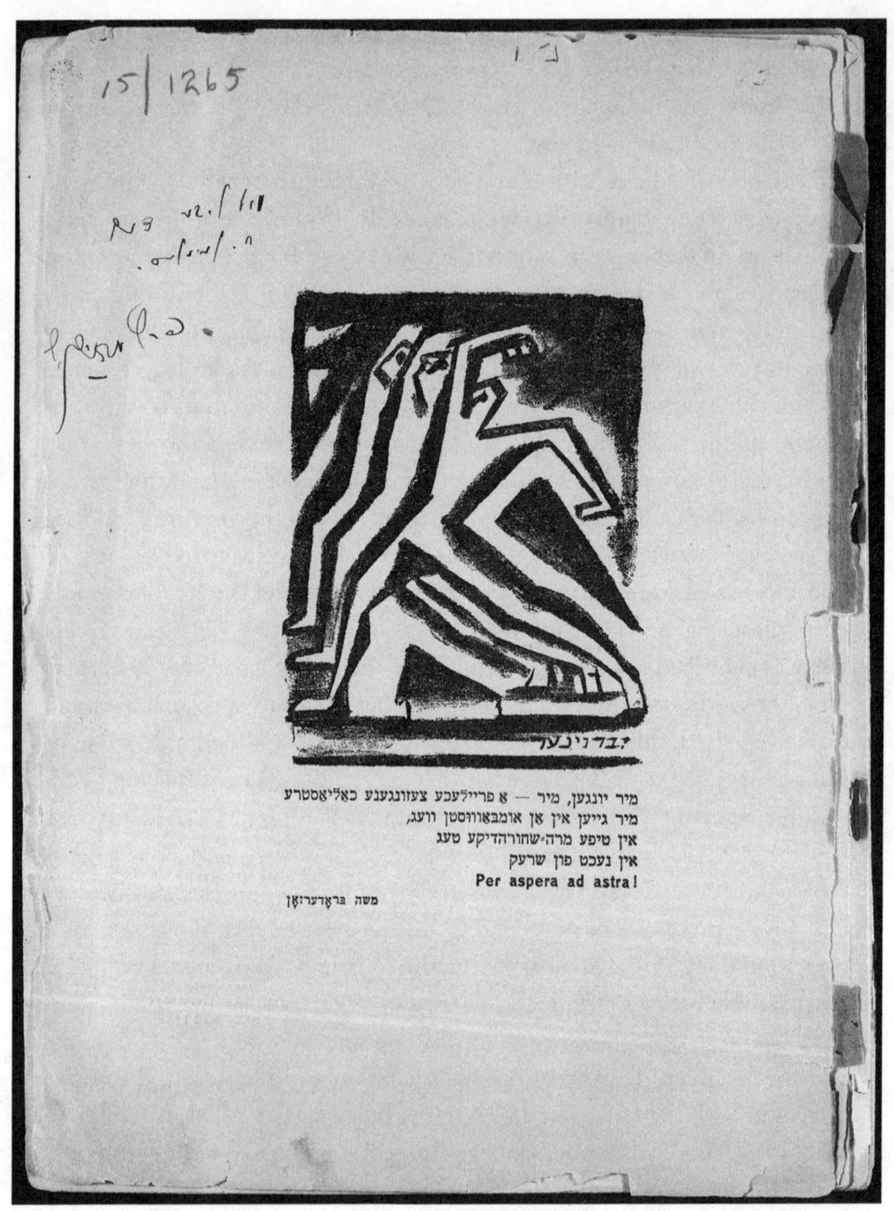

Yitskhok Broyner, "Striving," *Khalyastre* 1 (Warsaw, 1922). Inscribed by Perets Markish. Courtesy of the Library of the YIVO Institute for Jewish Research.

Linocuts originated in the light-industrial world of wallpapering, first deployed as an art form in 1905 by the expressionist group *Die Brücke* in Germany. The linocut print can appear simple, straightforward, of the moment, and—like the woodcut—often "brutal" in its detail; stylistically, it also suggests raw emotion, intense or dark interior states, and the appearance of "primitive" or folk art. The physical process, in which the artist must intensively work and rework the material to achieve the desired result, is complemented by the relative quickness of production—cut, ink, print. The entire process suggests a commensurate experience of tremendous emotion, the need to release some message or feeling onto the page, into public, as close to the moment of conception as possible. In the world of Yiddish little magazines, both woodcuts and linocuts were used to produce images that exemplify the exalted view of the print "as confession, as unconditional utterance."[65]

Khalyastre 1 (1922), Yitskhok Broyner's powerful image of a dense series of human bodies, includes silhouettes striding forward, arms outstretched with upraised fists and arms flung back, perhaps in despair or fear. This duality is born out in the effect of the linocut, dark and light stripes alternating in sequence, making it difficult to distinguish foreground from shadow in the repeating pattern of limbs that together make up "the gang." The image appears above the epigraph, an excerpt from "Tsu di shtern" (To the Stars) by Moyshe Broderzon: "We are young, we are a happy, singing gang / we go on an unknown path."[66] Broyner's work here, together with that of Jankel Adler in *Yung-Yiddish* and Marek Szwarc in *Albatros,* evidences an appreciation for print as a flexible, relatively affordable vehicle of artistic expression, one that combines sacred themes with secular motifs, as per Adler's manifesto, which called for a new "seventh day" to end the long "week of the commonplace." For example, in one of Broyner's prints, the human figure (perhaps Adam or Eve) is glimpsed from behind with a serpent coiled at his or her side. The figure's arms are raised toward the sun in wonderment, anguish, and/or prayer.[67] The human body in these prints is often distorted but always recognizable; the viewer's eye slowly works to make the rough pattern of ink cohere; the print retains the mark of the knife, the artist's hand remaining visible in the finished product. The effect is both fleeting—the two-tone designs feel dynamic and vital—and grounded—the solid panes of thick color lash the print to the page.[68]

In addition to their distinctive typography and characteristic prints, the Yiddish little magazines shared certain formal components of layout with other journals of the period. One such element is the grid, both a shape and an idea alluding to modernity and technology. As a design element, the grid belongs

Yitskhok Broyner, untitled print, *Yung-Yiddish* 4–5–6 (Lodz, Kislev, 1920). Courtesy of the Department of Special Collections, Stanford University Libraries.

equally to many modernist trends, including Futurism, constructivism, and Dadaism.[69] It is the location where affinity and style become most denuded, and perhaps where Yiddish little magazines most fully attach themselves to wider movements. In his study of the little magazines of Dadaism, Futurism, and imagism, Eric Bulson argues that "the grid was there to organize informa-

„Życie Żydowskie"

tygodnik społeczno-polityczny sprawom żydostwa i zagadnieniom sjonizmu poświęcony.

Zespół współpracowników:

Dr. W. Berkelhammer, Dr. Braude, Prof. Bromberg, Dr. Bulwa, Dr. Bychowski, H. Farbstein, E. Frenk, M. J. Freid, Dr. Gotlieb, Adw. Grynbaum, Adw. Hartglas, M. Jarblum, Inż. M. Koerner, Dr. J. Minc, Dr. S. Poznański, Dr. Ringel, Dr. Rosenblat, Adw. S. Seideman, A. Stand, A. Szejnman, N. Szwalbe, Dr. Szwarcbart, Dr. O. Thon, Z. Weicman, Dr. Zimmerman i inni.

Prenumerata: Rocznie Mk. 36 — Półrocznie Mk. 18, Kwartalnie Mk. 9 — Miesięcznie Mk. 3 — Numer poje[illegible]czy 85 fen.

Prenumeratę przyjmu[illegible] wszystkie związki sjonistyczne i biura [illegible]zienników i ogłoszeń.

Adres redakcji i administracji:
Warszawa, Senatorska 32.

Jedynym organem hebrajskim w Polsce
jest tygodnik

„HACEFIRAH"

Miłośnicy słowa hebrajskiego znajdą w nim, prócz bogatego materjału publicystycznego, utwory z nowej literatury hebrajskiej.

Pismo redaguje: **poseł I. Grynbaum.**

Adres redakcji: **Warszawa, Leszno 54.**

Przesyłki pocztowe adresować:
Warszawa, Skrzynka pocztowa № 158.

Czytajcie, popierajcie
i rozpowszechniajcie

„Dos Judisze Fołk"

centralny organ Sjonistycznej Organizacji w Polsce.

„DOS JUD. FOŁK" jest najlepiej in[illegible]rmowane o sprawach ż[illegible]ostwa i sjonizmu, Palestyny i djaspory.

Na czele redakcji stoją:
poseł I. Grynbaum,
Dr. J. Gotlib i N. Szwalbe.

Adres redakcji: **Warszawa, Leszno 54.**

Przesyłki pocztowe adresować:
Warszawa, Skrzynka pocztowa № 158.

Przyjmuje się prenumeratę na najstarszy i najbardziej rozpowszechniony **żydowski** dziennik prowincjonalny

„Lodzer Tageblat",

który wychodzi **2 razy dziennie.**

Cena prenumeraty rocznej 72 mk., półrocznej 36 mk, kwartalnej 18 mk., miesięcznej 6 mk., z wydaniem wieczornym 9 mk. miesięcznie.

Adres redakcji i administracji:
Łódź, Piortkowska 16, Tel. Nr. 47.

Back page grid. *Tel Awiw* (Lodz, 1919). Courtesy of the Library of the YIVO Institute for Jewish Research.

tion, but it was also an expression of being *in the network,* a way for magazines to identify their connections with and disconnections from one another."[70]

A typical back page from the New York journal *Otem* (Breath) (October–November 1923) lists the journal's editorial board members in Toronto, Chicago, Cleveland, and Newark and contains advertisements for a prep school (to learn English), a dealer of "Jewish books in all languages," a musician, an artist, and a restaurant called Russian Village, which promises the best food at reasonable prices. The back page of *Tel Awiw* (Lodz, 1919) is a neatly laid-out quadrant, each of four advertisements framed with a different style of line detail: *Jewish Life,* a Polish-language weekly; *Hacefirah,* devoted to Hebrew literature; a publication of the Polish Zionist Organization, and a daily paper in Lodz.

געדרוקט פון זאַך אין טויזנט
נומערירטע עקזעמפּלאַרן.
נײַנהונדערט (1000 — 101) װערן
פאַרקױפט.

נר. 778

RYNGEN (OGNIWA) □ □ □ □
□ □ □ ZBIÓR PRAC LITERACKICH
WYDAWCA: DR. MICHAŁ WEICHERT
□ □ □ WARSZAWA, 1922. □ □ □

SKŁADANO I ODBITO □ □ □ □
□ □ □ w DRUKARNI I. HENDLERA,
□ □ WARSZAWA, DŁUGA 26. □ □

Credit grid. *Ringen* (Warsaw, 1922). Courtesy of the Library of the YIVO Institute for Jewish Research.

Złożono i odbito
w drukarni
B. SZTROWAJSA
Łódź, Cegielniana 51.

געזעצט און געדרוקט
אין דרוקעריי פון
ב. שטראוויס, לאדזש
ציגל-גאס 51,

Credit grid. *Szweln* (Lodz and the Bronx, 1923). Courtesy of the Library of the YIVO Institute for Jewish Research.

Two small credit boxes, one in *Ringen* and the other in *Szweln,* provide basic information about the journal and its place of publication in Polish and Yiddish. The text is studded or surrounded by a pattern of small boxes. Both resemble architectural drawings of a floor plan or the façade of a building, alluding to the elegant yet rational urban grid of human-created forms.

One further shape demands some attention, as it seems a direct riposte to the events that precipitated Greenberg's, and *Albatros*'s, move from Warsaw to Berlin. Not exactly a grid, it is an enigmatic, funnel-like form that is used to convey an especially fraught message in the third issue of *Albatros.* The Yiddish text reads:

ALBATROS
Number 2 (Warsaw) was
confiscated by the
Polish authorities
due to blasphe-
my

The announcement seems an express jab at the Polish censorship officials who couldn't read Yiddish but were scandalized by the shape of a cross composed of Hebrew letters. In this instance, with the journal now based in Berlin, Polish censorship was no longer an issue. The funnel-shaped declaration is a benign geometric, abstract shape that appears to neither symbolize nor allude to anything but itself. The shape (apparently) no longer scandalizes; it no longer really matters—the journal endures, with the cast of characters more or less intact.

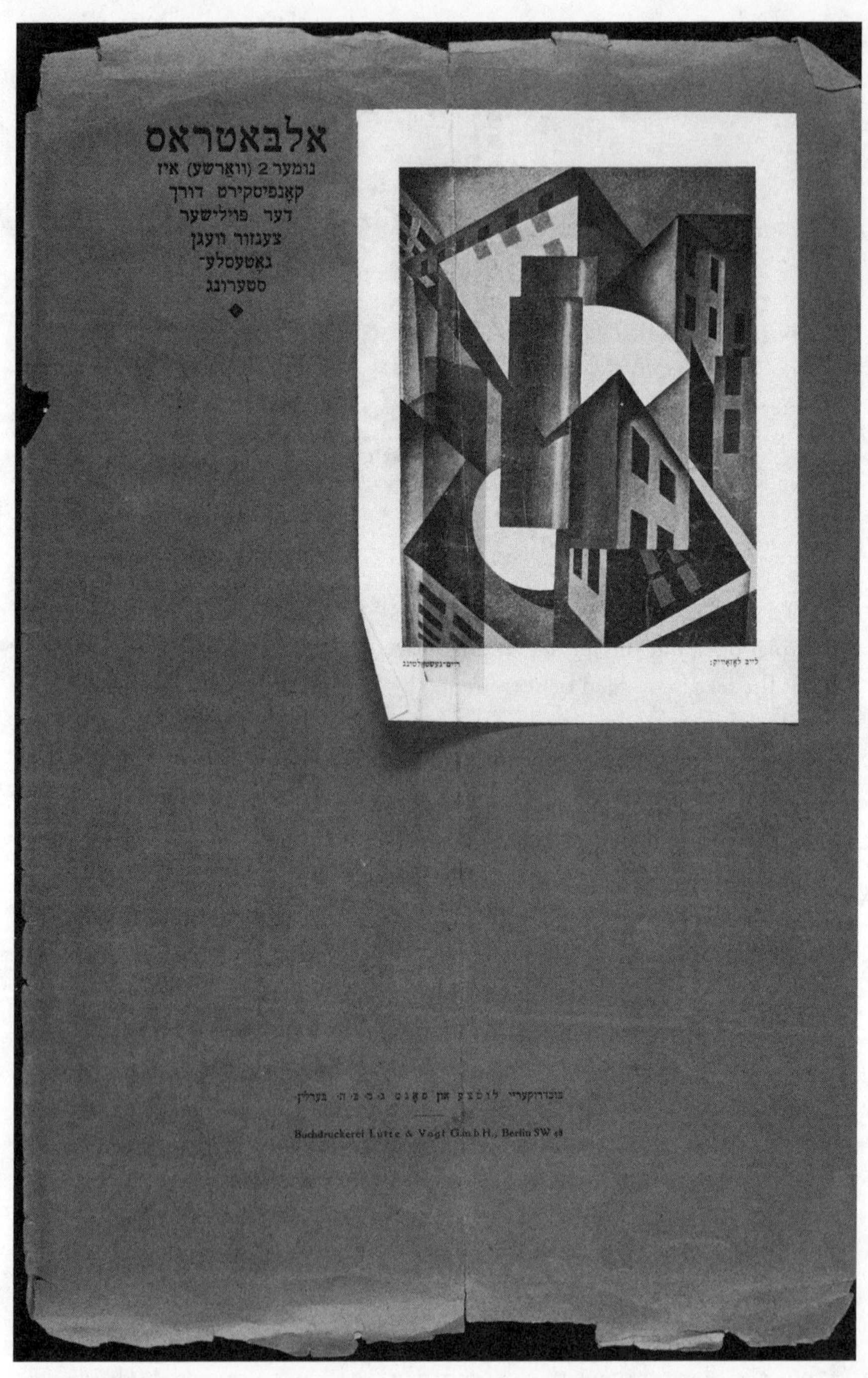

Funnel announcing censorship of *Albatros* 2. *Albatros* 3–4 (1923). Courtesy of the Library of the YIVO Institute for Jewish Research.

YIDDISH UNTETHERED

The distinctiveness and import of these little magazines are perhaps best appreciated within a comparative framework. Bulson's work provides an interesting counterpoint to a study of Yiddish journals, particularly his claim regarding the little magazines' "*decommercialized, decapitalized,* and *decentered*" form. According to Bulson, "There was never a single city to monitor or regulate movement, and even though Paris, London, New York, and Berlin were lightning rods for cultural activity, there was never any unified infrastructure between them, no international cadre of editors or translators or publishers with the power to regulate the flow of texts in every direction."[71] Though Yiddish titles also appeared in multiple urban centers, the condition of Yiddish little magazines seems to move against Bulson's paradigm in certain ways: for a short interval of time, a loose cohort of the same revolving cast of individuals was creating these journals, just in different locations and under a variety of titles. Moreover, some of these figures (most notably Berlewi, Lissitzky, and Chagall) became increasingly prominent and active in modernist art and design, in journals in other languages, and in more "universal" settings.

Some of the historical connections between these figures and the specifically Yiddish origins of their work have been erased. Indeed, translations of major essays by Berlewi and Lissitzky appeared decades later in a major anthology of interwar avant-garde manifestos; however, though the essays were attributed to *Ringen,* they were translated from Polish and German, without any mention of their original production and appearance in Yiddish. The erasure of Jewish participation seems retrospective: Jews were in fact highly visible as editors and contributors to little magazines in many avant-garde and modernist settings; and they were visible *as Jews,* even when the setting was not Yiddish.[72] Reinserting their Yiddishness into present-day discussion helps better contextualize their radical nature. Bulson does take issue with the Ezra Pound–centric nature of the field, noting that "part of what might open up research on little magazines is an examination of [the] minor networks in Western and non-Western countries alike and the transnational processes that neither Pound nor anyone else could possibly have discerned."[73] While Yiddish magazines may constitute one such "minor network," this is not the entire story. In their work on Jewish literature as world literature, Lital Levy and Allison Schachter note that Jewish languages "were at once local and transnational, crossing national borders while remaining confined almost exclusively to Jewish communities."[74] Literary production in these languages, including—and perhaps even especially—little magazines, was characterized by tremendous mobility: "Moving fluidly between local and transnational contexts, [Jewish literatures] negotiate literary influences from non-Jewish contexts while circulating texts among Jewish languages."[75]

Ultimately, Bulson seems skeptical of the ability of little magazines to establish connective networks across geography, citing the logistical headaches of transporting or mailing what were essentially relatively frail items. What he calls "transatlantic immobility" is an attempt to disrupt dominant critical models of little magazines; this counternarrative highlights the insularity of English-language claims, and asserts, or privileges, the margins.[76] Bulson's work shares with other postcolonial research a desire to retrieve those voices on the margins, valorizing the condition of diaspora or exile as a productive aesthetic position. Yet this project is quite different from Greenberg's call for "a bridge, four walls, and a rafter," essentially a kind of anchor (even if a relatively temporary one) within the tumult of Jewish "extraterritoriality." The concrete conditions of being a refugee—on the move, perhaps barred from returning to one's land, writing in a language that itself crosses national borders but has no territorial stake of its own, a language that seems, even, to reject that space as necessary or worthwhile beyond "a bridge, four walls, and a rafter": these conditions shape a different kind of experience. Perhaps Yiddish little magazines had a relatively greater degree of mobility, given the mobility of immigrants and the fact that they often carried with them personal libraries, including copies of these journals, thus transporting them to new locations. The transnational production and circulation of these Yiddish journals were part and parcel of the global phenomenon of modernist little magazines; at the same time, they traced a specifically Jewish network in that they necessarily addressed a different kind of audience than their European peers in other languages.[77] On the one hand, this audience was "limited" to Yiddish speakers; on the other hand, Yiddish was the lingua franca of millions of Jews across eastern and central Europe.

Furthermore, it's not clear how marginalized these Yiddish editors actually felt—and what they understood the position of their work in relation to "the world" to be. Someone like Greenberg, moving from Warsaw to Berlin and eventually to Palestine, seems to mapping a relative marginality, akin to *Inzikh*'s inscrutability for Harriet Monroe. At the same time, figures like Berlewi, Lissitzky, and Chagall moved toward the center—the first two through the development of an increasingly abstract set of principles (constructivism, suprematism, Prouns), the latter through a kind of global mythology of Jewish tropes, especially in the years before and after World War II.

Those little magazines edited by Pound and T. S. Eliot could aspire to worldliness precisely because they emanated from a position of power—of English, the language of empire. Yiddish's "strange" alphabet would always potentially stymie any true attempt at worldliness on the part of magazines that were created by people often in exile from some other location, on the move and in between.[78] At the same time, the fact that they operated on the same geographic landmass and in a common language across national borders may have actually shaped a set of conditions in which they were *less* isolated from one another. A short document by Henryk Berlewi, a review of a contemporary art exhibit in Dusseldorf, voices precisely this kind of connection. He calls for an end to "parochialism" or "particularism in art," specifically mentioning Lissitzky (in relation to suprematists and constructivism) and Chagall (in relation to expressionism). He notes: "A worldwide network of periodicals has appeared, propagating and arguing for new ideas and new forms: the organization of cooperatives on economic and ideological grounds; the generally international character of the whole movement—all these substantiate the claim that we are going through a period of transformation of traditional notions about art. . . . Art, which hitherto operated mostly on some sort of Olympus, isolated from the rhythm of everyday life, has been forcefully shoved out into the streets."[79]

When Berlewi calls for a "worldwide network of periodicals" in a document published in a Polish Jewish newspaper, perhaps he is not merely imagining a transnational, multilingual network but is also describing—or, at the very least, is inspired by—the example of Yiddish which, despite the ostensible limits of its reading audience, was in fact transnational. Furthermore, his observation that art is moving out of the "mortuaries called 'museums,' or 'art salons' and is erupting with unstoppable force into our everyday lives, becoming an article as necessary to us as any other on sale in Tietz's department store" echoes Hartlaub's call regarding "the new German print": printmaking "does not want to be stored motionless in portfolios. The print wants to fly, a broadsheet fluttering downward from spiritual heights to a great people with arms outstretched."[80] Though the little magazine may have begun as an ephemeral artifact—tied to a particular place and date, its existence superseded by the next issue—it paved the way for other genres whose contours would more forcefully blur the boundaries between text and image, and between book and object.

Chapter 3 "Good to think with": The Fictional Work of Objects

Early in Dovid Bergelson's *Nokh alemen* (The End of Everything, 1913), a modernist Yiddish novel set in a provincial town outside Kiev, Reb Gedalya, the shtetl's aging and increasingly outdated patriarch, encounters his daughter Mirel, his most precious possession: "Reb Gedalye had already returned from the Sadagura study house with his prayer shawl and phylacteries, and with Gitele [his wife] absent, felt very lonely in the empty house. He found Mirel standing all alone in her room, and . . . distractedly began fiddling with the knick-knacks on her dressing table."[1]

The passage's symmetry, its juxtaposition of religious and profane objects, is ironically tethered to the sense of a physical void: the house *feels* empty and Mirel is "standing all alone in her room." This perceived isolation is bracketed by a pair of object sets: the prayer shawl and phylacteries, on the one hand, and the knick-knacks or "trifles" (*kleynekeiten*) on Mirel's dressing table, on the other. Her father then tells her, in a "distracted" manner, that "the bailiff might call here today," to which Mirel responds by donning "her jacket and black scarf" and leaving the house. The narrative equivalence between the accoutrements of religious observance and the "knick-knacks" of Mirel's vanity seems to render them both equally unreliable as objects of comfort or sustenance; the handling of the prayer shawl and phylacteries should be treated with intention and devotion, the opposite of "distracted fiddling" (*arumtapn*), yet neither set of possessions will withstand the demands of the bailiff, who may or may not "call here today." The family is approaching bankruptcy, and within the provincial backwater that is the shtetl, financial concerns shape both traditional religious observance and the most mundane of possessions. The movement from religious objects to the contents of Mirel's vanity suggests that the former have been stripped of their functional value and are simply objects of idle distraction. This brief set piece, culminating in Mirel's abrupt departure, may be read as a cameo rendering of the entire narrative, from its granular exhaustion of traditional shtetl life and Reb Gedalya's bankruptcy and death to the eventual disappearance of Mirel, the novel's centerpiece. Indeed, the work of objects in Bergelson's novel seems to orbit around Mirel and her growing synonymy with the shtetl itself: both are fated to vanish by the novel's close.

The idea of the shtetl as a withering and diminished object is also implicit in Russian Jewish ethnographic work contemporaneous with *The End of Everything*. S. An-sky's great ethnographic project of 1912–14 was conducted in the same general vicinity as the setting of Bergelson's novel, the surroundings of Kiev. An-sky and his colleagues were determined to record and preserve material details about traditional Jewish experience, the minutiae of daily life that would be irretrievably lost in a rapidly shifting social and political landscape: "For An-sky, as for many other Russian-Jewish intellectuals of his time, the monumental and decisive changes that transpired in the late imperial period—growth of antisemitic ideologies, mass emigration, and the rise of conversion rates—led to the most significant cultural break in modern Jewish history, shattering the foundation of Jewish civilization."[2] In addition to photographs, data, and responses to an extensive questionnaire about shtetl life, An-sky collected examples of material culture including artifacts as well as *pinkasim* (communal record books). An-sky's goals were specifically contextual; he was not interested in creating a collection of highbrow items; his objective, "above all," was to capture "the narratives in which these objects figured."[3] One of the expedition's immediate results was a short-lived exhibit in St. Petersburg in 1914 of more than eight hundred objects and manuscripts, including common objects of everyday life as well as sound recordings and the *pinkasim*.[4] An-sky's collection was later dispersed, distributed to various institutions and archives in Russia and the former Soviet bloc. Much of it was destroyed. The dispersal of these objects prefigures the later brutal and systematic destruction of Jewish life and lives. The story of what ultimately happened to this vast record of shtetl life resembles in remarkable fashion what happens to Mirel at the end of the Bergelson's novel—she simply boards a train and disappears.[5]

The End of Everything is the first of three novels of modern Jewish life discussed in this chapter, chosen for their exemplary and distinctive attention to material culture and the meaning of things. In these novels we find a variety of things: that is, objects in relation to their human subjects, embedded in the physical and material transformations affecting Jewish societies in the early to mid-twentieth century. For Bergelson, his novel's elaborate deployment of personal and familial possessions points toward the demise of the shtetl; the diminished "use value" of traditional mores and behaviors is eventually focused in the figure of Mirel Hurvitz, the novel's putative heroine, whose own utility, or "exchange value," is increasingly attenuated.[6] In Henry Roth's *Call It Sleep* (1934), the detritus of a Lower East Side childhood become symbolic totems of a violent coming-of-age and budding artistic consciousness; the narrative's evolving treatment of a series of "evocative objects" highlights the charged relation between European, American, and Jewish cultural forms. In S. Y. Agnon's *Only Yesterday* (Hebrew, 1946), an epic historical novel of immigration and cultural renaissance set in Jaffa and Jerusalem, the novel's interlocking motifs related to the crafts of taxidermy and olive wood production underline a concern for art's significance in relation to the pragmatic work of nation-building. These novels offer us three different fictional landscapes in which the interaction between people and their stuff provides a sensitive measure of diverse material changes in midcentury Jewish cultures.[7]

Drawing on Marx's model of commodification, the symbolic value of the fetish from Freud and Claude Lévi-Strauss, postcolonial theories of the nation, and Bruno Latour's influential concept of the "hybrid," this chapter analyzes the materiality arising from the novel's generic performance. The novel, perhaps more than any other genre, gives us a sense of what Bill Brown describes as "the way cultural codes become objectified in specific material forms, the way people shape, code, and recode the material object world, the way they make things meaningful and valuable."[8] My material reading of the modernist novel by Jewish authors is indebted to Brown's work on the meaning of objects in American literature, an account of Gilded Age fiction that also resembles a "prehistory of the modernist fascination with things." By focusing on the treatment of objects in a series of canonical novels from the late nineteenth and early twentieth centuries, Brown explores how "different literary registers—naturalism, regionalism, and realism . . . dramatize the role of objects in American lives, and . . . the role of humans in the life of American objects."[9] Specifically, his

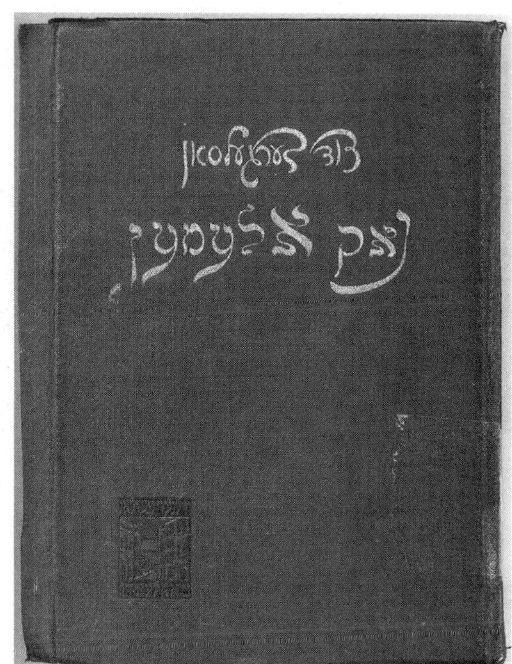

Dovid Bergelson, *Nokh alemen* (1913). Courtesy of the Library of the YIVO Institute for Jewish Research.

Henry Roth, *Call It Sleep* (New York: Robert O. Ballou, 1934). Custom cloth chemise and 1/2 suede slipcase. Courtesy of Swann Auction Galleries.

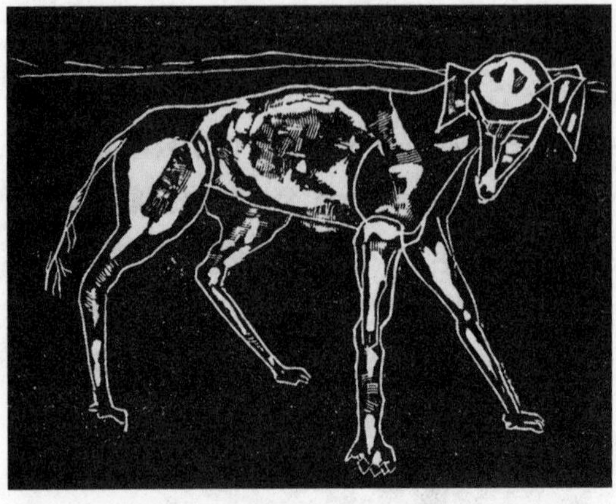

Balak, a walking book. Illustration by Avigdor Arikha, in *Kelev Ḥutsot: Parasha ketana shel Tmol Shilshom* (1960). © 2020 Artists Rights Society (ARS), New York / DACS, London.

analysis tracks the transformation of objects into "things" and examines their meaning for the people who make, handle, and possess them. Material culture, such as drawing room furniture or the extensive collection that is the putative subject of Henry James's *The Spoils of Poynton,* is the stage upon which plays a particularly American anxiety about class and social status in the first true age of consumer capitalism. That this fictional drama unfolds in both European urban centers and rural New England only underscores the degree to which "things," emblems of identity and desire, help American culture come to terms with its own status as both cosmopolitan and local. I am interested in how similar anxieties might be at play in novels by Jewish authors, with their transnational reach and native allegiances, tracing as they do the major trajectories of early twentieth-century migration.

Moreover, as a genre, the novel's *longue durée,* as well as its thick interweaving of character and plot, of psychological interiority with nuanced depictions of setting and landscape, provides an ideal medium in which to examine the meaning of objects and their production. Brown's work reminds us that the meaning of material possessions in fictional texts remains embedded in the particular social and economic milieus in which the texts are produced. Specifically, the three novels discussed in this chapter are all set in environments of tremendous material change, including migration as well as economic and political upheaval. Within these narrative worlds, objects—like Claude Lévi-Strauss's animals—become "good to think with" (*bonne à penser*), providing a vivid sense of how materiality matters for midcentury Jewish cultural forms.

Beyond the genre's plentiful description, novels are essentially indebted to the material form of the book.[10] We encounter the novel as a thing precisely because of its immersive quality: "The book's minute description of the material world is a device which tends to draw attention to the book as object."[11] This chapter explores this complementary set of conditions—objects in books, and the book as object—with an eye to the diverse social and material conditions within which these novels of modern Jewish life are produced and consumed. Broadly speaking, the novel's engagement with things, and its emergence as a thing, points to the arena in which writing competes with objects, fearing, while also taking pleasure in, its own commodification and immersion in the economic domain. For Marx, the commodity is defined by its exchange value, its worth in the marketplace in terms of other commodities; furthermore, exchange value supersedes use value (simply utility) precisely through an act of abstraction, one that (for Marx) involves the erasure of human labor and (for readers, fortunately), demands an imaginative act. In Marx's famous example, the transition from wood to table is even less remarkable than what happens after the table enters the marketplace: "It is as clear as noonday, that man, by his industry, changes the forms of the materials furnished by Nature, in such a way as to make them useful to him. The form of wood, for instance, is altered, by making a table out of it. Yet, for all that, the table continues to be that common, everyday thing, wood. But, so soon as it steps forth as a commodity, it is changed into something transcendent. It not only stands with its feet on the ground, but, in relation to all other commodities, it stands on its head, and evolves out of its wooden brain grotesque ideas."[12]

For the artist, commodification is two-faced: it potentially cheapens the artistic product but also makes art available to a wider audience, thus increasing one measure of its value; commodification, therefore, for our novelists, is both threatening and desirable. Modern Jewish writing had a special use-value problem, given its indebtedness to traditional Jewish forms and the preeminent theological, ethical role of those classical Judaic texts; Hebrew and Yiddish modernist poets resisted this ethical impulse through an adherence to the symbolist rallying cry of "art for art's sake." The novel continues this iconoclastic engagement with tradition through its treatment of material objects and its sense of self as a commodity within an economy of things.

Literature's entry into the marketplace—both "transcendent" and "grotesque"—occurs during what Benjamin famously termed "the age of mechanical reproduction," with the potential diminishment of art's authority. Modern Jewish writing's relation to tradition compounds this anxiety: indeed, according to Benjamin, "The uniqueness of the work of art is inseparable from its being imbedded in the fabric of tradition."[13] For Benjamin, "that which withers in the age of mechanical reproduction is the aura of the work of art . . . the technique of reproduction detaches the reproduced object from the domain of tradition."[14]

However, this "withering" of aura, while an inevitable consequence of technological advancement, is not to be mourned; that is, as "the criterion of authenticity" ceases to be the yardstick against which art is measured, the very function of art becomes radicalized, moving out of the domain of tradition and ritual and into another practice entirely: what Benjamin calls "politics."[15] The work of objects in these novels is a marker of the changing role of Jewish literary production in the twentieth century, in relation to both tradition and politics.

THE SHTETL AS DISAPPEARING OBJECT IN *THE END OF EVERYTHING*

Wherever she was she herself was the great piece in the gallery.
—Henry James, *The Spoils of Poynton* (1897)

Early twentieth-century Yiddish fiction had an uneasy relationship with realism; indeed, it often described an unstable sociological setting that seemed to be disappearing under the very pen describing it.[16] As early as 1911, the Russian Jewish critic David Frishman issued the following claim about the work of S. Y. Abramovitch (aka Mendele the Book Seller, 1835–1917), a foundational figure for both Hebrew and Yiddish fiction: "Let us assume, a deluge comes, inundating and washing away from the face of the earth the Jewish ghetto and the Jewish life it contains, not leaving behind so much as a residue, a sign, except by sheer chance, Mendele's four major works. . . . With these spared, the future scholar would be able to reconstruct the entire map of Jewish shtetl life in Russia in the first half of the nineteenth century in such a manner than not even one iota would be left out."[17] The veracity of Frishman's claim is, of course, beside the point.[18] More relevant is the anticipation of the flood, the ever-present premonition of destruction, and the belief in the text as a kind of material substitute. This trope in modern Yiddish fiction—the notion of the text as a material marker, a kind of map of the shtetl—is aptly summarized by David Roskies: "The smallness and self-containment of the shtetl, that which made it such a perfect vehicle for the exploration of the Diaspora Jew acting as a collective, alerted the novelists early on to its essential vulnerability, and they in turn, became the first to chart the ultimate disaster."[19] While Yiddish literature may have had its own internal, ideologically driven argument about its mimetic properties, the meaning of material detail became especially fraught in an era of change and uncertainty.

Bergelson's novel, like other Yiddish fiction of the first two decades of the twentieth century, is deeply shaped by the political, economic, and social upheavals of the time. Mikhail Krutikov underlines the particular importance of a sequence of events, including the pogroms in Kishinev and elsewhere in 1903, the Russo-Japanese War of 1904–5, and the failed revolution in 1905, as crucial to an emergent cohort of young Yiddish writers, including Bergelson (1884–1952) and other figures of the Kiev group, whose literary sensibilities were sharpened against the background of violent change.[20] Within this setting, Bergelson was seen as a "'poet of decline' of the wealthy merchant class of the Ukrainian shtetls, which was forced to abandon its leading position in Jewish society under the pressure of advancing capitalist urbanization."[21] The shtetl itself had ceased to function as an autonomous entity and would eventually "become a part of the city-centered system."[22] Bergelson's early short fiction is studded with scenes depicting the broken relationship between province and urban center, and the gradual dissolution of social ties predicated on the old economic order, disrupted by financial ruin and spiritual bankruptcy.

The novel renders the economic domain's pervasiveness in several ways: the repeated description of personal possessions and their value; the narrative treatment of Mirel as an object of exchange; and depictions of different kinds of labor in relation to the work of literature. The novel deploys the term *sokhrish* (commercial or related to business) to describe a whole range of objects and behaviors, such as *der shtum-sokhrisher shmeykhl* (the silent business smile), *sokhrishe koyles* (businesslike voices) and *sokhrishe moykhes* (commercial brains).[23] Indeed, Mirel's engagement to Velvl Burnes seems to be "irrevocably over" only after the financial agreements have finally collapsed and the promissory notes left as dowry are no longer worth their full value; "Velvl understood . . . that the three thousand rubles belonging to the man who should've been his father-in-law were lost for good."[24] The loss of Mirel's dowry also precipitates the family's eventual bankruptcy. This sense of Mirel as property is complemented and amplified by the novel's wide array of socially and economically marked objects.

The End of Everything is replete with domestic interiors, foremost of which is the Hurvitz homestead, the increasingly gloomy and dilapidated home where Mirel grew up. The household furnishings seem to possess a lively agency and desire otherwise lacking in the Hurvitz home: "Rose-colored curtains hung at the windows, velvet runners lay on the floors, all yearning for an absent joy. . . . A runner lay stretched out to its full length on the spotless floor of the salon, deeply envious of some other runner lying somewhere in some other house."[25] Mirel's home is contrasted with both the modern "furnished cottage" belonging to her ex-fiancé Velvl Burnes, filled with the accoutrements of the striving nouveau riche, and the snug cottage on the outskirts of the village where the midwife Schatz dwells in relative independence. The cottage offers

Mirel occasional respite, and it is within this relatively liberal space that Mirel first encounters the middling Hebrew poet Herz, who will capture her intermittent romantic attention until the novel's depressing conclusion. Within these houses as well as the quiet, newly furnished wing of her in-law's house at the edge of the Kiev suburb into which Mirel moves in the novel's long second half, the reader encounters a variety of objects and possessions, some personal, antique, or handmade, resonant with individual meaning or significance, and others machine-made, brought from outside the shtetl and indicative of modernity with its particular economy of labor, capital, and production.[26] The novel encourages readers to note the difference between antiques and religious ritual objects and books, on the one hand, and the more "new-fangled" items, such as Reb Gedalye's "nickel vaporizer he'd brought back with him from abroad," on the other.[27] Within these several domestic settings and amid all their material furnishings, Mirel, like the heroine of Henry James's *The Spoils of Poynton,* "was the great piece in the gallery."[28] Perhaps we should ask: which kind of an object is Mirel?

Indeed, Mirel is Reb Gedalye's most valuable possession, a precious commodity to be bid for and exchanged, the thing that may ensure his financial future, and with it the shtetl's viability as a social entity. The reliance on Marxist vocabulary here should not be read as an effort to retroactively identity Bergelson's Communism, despite the author's later, ultimately fatal, entanglement in Soviet politics. Marxist analysis describes a condition called "commodity fetishism," in which an object's commodification, the determination of its value in terms of other products, effaces the human labor that created it. Bergelson's novel does offer some comment on commodification's erasure of manual labor, especially as Mirel interacts with and responds to different kinds of work. However, the crucial difference between use value and exchange value, for the purposes of my analysis, concerns the role of the imagination and the power of symbolic meaning.[29] In the novel, Mirel is depicted as a mysterious beauty of middling intelligence and refinement, from a family once respected for the father's wisdom and religious piety. And yet, despite these relatively mediocre qualities, because of how Mirel is *imagined* by her peers and various lovers, her value skyrockets—for a while, at least—and she is pursued by a series of agents as a desired object of matchmaking.

Mirel's commodification is encapsulated in a set of scenes before and during a party held by the wealthy sugar refinery owner Nokhem Taraby, in which Mirel realizes what the reader has begun to suspect—"an awareness of her own fall from grace."[30] Before the party, Mirel stands on the verandah of her home as a sleigh carrying the Taraby children and their guests, students who have heard of her affair the previous summer with Nosn Heller, passes by, exposing her to their "lustfully voracious" and "lecherous, grinning" faces: "For some reason, his [the student's] lascivious glance aroused in her an unspoken, lustful excitement that intermixed prurient thoughts with deep inner dejection. The lustful arousal disappeared with the departing sleigh, but the dejection remained, grew stronger, and yielded to an innermost sense of emptiness and regret. All at once she appeared small and demeaned in her own eyes."[31] This amazing sequence moves quickly from Mirel's arousal at being the focus of attention to an "innermost" objectification, a realization of how "small" she has become.

On the very next page, another passage further increases the sense of Mirel's "devaluation": wrapped for warmth in her father's "rickety sleigh drawn by his emaciated horses," Mirel notices in the distance "the two expensive sleighs of those who were once to have been her in-laws, filling the silence of the fields with the jingle of their bells." The two sleighs eventually catch up to her own and, in a cruelly depicted scene, catch up to her, one on each side, before passing her. Velvl and his sisters—in the two different sleighs—carry on a conversation directly over Mirel in her sleigh: "They shouted calmly and busily across her, as though across an inanimate object . . . and swiftly left her behind." Mirel's fall from being the "greatest piece in the gallery" to a "lifeless thing" prefigures the eventual demise of her family, and with it, the shtetl itself.[32]

Mirel's transformation here exemplifies what Georg Lukács, extending Marx's work on commodity fetishism, theorized as "reification," a "cognitive occurrence in which something that does not possess thing-like characteristics in itself (e.g., something human) comes to be regarded as a thing."[33] For Lukács, commodity fetishism "stamps its imprint upon the whole consciousness of man; his qualities and abilities are no longer an organic part of his personality, they are things which he can 'own' or 'dispose of' like the various objects of the external world."[34] This well describes the novel's depiction of Mirel's relationship to her surroundings. As the story progresses, Mirel's fate as a "lifeless thing" is amplified by her increasing social isolation and detachment and her reluctant acquiescence to marriage: in the following passage, painters prepare the in-laws' house for the holiday, and Mirel is treated like a piece of furniture:

> One of the painters had occasion to pass through the adjoining room to collect some necessary piece of equipment and noticed something. Returning to his work fairly excited, he looked round carefully to make sure no one but his companion was there, and asked him with a suggestive wink:
>
> —The mistress of the house isn't bad-looking, eh? . . .
>
> In the disarranged room next door, Mirel went on lying on the sofa in her wide, low-cut dressing gown with its bell-shaped sleeves. . . .

> All around her stood the beds, both wardrobes with their mirrored doors and the armchairs from the salon together with the huge wash-tub from which the sodden floor-rag hadn't been removed for days on end.[35]

Her mother-in-law later enters and orders the furniture moved so the floors can be polished and the walls cleaned: "While all this was going on, Mirel never stirred from her place on the sofa."[36] Though she appears at points to resist, Mirel's behavior and especially her fate at the novel's conclusion largely mirror the effects of reification—the objectification of one's personal traits and social relationships—as it becomes routine: "a habit of mere contemplation and observation, in which one's natural surroundings, social environment, and personal characteristics come to be apprehended in a merely detached and emotionless manner—in short, as things."[37]

Another kind of language describing Mirel's diminished exchange value suggests a broader critique of Jewish society and the role of literature within it. Mirel's "utility" is broached again and again in the novel, as if she were some sort of old-fashioned instrument; she is harshly described by Herz as a "provincial tragedy" and "nothing more than a transitional point [*ibergang-punkt*] in human development."[38] The first reference locates her fate in the geographic margins neglected by modern commerce. The latter term reduces her to a point of reference whose meaning abides solely in relation to a now irrelevant past and a yet to be determined future. That this critique is offered by Herz, whose own precarious utility seems well represented in his short story "The Dead Town" (included in the novel in its entirety), suggests an anxiety regarding literature's place in the new economic landscape. Notably, Mirel's other occasional love interest, Nosn Heller, is also a literary failure; his attempts to publish a penny daily repeatedly flounder.

Against these abortive cultural endeavors and Mirel's passivity, the novel presents a stream of manual laborers whose industriousness is a rebuke to Mirel's (and her lovers') futility. A team of tailors and seamstresses descend with their shears and sewing machines to fit her for her wedding dress:

> And Mirel, it appeared, was fully aware that she'd recently come down a great deal in the world; was aware of it when she stood all afternoon in the stillness of a room bestrewn with linen; was aware of it when she gathered all this linen together and bent down to pack it into the open trousseau chest. All around her the wedding preparations went steadily forward, and from time to time through the stillness in the cool rooms could be heard the grating rasp of the large tailoring scissors. As he sat bowed over his sewing machine rapidly pumping its treadle with his foot, one of the young tailors' assistants attempted to break this silence. Wholly unexpectedly, he suddenly burst into full-throated song: O my beloved! / On a distant road / I take my way.

> Later the solitary rattle of the rapidly stitching machine was all that could be heard—heard at length, hoarsely and angrily, until it was finally silenced."[39]

The three-line ditty can be understood as a compressed rendering of Mirel's life and demise. The sounds echo in the following scene, where a young seamstress prepares one of Mirel's silk dresses; she "repeatedly picked up the hot pressing iron, sprayed the garment with water from her mouth, and heard one sewing machine pick up the rhythm of stitching from another indoors. Far, far away, near the town bridge to the east, the regular beats of the blacksmith's hammer died slowly away one after the other, and the shtetl fell silent."[40] Mirel's utter passivity in these passages, her lack of purpose and utility, her reduction to a kind of faded, pure exchange value is juxtaposed with the concerted, rhythmic, and embodied efforts of the work around her.

More sophisticated machines will eventually replace the tailor's feet, the seamstress's spit, and the strong arms of the blacksmith; the carefully wrought objects of what James calls "the more labouring ages"—"the upholsterer's and joiner's and brazier's work, the chairs and tables, the cabinets and presses, the material odds and ends" will become desirable antiques.[41] Indeed, in an era of technological change, antiques demonstrate both status and nostalgia for an ostensibly simpler time. There don't seem to be any antiques per se in *The End of Everything*. Rather, the shtetl itself, a fetishized literary object, is the antique, a remnant of the laboring ages. Indeed, the novel's main characters are alienated from that older way of life, viewing it, from "the outskirts of the shtetl," almost like a tableau: Mirel spies Herz, his critical glance—the always "twinkling" or "glinting" eyes—turned toward the shtetl's spiritual and agrarian setting.

> [He] looked attentively at those Jews who'd just returned from the bathhouse and were standing about here and there next to their widely opened front doors preparing to welcome the Sabbath in the synagogue. . . . Noticing Mirel, he took several steps toward her and directed her attention to the shtetl:
>
> —She ought to look closely. This was truly a Sabbath sky; there on the western mountain even the green fields all around looked as though they were welcoming the Sabbath.
>
> Glancing mechanically in that direction, Mirel saw nothing but a weary peasant still plowing his fields as twilight drew on. A great band of plowed earth stretched across the entire face of the verdant mountain, encircling it as though with a broad black belt.[42]

Herz and Mirel may stand apart from the shtetl, each in their own way: Herz's itinerant career as an admired but minor poet, and Mirel's resistance to the conventions of marriage. However, they are both far too passive to really be considered defiant; rather, their interaction here provides one of the novel's clearest articulations of the gap between the shtetl and its dissatisfied, unsettled youth. In this passage, Herz, though alienated from religious orthodoxy, seems genuinely moved, and takes a noble, if somewhat ironic, stab at spiritual uplift. While he may not abide by the preparatory rituals for the Sabbath, he appreciates their aesthetic, pantheistic value. None of this seems to help his work very much: any novel that ends with its main writer figure suffering from having his tonsils removed and unable to speak leaves a sense of writing as maimed and voiceless. Mirel, on the other hand, ever her father's daughter and attuned to finances, understands how impoverished, even naïve, this romanticized version of Jewish life is: in her perfunctory, "mechanical" glance, the anticipatory green fields are plowed under, pinned down by the broad belt of drudgery, the peasant's physical labor.[43]

Ultimately, Mirel's utility and the viability of the shtetl are one and the same. Unlike the case of Emma Bovary (a possible inspiration for her character) or even Lily Bart, her contemporary from Edith Wharton's *The House of Mirth* (1906), when Mirel disappears at the end of the novel, her demise signals the end of an era; Bovary's and Bart's respective milieus simply carry on without them. Mirel's final disappearing act may seem an act of supreme agency, yet one whose pragmatic parameters have grown narrower and narrower as the plot progresses. Having determined that married life is not for her and having aborted a child whose paternity was in doubt, Mirel takes the eighteen-hour train journey back to the shtetl she had left when she became a married woman, only to find herself moving from location to location (the rabbi's house to the inn by the railway station), strung between waiting at the home of a family friend and visiting the post office looking for letters that never arrive.

Bergelson's novel is not unique in its treatment of the shtetl, or Jewish community, as a feminized object. Within Yiddish fiction, the *agunah* (a woman abandoned by her husband who may not, according to Jewish law, remarry) connects the demise of shtetl life to other catastrophes in Jewish history as well as to the concrete effects of modernity on the family unit.[44] Indeed, the figure of the city as an abandoned or wayward woman has a long tradition in Hebrew writing, going back to the biblical book of Lamentations, where Jerusalem (Zion) is vividly mourned in precisely those terms. The shtetl as a feminized object is thus grounded in both reality and symbol. Notably, Mirel suffers some of the social stigma of the *agunah*, though it is she, technically, who is the agent of her own desolation, as she leaves "on the train that traveled to the border" in the novel's closing pages.[45]

BRICOLAGE AND EVOCATIVE OBJECTS IN HENRY ROTH'S *CALL IT SLEEP*

To move from *The End of Everything* to Henry Roth's *Call It Sleep* involves encountering a radically different set of spaces. David Shearl's parents Genya and Albert, eastern European Jewish immigrants in early twentieth-century New York, may come from the pastoral environments described in Bergelson's novel, but *Call It Sleep* is largely set in the gritty and teeming streets of Brooklyn and Lower Manhattan. The two novels are both emblems of modernist style, with an elliptic, fragmented, and often opaque narrative. They also share a partially omniscient point of view, with the motives and desires of the main characters driving the plot while remaining largely hidden to the reader. If for Bergelson the material world is funneled through the vehicle of Mirel as a commodity and disappearing object, the objects of *Call It Sleep* endure as stubborn reminders of what was as well as complex symbolic artifacts marking a yet unconstituted future. The relatively spare apartment of the new American family is almost a rebuke to the richly decorated, labyrinthine domestic quarters in Bergelson's novel. *Call It Sleep* capitalizes on a quality referenced by another American writer, Willa Cather, in her landmark essay "The Novel Démeublé" (1922), where she accuses the contemporary novel of being "over-furnished." Cather's critique of extraneous detail and "mere verisimilitude" is in keeping with a modernist objection to ornament; in contrast, domestic objects should be fused with feeling, existing within the novel's material world as central to the characters' "emotional penumbra," lending a kind of visible depth to the text in which they operate.[46] Cather's evaluation reaches for something beyond symbolism; in other words, not just things, and not even ideas in or about things, but rather the emotional residue that resides between people and their stuff.

Though first published in 1934, *Call It Sleep* entered the American literary canon as a classic tale of immigration and acculturation only after a 1964 review by Irving Howe of a newly released paperback edition.[47] The author's own virtual silence and relative disappearance from the literary scene added to the book's reception as a unique event.[48] The novel may also be read as the depiction of an aesthetic education in relation to institutions of family, religion, and nation in the spirit of James Joyce's *A Portrait of the Artist as Young Man*. Certainly the novel's dense polyphonic weave of different languages, voices, and registers, out of which David emerges as a kind of maestro, supports this view.[49] Indeed, from a young age, David successfully navigates the novel's relatively strict demarcation of language and space. Scholars have noted that details of

David's young life resemble Roth's (1906–95). David speaks Yiddish at home, English in the street. Roth renders Yiddish, especially that of David's parents, as a richly allusive, ornate, stylized speech, full of detail and nuance. However, their English, like David's, sounds like the flawed, accented, partial, or broken street English of a new immigrant. Hebrew is the language of Jewish learning; and Polish is for secrets between his mother Genya and her newly arrived sister. David works through the linguistic contours of his world to create a sense of self and fashion a set of explanations about his parents' past, which is also his own origins story. His reflections are triggered by a specific set of objects associated with his parents' lives in Europe (a cornfield painting and a pair of bull horns) as well as important talismans from their shared lives in New York (the whip, the rosary). This work of objects enables David's gradual mastery of language as a malleable, even dangerous, material element. The practice in both instances—that is, in relation to both physical objects and the treatment of language as material—is one of *bricolage.* I describe the novel's distinctive reliance on objects drawing on both Freud's idea of the fetish as an object representing an absence or something that cannot be said, and Claude Lévi-Strauss's explication of the practice of bricolage.[50] While in Bergelson's novel, Mirel's emergence as a commodified object highlights both the shtetl's demise and an anxiety over writing's entry into the economic sphere, the focus of *Call It Sleep*'s engagement with materiality inheres almost entirely in young David's relation to the object world he inhabits. Both Freud and Lévi-Strauss provide fruitful models for understanding this complex relation, particularly as an indicator of David's aesthetic awakening.

Bricolage is a creative form of composition and assembly. In Lévi-Strauss's terms, the activity of the bricoleur is distinct from, and even oppositional to, that of the engineer: the domain of the former is the science of the concrete, that of the latter, the abstract.[51] Bricolage's relatively limited repertoire, like the stable, "constitutive units of myth," ironically allows for more creativity: "Consider [the bricoleur] at work and excited by his project. His first practical step is retrospective. He has to turn back to an already existent set made up of tools and materials, to consider or reconsider what it contains and, finally and above all, to engage in a sort of dialogue with it. . . . He interrogates all the heterogeneous objects of which his treasury is composed to discover what each of them could 'signify.'"[52]

Lévi-Strauss's observations may well describe many forms of childhood play, wherein a closed set of objects is tinkered with to create new combinations. David's tendency to assemble his world through certain objects is certainly evident early on in *Call It Sleep.* As a young boy, he turns to his box of "trinkets" when left alone with Luter, a friend of his father's whom he doesn't trust: "Hurt, David had turned away and gotten out his box in the pantry in which he saved both the calendar leaves he collected and whatever striking odds and ends he found in the street. His mother called them his gems and often asked him why he liked things that were worn and old. It would have been hard to tell her. But there was something about the way in which the link of a chain was worn or the thread on a bolt or a castor-wheel that gave him a vague feeling of pain when he ran his fingers over them. They were like worn shoe-soles or very thin dimes. You never saw them wear, you only knew that they were worn, obscurely aching."[53]

David's treasures consist of pages marking the passage of time as well as found industrial detritus; their visible, tangible evidence of being "worn and old" comforts David in vulnerable moments. The self-soothing motion of running his fingers along their surfaces, themselves worked through use and handling, seems expressly directed toward the absence of his mother, in whom Luter has displayed a prurient and confusing (to David) interest. Arguably, David turns to his box of stuff in Luter's presence to find an objective correlative for his own "obscure aching"; like a fetish, the objects potentially reanimate the presence of his mother, who is with his father on a rare evening out. David's engagement with these objects is notably different from Reb Gedalya distractedly "fiddling" with the things on Mirel's vanity. Reb Gedalya's handling of his daughter's objects is ultimately a meaningless, idle act; it brings neither him nor Mirel any real comfort and does nothing to prevent his family's catastrophic undoing.

David's relation to the world of objects, on the other hand, is productive, tactile, and autoerotic; like the bricoleur, he relies on an "already existent set made up of tools and materials" and plays with "whatever is at hand."[54] In an earlier sequence, on the street with his friends, handling a small cog from an alarm clock mesmerizes David—he is "engrossed in the rhythmic, accurate teeth of the yellow cog in his hand"—until he yields to a transcendent vision that prefigures his budding aesthetic development: "His body relaxed. . . . Within him a voice spoke with no words but with the shift of slow flame."[55] In these early scenes, he intuitively draws on the resonant and productive profundity latent in what Sherry Turkle calls "evocative objects"—"companions" to our intellectual and emotional lives.[56]

David's development within the home as well as in external settings such as school and the street is littered with the depiction of such evocative objects and David's meditative grip on them: pennies received from a neighbor for lighting her *shabbes* oven; the apple and cake he is given at the police station after getting lost; the rabbi's sharpened wood pointers in *cheder* (religious school); the zinc and wire "sword" forced on him by some local toughs; and the skate key belonging to his new friend Leo. David's relation to these objects infuses them with emotion and diverse symbolic power: they are tokens of the unfamiliar, the American, the roughness of the street. Some represent access to Jewish textual study, which is itself fraught with both random punishment and transcendent beauty. Ultimately, these items point toward David's emergence as an artist and a sexual being, separate from his mother's suffocating tenderness as well as his father's abusive anger and brutal violence.

His brief friendship with Leo, whom David meets one afternoon on the roof of his building, sets in motion the novel's concluding series of dramatic events. While Leo's confidence runs rings around David's juvenile adulation, the older boy's magnetism is also depicted in relation to stuff: home alone with David and snacking on forbidden non-Kosher crab legs in his kitchen, Leo "climbed up on the pantry ledge" and retrieved his own box of "trinkets, rings, lockets, cameos":

> Leo fumbled among them. . . . He pulled out a broken string of two-sized black beads near one end of which a tiny cross dangled with a gold figure raised upon it like the one on the wall. "Dat's de busted rosary me ol' lady foun', dere's on'y a coupla beads missin'. I'll give it tuh yuh. Come on it's real holy."
>
> David stared at it fascinated. "C'n I touch id?"
>
> "Sure yuh c'n, go on."[57]

David notices the dusty box's sliding cover with the word *God* "printed in bold, black letters."[58] Among the jewelry and other knick-knacks, the rosary is both decorative ornament and ritual object. The scene is deftly tied to the above-cited depiction of David's "gems" through the casual mention of the mother; Leo's fumbling here will be exchanged in later scenes for physical dexterity, even deception, as he tricks David into arranging a compromising rendezvous with Esther, David's older cousin. Both scenes trade on the comforting caress of the evocative object to displace or repress anxiety provoked by the idea of his mother Genya and cousin Esther as sexual beings. The passage also contains some of the novel's typically vivid rendering of the colloquial speech of its two speakers, both young, ethnically tagged New Yorkers. David's request to touch "id" may be read as Freudian pun: in order for his own creative, erotic side to truly blossom, David will need to get close to his "slow flame" and allow it to burn higher and brighter as it does in the novel's apocalyptic closing section, when David is electrocuted by the streetcar's third rail.

Both the soothing function of David's box of stuff and the revelatory encounter with Leo's rosary are undermined in the novel through David's experience of two special items belonging to his parents, objects that recall troubled, unresolved aspects of their past. Indeed, despite their different personalities, both

Genya and Albert are tightlipped in relation to their lives "back home," and David tries to glean what he can from his mother's long conversations in Polish with her sister and from his father's rare comments. Two newly acquired items, purchased simply for decorative purposes, stir up memories of the past, and both objects become the subject of fascination and fixation for David. First, his mother brings home a small painting: "It was a picture of a small patch of ground full of tall green stalks, at the foot of which, tiny blue flowers grew."[59] The painting reminds Genya of the cornfields of her childhood landscape—"David had hardly ever seen his mother so animated"—and is later connected by the paranoid Albert to Genya's supposed infidelity. As if in response to the painting's idyllic pastoral scene, Albert, who has recently found steady employment as a milkman, brings home a new whip and a mounted set of bull horns. David discovers these items as he enters the apartment: "On the wash-tub lay a bulky package, the strings cut, but the heavy brown paper still covering it; and beside it, crossing each other, a new white-handled whip and the butt of the old broken black one."[60]

David had witnessed his father break the whip while beating a milk thief, an episode—during which Albert also threatened his son—seared in his memory. The new whip is clearly a reminder of his father's explosive violence, while the second item signals something else, a message just as ominous but more opaque: "Before him on a shield-shaped wooden plaque, two magnificent horns curved out and up, pale yellow to the ebony tips. So wide was the span between them, he could almost have stretched his arms out on either side, before he could touch them. Though they lay there inertly, their bases solidly fashioned to the dark wood, there pulsed from them still a suggestion of terrific power, a power that even while they lay motionless made the breast ache as though they were ever imminent, ever charging."[61] The plaque is a reminder of Albert's work with cattle as a young man; it is also linked to the death of his father, who was trampled by a bull while working with Albert. Juxtaposed against the delicate, tiny blue flowers of his mother's painting, the massive horns, which David cannot even touch, point toward an unattainable strength and masculinity belonging exclusively to his father.

David's evocative objects and his parents' emotional baggage, symbolized through the commodified aesthetic objects of the painting and plaque, collide in a climactic scene toward the novel's conclusion. Confronted by Albert about David's true paternity, Genya tries to shield her son from his father's wrath. During his parents' escalating quarrel, David retrieves the broken whip from the kitchen and presents it to his father: "'This?' The lids dropped over his father's consuming eyes. 'Why do you—? Why is this given? You know what happened to this? Is it your fate you're begging for?'" Before he can be stopped, Albert attacks his son, and the rosary beads fall from David's pocket: "There, stretched from the green square to the white square of the checkered linoleum lay the black beads—the gold cross framed in the glimmering, wan glaze. Horror magnified the figure on it."[62]

Within the context of the novel's discursive treatment of religious tropes, David's admission of guilt and offering of himself as a sacrifice seem to combine the compassion of the rosary with the wrath of Old Testament Judaism. Cast into the street by his mother to save him from Albert's rage, traumatized and badly beaten, David escapes into the neighborhood. He is determined to overcome his fear and face the transformative power within the streetcar tracks.[63] The weapon of choice emerges associatively from his racing mind: "Here I am Mama! By cans I'm hiding. . . . Store-spoon, milk-spoon. . . . Even if it ain't a sword, could go in the crack. Where it splashes, hold cup like where you held sword."[64] The dipper combines this mother's love (milk) with his father's wrath (his workplace): "David picked up the dipper, crept out the store entrance, and with the scoop of the dipper under his armpit, long, flat handle in his hand, he slunk quietly toward Tenth Street." The text's erotic images ("the wavering point / of the dipper's handle found the long, / dark, grinning lips") coexist with a sense of the dipper as a pen, caught in David's "frozen fingers."[65] He eventually succeeds in slipping the dipper in the streetcar tracks, igniting the third rail; the long poetic passages that synthesize the voices of the street—the "multitudes"—mark his own debut as an artist:

> *Power! Power like a paw, titanic power,*
> *ripped through the earth and slammed*
> *against his body and shackled him*
> *where he stood. Power! Incredible,*
> *barbaric power! A blast, a siren of light*
> *within him, rending, quaking, fusing his*
> *brain and blood to a fountain of flame.*[66]

Ostensibly moving beyond the fetishized objects of his childhood, the "trinkets" of the absent mothers' pantries, the work of bricolage in the these passages is rendered as a hands-on engagement with the full-throated voices of the street—the profane argot, colloquial jargon, and accented English of commerce and neighborhood. While the novel had earlier deployed a more express intertextuality to underline David's exposure to traditional Judaic sources, here the pastiche of casual conversation (about card playing and family life) and particular cultural references (to the Statue of Liberty and the New Testament) are funneled through David's gradual regaining of consciousness. Bricolage here approaches a kind of acculturation: David absorbs the dense particulars of his cultural environment and rearranges them to satisfy, if only temporarily, his own existential need to belong, to feel whole and rooted. After being resuscitated and brought home by a policeman, David sees his father: "For the briefest moment David felt a shrill, wild surge of triumph *whip* within him" (emphasis added).[67] David's acknowledgment of his brief challenge to the whip's authority is embedded in an awareness of the power of language as that set of materials "at hand." Like the material sense of language in imagist poetry, here too language is gradually revealed in Roth's novel as a malleable, yet persistent, substance, equally shaped by the concrete circumstantial conditions of its production and those actor-agents who speak and work with it.

In the novel's concluding paragraphs, as he begins to fall asleep, David feels he has "the power to cull again and reassemble the shrill cry, the hoarse voice, the scream of fear, the bells, the thick breathing, the roar of crowds and all sounds."[68] He recognizes the potentially regenerative property inherent in the creative process—the culling and reassembling. Roth's project, then, represents a near note perfect iteration of the modernist writer's coming-of-age in the metropole, an artistic working through of the cultural materials at hand. Regarding the influence of modernism on transnational, postcolonial poetic forms, Jahan Ramazani's observation about Anglo-American writers rings true here: "The modernists—many of them exiles and émigrés themselves—were the first English-language poets to create a formal vocabulary for the intercultural collisions and juxtapositions, the epistemic instabilities and decenterings, of globalization."[69] This "modernist bricolage" consists of a heteroglossic engagement with an array of cultural sources. Roth's David, as a figure for the author himself, is a direct descendent of the early Objectivist poetry of Charles Reznikoff and Louis Zukofsky, and he anticipates the postwar Hebrew-Yiddish work of New York poet Gabriel Preil. To the degree that language remains an important theme for contemporary American Jewish authors such as Michael Chabon and Nicole Krauss, Roth's David—with his evocative objects and tactile relation to the materials at hand—remains an exemplary and foundational figure.

BETWEEN OLIVE WOOD AND TAXIDERMY IN S. Y. AGNON'S *ONLY YESTERDAY*

With our discussion of S. Y. Agnon's novel *Only Yesterday* (Hebrew), perhaps best known for the canine hero who narrates much of its second half, we pivot to one final geographic setting: Palestine of the early twentieth century. Though all three novels comment on the emergence of modernist Jewish culture, perhaps nowhere is the role of the artist more expressly at the center than in Agnon's novel. Shmuel Yosef Agnon (1888–1970) is renowned for his deft weaving of modernist irony with traditional Judaic sources and motifs; his writings treat a broad range of the epistemological questions and material conditions shaping modern Jewish life.

The author's interest in economic concerns and his knowledge of contemporaneous critical writing about financial and monetary matters are the subject of a recent monograph by Yonatan Sagiv. While Sagiv's study does not address *Only Yesterday,* his attention to the function of economic and commercial discourse in Agnon's work helps frame our analysis of that novel's extended meditation on the ideal materials of new cultural formations. According to Sagiv, the discussion of economics is inseparable from other core elements of Agnon's work, including his incisive depiction of the cultural and social fissures of early twentieth-century Jewish experience: "Agnon's writing demonstrates that while discourses such as religion, language, or psychoanalysis seem separate from the operations of the monetary economy, these discourses at the same time cannot escape being caught up in an economy of their own, subjected to rules of exchange, calculation, profit, and loss."[70] Indeed, the economy of artistic production receives extensive treatment in Agnon's novel. Of the works discussed in this chapter, *Only Yesterday* contains the most extended meditation on art's role in modernity's new economic order. The novel's discursive treatment of materiality differs from that of *The End of Everything* and *Call It Sleep,* both of which depend on an imaginative act of abstraction—the gap between object and narrative, between thing and meaning. The earlier novels pay careful attention to material objects' relation to temporality and loss, and their tendentious capacity to constitute physical markers of presence—whether for the disappearing shtetl, the lost secrets of Genya's and Albert's pasts, or the emergent force of David's aesthetic awakening. A different sort of material mediation shapes the heart of *Only Yesterday.*

In *Only Yesterday,* the question of raw material itself—and what can be made of it—constitutes an essential narrative thread. Yitsḥak Kummer, the novel's young Galician protagonist, travels to Palestine and finds gainful employment in Jerusalem as a housepainter. His training and practice are embedded in the depiction of other kinds of thing-making and the material conditions shaping their production, circulation, and consumption. Yitsḥak meets artisans from the Bezalel School of Arts and Crafts, who make olive wood products sold as "Holy Land" souvenirs as well as the taxidermist Arzef, a Jerusalem native. Both of these domains are clearly metonymic representations of the possibilities and limits of Jewish cultural production in prewar Palestine. Moreover, their hybrid status as both natural and man-made foregrounds the degree to which objects mediate human relations and potentially shape the production of a national self. The olive wood frames, books, and ritual objects are purchased by Christian pilgrims, and Arzef's stuffed animals are displayed in European museums, thus embedding an emergent national Jewish culture within a transnational setting of creation and exchange.

At the same time, these creations serve as foils for the novel's chief figure of nonhuman thing making—Balak the dog.[71] Balak's animal pedigree is undeniable; however, given the presence of script written by a human hand on his skin, Balak is also a book—specifically, a scroll, prepared by Yitsḥak Kummer, the scribe, and treated as such by the various communities in Jerusalem who are challenged to interpret him. The novel's complex rendering of the artistic process across a wide range of materials reaches its peak in Balak's wandering through the city, a movement that demonstrates how both animals and ostensibly inanimate objects may display agency and become, borrowing Ian Hodder's term, "entangled" with their implicit subjects.[72]

Animals and objects are both examples of what Bruno Latour has termed "hybrids."[73] Insisting on the principle of relationality rather than essential dualisms and distinct, stable entities, the hybrid exists at the seam between animal and human, as well as that between the social and the material or technological.[74] While crafted objects may be the products of human labor, they continue to exist in and of themselves, mediating the hands that made them and producing their own proliferating meaning. As we have seen, this distinction between material and ideas is at the heart of Marx's description of a commodity. Within *Only Yesterday,* the narrative turns on attention to things created from "Nature" through an act of imaginative abstraction; the objects of taxidermy and olive wood craft support the novel's discussion regarding a new, national Jewish culture in Palestine—a discourse that culminates in the creation and circulation of Balak the dog. Agnon's novel builds on our discussion of materiality in the following way: as we have seen, for both Freud and Lévi-Strauss—and to a lesser extent Marx—the meaning of the material object resides in some relation to human activities. Indeed this, according to Brown, constitutes the very essence of thingness: "The story of objects asserting themselves as things, then, is the story of a changed relationship to the human subject and thus the story of how the thing really names less an object than a particular subject-object relation."[75] Though subject-object relations shape the narrative meaning of materiality in *Only Yesterday,* we find something else as well—sustained attention to the relation itself, and its eventual dissolution in the presence of the hybrid.

Yitsḥak first learns of olive wood crafts through the figure of Shimshon Bloykof, who excels as a creator of olive wood objects, especially picture frames.[76] Bloykof, who trains Yitsḥak as a housepainter, has a pragmatic attitude toward his craft, noting, "I was foolish and I thought everything preceded from ideas and I didn't know that the main thing about painting is painting."[77] There is a family resemblance here to Marx's distinction cited earlier regarding the play between materiality and ideas, the way in which the chair's wood becomes "transcendent" through its commodification and entry into the marketplace. Bloykof's devotion to "painting as painting" is evident as he trains Yitsḥak to support himself through commercial signs and domestic interiors—as a result of which he becomes financially self-sufficient, an independent laborer and, ultimately, a more eligible bachelor.

Yitsḥak also encounters students from the Bezalel School of Arts and Crafts, founded in 1906 out of a belief that art could contribute to the national enterprise. Bezalel's program conformed to maskilic notions of art's rehabilitative utility as well as the desire to help Jews become productive by teaching them skills and finding them work, freeing them from the charity of Jerusalem's *haluka:* "The assumption was that education in crafts and trade would give the population not only work but also an outlet for individual expression; it would add value to the products and thus increase their competitiveness."[78] Bezalel trained students in a variety of decorative crafts and religious objects meant for domestic and foreign markets; sold to pilgrims and tourists as souvenirs and exported to markets abroad, olive wood frames inlaid with seashells were one of the school's early areas of specialization.[79] Some of the school's early supporters specifically understood its virtues to reside in a devotion to traditional handicraft. Writing in 1907 in the British newspaper the *Jewish Chronicle,* Dr. Otto Warburg claimed that "in this age of large industries dominated by machinery . . . the individuality of the workman is dying before the mechanical contrivances which turn out all kinds of work to a given pattern in a given time."[80] Warburg's comments recall Benjamin's analysis of the fate of art's "aura" in the "age of mechanical reproduction" and demonstrate how transnational economic forces shaped modern Jewish cultural expression.

Bezalel's origins were understood as emblematic of the Zionist movement's desire for a new Hebrew culture, one expressly rooted in the new-old geography of Palestine/The Land of Israel. However, the school's emphasis on the production of Arts and Crafts was subsequently perceived as outdated by later generations of modernist Israeli critics and artists. This untenable paradox, in which Bezalel simultaneously represents both the epitome and the antithesis of Zionism, resembles Zionism's own conflicted origins—an ostensibly secular political movement entrenched in Judaism's theological messianic beliefs.[81] The objects produced in Bezalel's workshops also mark Zionism's ambivalent relation to Orientalism, a complex field in which "the Jew becomes simultaneously colonized and colonizer."[82] These competing tensions are well served by the novel's generally ironic depiction of Bezalel as well as its extended engagement with the making of objects.[83]

One long chapter describes the plight of Bezalel-trained Jewish artisans working for a German Christian business owner who sells the objects abroad; the artisans try to raise funds to organize their own shop, but their efforts are ultimately defeated, in part by accusations of blood libel. The local production of religious artifacts from olive wood, ostensibly part of a new economic regime, is thus mapped onto relations between Jews and gentiles in Europe in which the threat of commercial disruption is quelled through antisemitic violence. Jerusalem's olive wood industry seems to be a special case of what Arjun Appadurai calls "tourist art," that is, "objects produced for aesthetic, ceremonial, or sumptuary use in small face-to-face communities [that] are transformed culturally, economically, and socially by tastes, markets and ideologies of larger economies."[84] While these objects of religious ritual art were products of a colonial enterprise, with the production and exchange of indigenous materials marking a relation between East and West, they were also part of the local cultural economy.[85] Specifically, the novel's formal structure, with the first half taking place largely in Jaffa and the second unfolding in Jerusalem, places two formidable, potentially competing cultural options front and center. Indeed, Bloykof's frames are ubiquitous items in early Zionist Palestine: "[They] are found in the home of every Hebrew writer in Jaffa and Jerusalem. Those frames are made of olive wood in the shape of a Magen David inlaid with seashells, but the teachers of Jaffa who have a literary bent put the pictures of our writers and poets in them, the greatest one in the middle and his satellites around him, including pictures of themselves, for there isn't one single teacher in Jaffa who doesn't see himself as a writer, unlike the teachers of Jerusalem who see themselves as sages and who put pictures of our great sages including pictures of themselves in those frames."[86]

The literal framing of writers in these souvenir objects embeds authors within the material world of commerce and exchange. The equivalence between the two groups of writers—one (in Jaffa) presumably "secular" and the other (the Jerusalem sages) presumably devoted to "religious" matters—is commensurate with the novel's staging of an emergent national culture through distinctions between these two cities and their populations. Yitsḥak eventually rents a room from one of the Jewish artisans who had tried to open their own shop. That these craftsmen are described as starving dogs creates a link between the olive wood craftsmen and dogs, a proposition borne out in the novel's elevation of Balak as a philosopher-dog, a true artist, thoughtful and creative and even textual, but also concerned with the material world of food and fleas.

Both the olive wood industry and taxidermy rely on materials of the natural world. Readers are first introduced to Arzef and his work when Yitsḥak moves from Jaffa to Jerusalem:

> What made Arzef choose that strange craft of stuffing the skins of animals and birds and insects and reptiles no one knew. Arzef lives alone like the First Adam in the Garden of Eden . . . among all kinds of livestock and animals and birds and insects and reptiles and snakes and scorpions. He dwells with them in peace, and even when he takes their soul, they don't demand his blood in exchange, since they enter the great museums of Europe because of him. . . . Important to Arzef are the livestock and animals and birds and insects and reptiles mentioned in the writings of the Holy Ones and in the two Talmuds, that dwell in the Land of Israel. Arzef hunts them and throws away their flesh and fills their skin so they will be preserved.[87]

If Arzef is "the First Adam," then naming—Adam's primary obligation toward his animal fellows—is figured in this passage as both death and memorial practice: he "hunts them and throws away their flesh and fills their skin so they will be preserved." Language ironically both destroys and enacts a kind of presence, a material marker of the animal's absence. Arzef's work is also implicitly connected to the Zionist project of inventing a "Hebrew landscape" through its attention to Talmudic flora and fauna.[88] Indeed, taxidermy has historically acted as a point of negotiation between old and new worlds, between ostensibly established European orders and colonial projects, whether in the Americas or in the Middle East.[89] The "strong colonial resonance of taxidermy as a form" is borne out, in part, through the depiction of Arzef's work being displayed in "the great museums of Europe" and the professional, financial attention of (presumably) Orientalist scholars.[90] The trade of taxidermic specimens within the novel's commercial realm also allows their essential ambiguity to be directly referenced. For example, Arzef debates a customs official "who had trouble assessing how much customs duties to impose on them [a pair of stuffed skins], either the rate for live animals but they weren't alive, or the rate for inanimate objects but they did have skin and they did have bones."[91] This stubborn ability to exist simultaneously as part of both nature and culture is, according to Rachel Poliquin, "the irresolvable tension that defines all taxidermy."[92] There is also, arguably, something quintessentially "transcendent" and "grotesque" about taxidermy as an art form—extending, even eternalizing the life of a natural being (more powerful, perhaps, than the First Adam!) but in a form that also always reminds the viewer of death.

The character of Arzef appears to have been modeled, in part, on the zoologist Yisrael Aharoni. A photograph from the 1940s at the Hebrew University, Jerusalem, features Aharoni in the classroom: a lab-coated professor holding a bone, a zoological lesson in Latin, Hebrew, and Arabic on the blackboard behind him.[93] He is framed by two complete specimens (a bird and a rodent), literally, "arranged skins" (taxidermy), and surrounded by smaller pieces of skeleton; these fragments, partial souvenirs, hint at some once-vibrant whole. Bird and rodent are also each potentially related to some larger collection, classified by species and type. These calibrated differences between the animal remains potentially destabilize the seemingly ironclad distinction between animal and human; by recognizing the multitudes contained within the former term, we are asked to interrogate the possibilities for difference within the latter—a quality also alluded to in the blackboard's polyphonic linguistic terrain.[94] However, these observations are possible when we turn away from the man in the lab coat and the etymological lesson on the blackboard to consider the thing itself, and not, to paraphrase Williams, the ideas in it.

Arzef is linked to Balak in the novel through the practice of taxidermy, and the fatal focus on Balak's skin, upon which Yitsḥak has—on a whim—painted the Hebrew words *kelev meshuga* (crazy dog). The word for dog (*kelev*) read backwards is Balak. Though dogs are expressly exempt from Arzef's reach, Balak's presence in the novel—the dog is also a walking signifier of sorts—should remind readers that books, historically, have been made from animal corpses.[95] Well into the early modern era, animal skins were used to create vellum or parchment, and animal bones were the source of the glue used in binding. Balak has Hebrew letters written upon his fur, and is perceived via this holy script by those who encounter him. So too, Arzef is not only a taxidermist but also a kind of bookmaker—an artisan working with animal skin.

I offer this reading of Balak as a scripted hybrid or walking book because it embeds him in the novel's concern with made objects—specifically objects that straddle the relation between nature and culture. Capitalizing on and complicating Agnon's treatment of materiality in taxidermy and olive wood craft, Balak is the novel's greatest "thing" as well as its most memorable rendering of the hybrid—an entity who fully embodies, and suffers, the dissolution of the nature-culture divide. Balak's symbolic value is so prolific (notably spoofed within the journalistic accounts and rumors regarding the dog's meaning), the imaginative investment in his skin and perambulatory habits so great—yet Balak himself remains ultimately inscrutable, irreducible, and beholden only to himself.[96] As a made object, he succeeds in escaping the market's commodified logic, given his uniqueness and his residual and mobile aura.

Agnon's modernist novel is not as directly implicated in the slaughter of animals as medieval parchment manuscripts; however, the novel seems to suggest that certain traditional norms regarding the text's embodied qualities may endure in modern settings. Just as olive wood crafts may preserve substantive traits of premodern art (their status in religious ritual, their potential aura as individual, hand-made creations), so too the book—in Agnon's hands—struggles to retain some of its status as a document of communal consequence even as it becomes an object of economic exchange. Certainly the figure of the writer in Agnon's work is a complex synthesis: the solitary modernist genius, alone in his room—Hemdat, in the earlier stories—as well as the scribe, a more traditional figure embedded in his community and in a world of craft, of writing as a kind of physical, artisanal extension of the author's hand.

In the years following the publication of *Only Yesterday,* Agnon was involved in the writing of *Sefer Buczacz* (1955). *The Buczacz Book* is a *yizker* (memorial) book, a new-old genre whose function goes beyond the memorialization that typified its premodern antecedents; earlier documents such as *pinkasim* (registers) included anecdotal, impressionistic accounts alongside lists of important events and personalities associated with a particular town, often in the wake of disaster or antisemitic violence. *Yizker* books, however, offered more than just a postwar historical record of towns that were largely wiped out in the Shoah; they were conceived as artifacts, often referred to by their authors as objects such as a gravestone or memorial candle for the destroyed town. As a genre, they confirm Barbara Benedict's observation that "historically, literary genres have always emerged from the conditions of their production."[97] As such, *yizker* books constitute compelling evidence regarding the immense importance of material forms for midcentury Jewish cultures, during precisely those years in which the material foundations of many Jewish communities were under attack. The ethnographic project of S. An-sky privileged objects and photographs over written accounts as a way to preserve a vanishing civilization and connect an alienated intelligentsia to its cultural roots. Chapter 4 will explore how the *yizker* books extend this prewar work, creating a new transnational genre wherein writing itself becomes an object. Understood in relation to the material concerns of fiction discussed in this chapter, *yizker* books represent a deepening of the anxiety over writing's value during an era of tremendous social and political instability.

The material preoccupations of novels by Bergelson, Roth, and Agnon, with their commodified, evocative, and hybrid objects, may be read in relation to those cataclysmic changes that shaped Jewish modernity. The novel's generic conditions offer an arena in which people and their stuff may be observed and coded in the widest possible terms; that is, the novel's formal affordances allow for a certain set of object lessons. These novels, whose writing and publication straddle the horrors of midcentury, therefore exemplify one way in which modern Jewish literature has been reconceived as material form.

Chapter 4 Between *Sefer* and *Bukh*: Holocaust Memorial Books

Korets, Karlin, Bratzlav, Lubavich, Ger, Lublin—hundreds of little towns were like holy books.
—A. J. Heschel, "The Inner World of the Polish Jew" (1947)

In more ways than one, these memorial books are a species of fiction.
—David Roskies, *The Jewish Search for a Usable Past* (1999)

Historically, literary genres have always emerged from their conditions of production. The way they were performed and produced, by and to whom, and how they were preserved for future audiences together make up their form.
—Barbara Benedict, "The Paradox of the Anthology" (2003)

MEMORY AND GENRE

The *yizker* book, a form that emerged largely after World War II and the Holocaust, although it has important antecedents in the interwar period, further exemplifies the material turn we have been seeing unfold in Jewish writing.[1] Composed in locations from Buenos Aires to New York to Tel Aviv, each book narrates the history and demise of an individual Jewish community—across eastern and central Europe and into the Balkans. These multilingual books were conceived as objects to commemorate the absence of those murdered populations and destroyed communities. Though related to premodern examples of Jewish writing about memory in the wake of trauma and catastrophe, the sheer number of memorial books—between nine hundred and fifteen hundred—sets them apart, as does their often staggering physical size and weight.[2] The heft of the memorial book is achieved in two ways: generally oversized dimensions—somewhere between a quarto (twenty-four by thirty centimeters) and a royal octavo (seventeen by twenty-five centimeters)—combined with prodigious page lengths. For example, *Pinkas Zamosc* (1957) clocks in at a staggering 1,265 pages, but 500 pages is not an unusual length for these books. Page after page, text appears in tightly spaced double columns or as a single block, with relatively scant room for illustrations, photographs, or chapter breaks. Variously catalogued as history, memoir, autobiography, and local field guide, the memorial book suggests a capacious genre that defies easy categorization. The very question of naming them points to their fundamentally hybrid status and their generic instability: note the plethora of terms in Hebrew and Yiddish used in their titles—*pinkas, sefer, megile, zamlbukh, gedenkbukh, geschichte.* More frequently, simply the name of the town commemorated serves as the complete book title. Often edited by committee, the materials are composed by an array of people connected to the town—survivors as well as descendents. The books are, quite literally, "collected memories," blending different modes and methods: folklore, anthropology, history, ethnography, reportage, memoir, lists, charts, maps, and statistics.

While their large number renders them sui generis, the memorial book is also a descendent of earlier forms of Jewish textual memory.[3] These "precursors" included the early modern *pinkas* (literally, pamphlet or notebook), those town records often compiled in the wake of antisemitic violence, as well as interwar ethnographies.[4] The *zamlbikher* (almanacs) are another important precedent for the memorial book form. These accounts of the minutiae of lived experience, the earliest of which date to 1916, were a kind of local history, exploring both the shtetl and cosmopolitan, urban life. Compiled by editors in Vilna's newly founded YIVO (Yiddish Scientific Institute), the *zamlbikher* were made possible by the work of hundreds of *zamlers* (collectors), themselves expressly "of the folk," who collected material with zeal and ingenuity, often working and sharing sources in local *zamlerkrayzen* (collectors' circles).[5] Like An-sky's work, these projects were conceived as fundamental records of life; it is only in retrospect that we have come to appreciate them as memory work.

A similar duality informed the production of the *Oyneg Shabes* archives, the enormous cache of documents written in the Warsaw Ghetto during the war, collected by the historian Emanuel Ringelblum.[6] Indeed, in his magisterial study of Ringelblum, his circle, and his life's work in Warsaw, Samuel Kassow points to the *zamlbikher* as possible antecedents for the *Oyneg Shabes* project.[7] Ringelblum and his comrades hid their extensive written record, including a myriad of documents, from personal notes and letters to lists of work assignments, descriptions of cultural gatherings, and official documents having to do with ghetto life and its restrictions, in a group of milk cans and metal strongboxes, and buried them in several locations shortly before German forces destroyed the ghetto in 1943. Some of the caches were miraculously recovered after the war and eventually published. Given their insistence on writing as an act of survival, on collecting as a prelude to re-membering, the *Oyneg Shabes* archives constitute an essential conceptual precursor to the *yizker* book.[8] The examples of both the *zamlbikher* and the *Oyneg Shabes* archives help us better understand the work of the *yizker* books, a corpus composed after the war and usually at a considerable geographic remove from their substantive locale—the object of their memory.

The memorial books themselves are more than acts of historical writing; they are expressly a form of collection and assemblage, as they are constituted through the gathering and collation of other texts, visual artifacts, and data. Each individual *yizker* book seeks to rescue something of the intimate particular, to concretize and commemorate the particular habits, behaviors, streets, histories, figures, and events, small and large, of a single community. Each book summons the unique, singular space of its titular location; like the souvenir, it possesses an incomplete relation to the past, demanding supplementary narrative.[9] At the same time, these books inevitably exist for the contemporary reader as a collection, a corpus of postwar work that presents a record of prewar European Jewish life.[10] Indeed, many of the books have been digitized and are available for download from the Yiddish Book Center in Amherst, Massachusetts. A printed collection of these bound facsimile volumes resides in the New York Public Library, available to the general public, including those searching for information about their ancestry. The digitized preservation process has potentially homogenized the history of these towns, ignoring the individual particulars of lived experience as well as the significant material features characterizing each individual book—its size, contours, iconographic and visual qualities, those traits that constitute its existence as a particular object. Bound within the institutional frames of those archives, libraries, and museums that house them—themselves also postwar constructions—these collections strive for completeness through forms of classification such as geographic area, language or genre, but necessarily remain incomplete and broken, like the past they seek to represent.[11]

The memorial book's desire to be representative or paradigmatic is inevitably shadowed by the original object, the town itself—"the city in its fullness."[12] Scholarship about the *yizker* books has typically focused on their reception as vehicles of memory and history. According to Jonathan Boyarin and Jack Kugelmass, historians have been wary of these books because of the potentially skewed or selective nature of their accounts.[13] A pair of reviews from the 1950s by the historian Yankev Shatzky offers a characteristic indictment of the books for their "unreliable" status. Most of Shatzky's comments address the "professionalism" of the volumes—specifically their reliability as historical documents—and he employs the descriptions "simple," "folksy," or "primitive" for books that do not, in his view, measure up. For example, regarding the *Pinkas Kowel*, Shatzky claims that "this must be an example how *not to gather together such a publication*. It is too primitive and too rough," while "the Belchatow memorial book may serve as an example on how such a volume should be compiled. It must be read by all who would like to learn what the surviving Jews experienced as they expressed their feelings about the destruction of their town in writing."[14] Here, Shatzky's view of the true purpose of these books becomes clear: to present a picture of the town's recent past and to provide impressions about the meaning of its destruction are more important than the town's history. In another essay two years later, Shatzky reviews a second group of volumes. Regarding the *Yizker-bukh Ratne*, he regrets "that so much effort went to waste, for it is doubtful whether even compatriots from Ratne will be able to read such a big and in essence boring book."[15] On the other hand, the *Yizker-bukh fun der Zhelekhover yidishe kehila* is "richly illustrated and attractively published. It was assembled with great culture, love, and reverence."[16]

Clearly, Shatzky's observations regarding the books' historical veracity demand critical context. Take, for example, his assertion that the memorial books are largely gravestones and, "as is well known, no one reads gravestones."[17] There is ample evidence for the first half of this claim—prefaces to many volumes refer to themselves as a *matseyve* (gravestone), and commensurate imagery appears on their title pages. However, gravestones may indeed actually be read, quite carefully, for both their iconic, locational qualities and their textual features. The memorial book's metaphorical status as a gravestone highlights its hybrid status, imagined as both a concrete, physical marker and a textual record of what has been destroyed—literally, a "giant paper cemetery."[18] Moreover, these books were written not as positivist accounts of a historical past but

Nota Koslowsky, title page illustration for A. Trus and J. Cohen, *Braynsk, sefer hazikaron* (1948). Courtesy of the Library of the Jewish Theological Seminary.

as emotional narratives, embedded in their present-day composition and compilation, for an intimate audience of Yiddish speakers and readers; survivors and descendents created the books, often within the communal structure of the *landsmanshaft* (mutual aid society) organizations, in order to commemorate the history of their town and its destruction and to honor the memory of their murdered neighbors.

The Yiddish historian Nachman Blumental delivers a more appreciative account of the memorial book in a series of twelve review essays appearing under

Nota Koslowsky, title page illustration for *Felshtin: Zamlbukh lekoved tsum ondenk fun di Felshtiner kdoyshim* (1937). Permission courtesy of Sidney Shaievitz, The Felshtin Society. Image courtesy of the Library of the Jewish Theological Seminary.

the title "A New Literary Genre—the *Yizker* Book" in the Israeli Bundist publication *Lebns-Fragn* in 1960–61. Blumenthal offers some general remarks regarding what he calls a "genealogy of literary genres," comparing their emergence to evolution in the natural sciences, and then proclaims: "It is a fact, that we in our time, after World War II, are living in a period in which a *new literary genre* is emerging and developing in mass proportions [scale]: the *yizker-bukh*" (emphasis added). Blumenthal lists a number of features that characterize the memorial books as a genre and distinguish them from other writing about the war. Chief among these is the strong tie between memory and place: the memorial book is a commemorative project, memorializing, like a tombstone, the life of the Jewish community it purports to describe. Furthermore, the books are authored collaboratively by people who "lived there, are from there, and lost their near and dear ones there." Notably, these authors are not professionals—"not necessarily intellectual or blessed with writerly talent"—but simply individuals who "have the need to express themselves and have something to say."[19] The importance of the first-person account is also noted by Rosemary Horowitz, who suggests that the "genre of autobiography, a relatively new one among eastern European Jewry, also exerted an influence on *yizker* books."[20] For Blumenthal, the memorial book is thus both the product of the "folk," the "nonwriter," as well as itself a *kol bo,* a miscellany of memories with neither ideology nor platform. The result is "colorful and not monochromatic."[21]

With the production of memorial books in Israel, Hebrew was introduced as a second language, eventually eclipsing Yiddish as the primary language of Holocaust memory, a choice at once ideological and pragmatic. For example, in *Pinkas Bendin* (1959), published in Israel, the editors expressly address the question of language: "Sons of our city in Israel—and they are the majority—demanded that it [the book] would appear in Hebrew, while sons of our city abroad demanded that it be composed in Yiddish, so that they would understand everything written in it."[22] Their solution, which was adopted by other volumes as well, was to produce two sections of equal length, one in each language, containing largely the same material. As Hebrew, and later English, emerged as dominant languages of memory about eastern Europe, Yiddish receded and the audience necessarily changed; in fact, language change was dictated by audience, or at least the idea that the books were produced for a specific posterity, and not only "in memory of." In recent years, some books have been translated for English-language readers, whose own approach and needs—several generations removed from the memorial book's "home" landscape—are somewhat different. Thus the books became less a memorial and more a memory text, part of the broad canon of scholarship and belle lettres related to the war and the Holocaust. Some have even been translated into Polish for Polish audiences wanting to learn about their own history in the wake of the Communist era, during which many local histories were wiped clean. These histories were preserved—in prolific detail—in memorial books.[23] As early as the 1970s, the memorial books became increasingly homogenous in form, especially those volumes published in Israel and edited by S. Kanc (at least thirteen volumes) and Dovid Shtokfish (at least sixteen volumes), which use some of the same visual material in different books.

I move beyond arguments about the memorial books' veracity as historiographic documents and build on Blumental's sympathetic evaluation of them as a "literary genre," focusing on their unusual generic status and relation to material form. Contextualizing claims about the memorial books in relation to their status as objects allows for a wider sense of the memorial book as a genre, an approach that itself leads to a fuller appreciation of the memorial book as both text and thing. In fact, the books were envisioned as possessing this dual function—resembling both the commemorative performance of the *Yizker* (the traditional memorial liturgy) as well as memorial objects, particularly those associated with Jewish rites of mourning: the lighting of a *ner tamid* (memorial candle or eternal light in a synagogue); a chronicle or list of people and places (similar to that of a traditional *pinkas* or chronicle); a *sefer* (sacred text). The memorial books put pressure on the boundaries of literary genre, as they are experienced both temporally, as a narrative, linguistic form, and spatially, as a three-dimensional object possessing a specific, repeated series of material and visual traits. Being appreciated for their objecthood complicates the received notion of these books as *only* textual vehicles of memory and history; understood as things, they expand the repertoire of artifacts whose analysis shapes our sense of the past.[24]

The memorial book may be a paradigmatic example of a genre that emerges from within the specific pressures of historical trauma, and displays an even wider variety of material affordances than any of the genres discussed thus far in this study. For example, Barbara Benedict notes that the new literary genre of the anthology, miscellany, or collection emerged during the long eighteenth century in a period of crisis characterized by the "decay of aristocratic and ecclesiastical authority during the Renaissance, Reformation, and Commonwealth," prefiguring what Habermas described as the emergence of the public sphere.[25] The Holocaust as a set of discrete historical events was characterized by the ongoing transformation of material experience—that is, the violent destruction of bodies, possessions, and places. It is not surprising, therefore, that a genre emerging in the wake of these events, within precarious and vulnerable conditions, might engage the terms of its own existence as a material object. Though the genre's postwar emergence may be observed in different locations, the prewar example of two memorial books related to the Ukrainian pogroms of 1919–20—*Khurban Proskurov* (1924) and *Felshtin* (1937), both discussed below—suggests an earlier, incipient awareness of writing's particular vulnerability to physical destruction and change. Both books anticipate the tone and substance of the postwar volumes: their distinctive size and formal features; the mix of narrative history, testimony, and images; and the collaborative nature of their production, distant from the events and places they describe.

But despite its resemblance to earlier forms, the genre of the memorial book seemed to appear out of whole cloth in a range of geographic locations. Perhaps, however, it is the nature of a literary form to percolate below the surface until it appears, given the right set of historical circumstances. We may therefore understand the emergence of new literary genres as a Kuhnian paradigm shift: the appearance of a new one represents the surfacing of something long in formation—the visible codification of practices, temperaments, and tendencies that have long been brewing. In the case of the memorial books, these "precursors" include the early modern *pinkas* and *zamlbukh.* Reading the memorial book as an emergent genre allows us to perceive these strands of continuity but also to appreciate its new and particular material features—the magnitude of its reach as well as its unique combination of visual, iconic forms.

Identifying these material features also underscores the possible relation between the memorial book and the other literary genres discussed in this study's earlier chapters—poetry, little magazines, and the novel. Indeed, the memorial book represents the most striking manifestation of my project's claims about the emergence of secular literary genres within Jewish culture—it is the spine around which my book revolves. Those material affordances discussed earlier—more material poetic language in a secular mode; a sensitivity to the alphabet's iconic value and the power of text and image together; an awareness of literature's own vulnerability to physical destruction and change—were part and parcel of their generic formation, embedded in the particular historical conditions of their production and consumption. The postwar emergence of the memorial book is a central juncture in this historical process, one that sets the stage for postmodern engagements with the book as a material form, especially mixed-media corpora such as graphic novels and artists' books. Indeed, viewing literature through the lens of materiality not only expands the canon; as we have seen, it also shifts our appreciation of more historically normative genres such as poetry and the novel.

Approaching the memorial books as a literary genre represents a unique opportunity to explore what Leora Auslander describes as "the two boundaries that scholarly production of the last generation has shown to be particularly fraught . . . those between the material and the linguistic and the material and the visual."[26] In considering these books with attention to their material and visual qualities, I focus largely on the earlier volumes. Having reviewed (that is, physically handled and paged through) over two hundred volumes, I recorded important details about fifty-six individual volumes.[27] Of that selection, published from 1924 to 1977, most appeared from 1941 to 1959, with smaller groups from the 1960s and 1970s. Given my desire to address their material generic features, I sampled only those with illustrations or some other iconographically noteworthy feature, including the two important prewar examples, *Khurban Proskurov* and *Felshtin.* In this chapter, I turn first to the visual architecture of the memorial books, focusing on drawings and visual features common to many of the books as well as maps of the towns and their surrounding area. I then consider the books themselves in relation to the broader context of "Holocaust objects" during and after the war, and finally, the "afterlives" of the memorial books in contemporary fiction.

THE VISUAL ARCHITECTURE OF THE MEMORIAL BOOKS

With the notable exceptions of Boyarin and Kugelmass's introductory essay to their anthology and selections from Rosemary Horowitz's edited volume, *Memorial Books of Eastern European History: Essays on the History and Meanings of Yizker Volumes,* scholars have largely overlooked, or even dismissed, the material and visual dimensions of these books.[28] Their comments typically treat the memorial books as a "research source" and the illustrations as supporting the text. For example, Abraham Wein notes that "illustrative material occupies an important place in memorial books. Sometimes there are hundreds of photographs, maps, sketches and other types of illustrations in a single book. That material complements the written word, capturing the general atmosphere of the town, its synagogues, institutions, and organizations, and personalities and types that characterized Eastern European Jewry."[29] What would it mean to go beyond this cursory observation to consider the illustrations as more than merely "complementing" the narrative?

Some memorial books contain a dizzying abundance of photographs of life before, during, and after the war, grouped by family, class in school, sites, landmarks, community celebrations or events from before war, images of ghetto life during war, postwar visits to ruins and remains. Daniel Magilow astutely distinguishes between memorial book photographs and Holocaust photography more broadly, noting that more well-known images of the Shoah were often taken by the perpetrators, while the images in memorial books were usually from personal collections, addressed to a specific audience—the community of loss.[30] Indeed, books about Ciechanowiec and Lomza are especially profusely

יזכור

המנציחה:
שלכטר (פטשק) חנה — ישראל
הנספים:
פטשק אלקה (לבית ליס) אם
פטשק יצחק אח

אלקה פטאַשק יצחק פטאשק

המנציחה:
שפרעכער (פיאנקה) גיטל — ישראל
הנספים:
פיאנקה רחל־לאה סבתא
פיאנקה משה אב

יושבים מימין לשמאל: משה פיאנקה רייזה פיאנקה
עומדים: בנימין פיאנקה דבורה פיאנקה

פיאנקה רייזע (לבית גרודנר) אם
פיאנקה יונה אח
פיאנקה דבורה אחות
פיאנקה בנימין אח
פיאנקה יהושע אח
פיאנקה רוזה (אשת יהושע) גיסה
פיאנקה שרה־פאיע (בת יהושע)

יונה פיאנקה יהושע פיאנקה

המנציח:
פיורה אלתר — ישראל
הנספים:
פיורה רייכל (לבית קופיטובסקי) אשה
פיורה מרדכי בן
פיורה מינה בת
פיורה דבורה בת
(ר׳ תמונה בעמ׳ 777)

המנציחים:
פיורה אלתר — ישראל
פיורה נתנאל — ישראל
הנספים:
פיורה שלמה אב
פיורה מנוחה אם
פיורה יצחק־יוסף אח
פיורה חיים־פסח אח

776

Memorial page from *Ciechanowiec, mehoz Bialystok, sefer edut ve-zikaron* (1964). Courtesy of the Library of the Jewish Theological Seminary.

illustrated, with photographs of the town, notable figures, and group portraits related to school, political affiliation, or cultural activities appearing on nearly every page.[31]

Some books include an alphabetized list of individuals and families killed during the war, alongside their photos. As Blumenthal notes in his appreciation of memorial books as a literary genre, the photographs contribute to their "truthfulness," their focus on "the concrete person, the concrete family, who are named with the true first and family names."[32] *Sefer Radom* (thirty-two centimeters tall) contains a lavish section entitled "Radom in Pictures," structured like a historical narrative and bound in between the Hebrew- and English-language sections of the book, 451 pages and 117 pages, respectively.[33] The introduction to the 75-page "supplement" offers a comprehensive goal for this extensive set of photographs, nothing less than a "mirror" of the war's horrors as well as the good times that preceded it:

> This part of the present volume, called "Radom in Pictures," is to visualize—as far as material has been available—the great institutions of that community and their important activities in all fields of life, in the course of the long history of Jewish Radom. It is also to perpetuate the memory of our community's public figures, writers and poets, rabbis and leaders and social pioneers; to show in pictures, as far as can be shown, the holocaust and the ghettoes, with all their sufferings and human misery. Thus it will be a true mirror of a community, once full of life and effervescent, a community of pathfinders of truth who believed in their philosophy of life, until struck down by cruel fate.[34]

Within the context of the memorial books, photographs exemplify Susan Sontag's maxim that "images do not seem to be statements about the world so much as pieces of it, miniatures of reality that anyone can make or acquire."[35] Their very presence alludes to the absence of the spaces and people they represent.[36] Alongside the other illustrations, the photographs add to the memorial book's significance as a material artifact: they seem to be concrete "pieces" of the world, a new kind of "thing."[37] Their vernacular quality—"that anyone can make or acquire"—augments their distinctiveness; however, the photographs also share in the books' iterative quality—that is, they are nominally devoted to a specific town but exist as part of a larger, even infinite, series of similarly conceived, and remembered, photographs.[38]

In Blumenthal's terms, there is something concrete and "truthful" about these photographs, but what of the illustrations, what kind of concreteness might they contribute? A preliminary typology of the volumes' illustrations would include a fallen menorah with flames threatening a nearby prayer book; a freakishly large candelabra, with letters of the town holding up the candles, and row after row of gravestones in the background; a small tree stump with a single branch clinging to the side; a town's physical form engulfed in flames; a cloaked mother and child watching a long line of refugees as their town burns on the horizon.[39]

These images were created using a variety of media, including pencil or charcoal drawings, watercolor sketches, and linocut or woodprints; though they

Title page of *Sefer zikaron le-kehilat Zborow* (1975). Courtesy of the Library of the Jewish Theological Seminary.

are placed alongside and usually work in tandem with the narrative, they may also be understood as a kind of visual code operating laterally across these books, alerting readers to the volumes' memory work even before they read the textual particulars.

Scholars agree that *Khurban Proskurov* and *Felsthin* set the tone and format for postwar memorial books, and both volumes contain especially distinctive and relatively extensive visual components.[40] However, the books' styles could not be more different; as described below, each book's visual domain shares certain formal features with other genres, other illustrated forms of Jewish writ-

Title page of *Rowne: Sefer zikaron* (1956). Permission granted by Henry Sapoznik, First Rovner Landsmanshaft. Image courtesy of the Library of the Jewish Theological Seminary.

ing, embedding the memorial books in the wider domain of midcentury Jewish visual culture. This process of borrowing features from visual culture shapes the memorial books' emergence as a new genre. *Khurban Proskurov* was published in memory of that Ukrainian town's pogrom victims; in comparison with the length of later *yizker* books, it is relatively on the slim side, just 112 pages of thick, semi-glossy paper; but the book's visual dimension is striking—every page of text is enclosed within a dark black frame like those used in traditional mourning announcements. Michael Loeb's art nouveau illustrations reference iconographic staples of bereavement—a pastoral graveyard scene; a fallen menorah

Title page of *Pinkas Kolomey* (1957). Courtesy of the Library of the Jewish Theological Seminary.

streaming flames next to a book titled *yizker*; a single tombstone with a long textual dedication; a delicate floral pattern whose petals are interwoven with the letters of a stylized rendering of the word *yizker.*[41]

The illustrations recall the drawings of Ephraim Moses Lillien (1874–1925), whose work was known for its biblical themes and who taught early classes at Jerusalem's Bezalel School of Arts and Crafts. *Khurban Proskurov*'s full-page frame of a burning candle and roses laid over a mix of foliage and thorny stems resembling a wire fence, with sunlight streaming from a hilltop set of structures in the upper right corner seems to expressly reference Lillien's well-known images created for the 1901 Zionist Congress in Basel and a series of illustra-

Title page of *Sefer Deblin-Modryzc* (1969). Courtesy of the Library of the Jewish Theological Seminary.

tions for *Lieder des Ghetto* (1903), a German translation of Morris Rosenfeld's Yiddish poetry.

In fact, seven of Loeb's illustrations were originally part of another context entirely. *Yizker: Tsum ondenken di gefalene vekhter un arbeyter in Erets Yisroel* (In Memory of Fallen Workers and Guards in the Land of Israel, 1916) was published by the New York–based Po'ale Tsiyon Palestine Committee. This volume

Michael Loeb, Menorah, in *Khurban Proskurov* (1924). Courtesy of the Library of the Jewish Theological Seminary.

Michael Loeb, art nouveau floral, in *Khurban Proskurov* (1924). Courtesy of the Library of the Jewish Theological Seminary.

was itself an expanded Yiddish version of a Hebrew edition of the book, which had appeared in Palestine in 1911.[42] The 1916 Yiddish edition was compiled by a group associated with the earlier book, whose members had found themselves in temporary residence in New York.[43] Loeb's illustrations appear in both books, and it seems likely that the drawings were prepared in a style that would suit the first publication's Zionist tenor—thus their resemblance to Lillien's

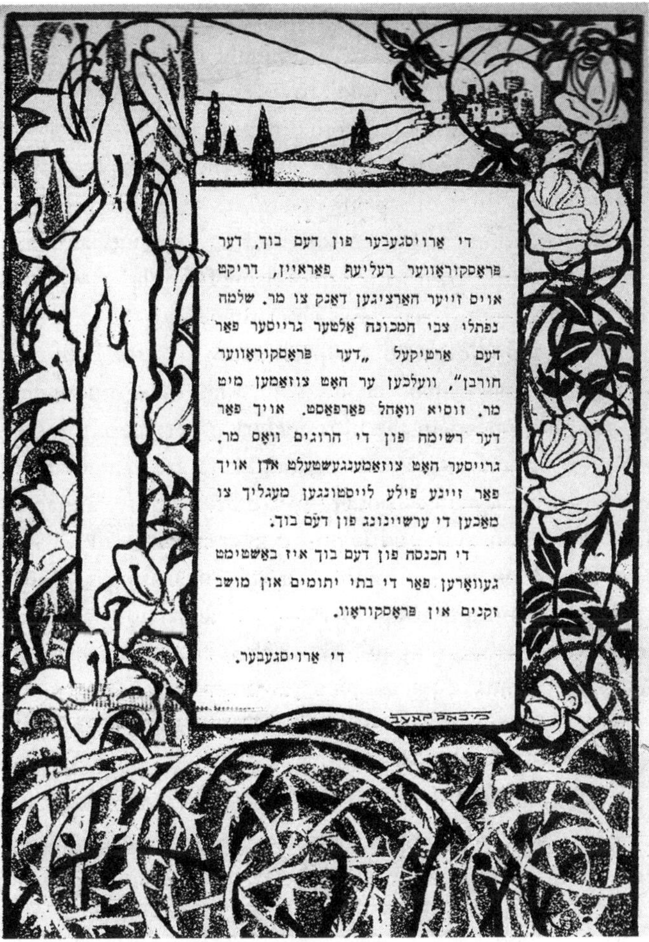

די אַרויסגעבער פון דעם בוך, דער
פּראָסקוראָווער רעליעף פאַראיין, דריקט
אויס זייער האַרציגען דאַנק צו מר. שלמה
נפתלי צבי חמכונה אַלטער גרייסער פאַר
דעם אַרטיקעל „דער פּראָסקוראָווער
חורבן", וועלכען ער האָט צוזאַמען מיט
מר. זוסיא וואָהל פאַרפאַסט. אויך פאַר
דער רשימה פון די הרוגים וואָס מר.
גרייסער האָט צוזאַמענגעשטעלט און אויך
פאַר זיינע פילע לייסטונגען מעגליך צו
מאַכען די ערשיינונג פון דעם בוך.

די הכנסה פון דעם בוך איז באַשטימט
געוואָרען פאַר די בתי יתומים און מושב
זקנים אין פּראָסקוראָוו.

די אַרויסגעבער.

Michael Loeb, homage to E. M. Lilien in *Khurban Proskurov* (1924). Courtesy of the Library of the Jewish Theological Seminary.

well-known drawings.[44] The repurposing of these images in *Khurban Proskuruv* creates a visual intertext and speaks to the fluidity of generic forms among different locations of memory: the "original" memorial book of 1911 is the first of what will become a veritable industry in modern Israeli culture, with its plethora of memorial sites and institutions. Though both the 1916 and 1924 volumes are enmeshed in other locations, the site of New York, with its relative stability and abundance of supportive, well-funded cultural institutions, seems essential to this network of exchange.

Like *Khurban Proskurov, Felshtin* is dedicated to the memory of Jews who perished during the Ukrainian Civil War; about a third of the town's population was murdered in a 1919 pogrom. However, *Felsthin*'s illustrations, created by Nota Koslowsky, could not be more different. Delicately drawn in a naturalistic style that conveys both a literal sense of the town's physical space and a dark, almost gothic, hint of its fate, *Felsthin*'s extensive illustrations have a simple, emotive quality.[45] The book's front cover, spine, and title page all contain the name of the town with flames rising from the crown of each letter. Inside, the full-page frontispiece shows a tombstone with the town's name looming over a forest of candles and dimly perceived structures. Four different renderings of a hand-drawn map of the shtetl punctuate the text in slightly different iterations: the first appears in the introductory pages above the caption *Bildliche mapa* (Pictorial map)—resembling an illustration in a picture book more than other *yizker* book maps. Though it is technically also a map, I therefore treat it here in relation to the other drawings created specifically for this volume. As an illustration, it seems more interested in creating a mood for readers than in actually communicating anything particular to the place—a mood that is both nostalgic and sanguine about the violence perpetrated upon the town and its inhabitants.

Koslowsky's "bird's-eye" map of Felshtin invites the viewer in but contains little sense of concrete geographic space; instead, the simply rendered homes and larger structures, including two churches, depict an orderly and intimate community life, clustered around a short main road leading in and out of town. Two other versions add contrast and adjust the town's features, creating the impression of a skull with two large sunken eye sockets. One such map is punctured by a bayonet and features a large overlaid caption "The Slaughter," letters dripping with blood. The other juxtaposes the town map with a cluster of skyscrapers and city streets, alluding to the book's provenance in New York; the two scenes are linked through the overlaid words "Felshtin United" and a dense crowd of human figures gathered in front of a speaker to honor the town and its memory. The fourth rendering of a "bird's-eye view" of the town, included in the volume's short English-language pages at the back, contains the fullest version; it retains the skull-like visage and the town's main features are complemented by more surrounding pastoral detail.[46] The skull appears more explicitly in another drawing, floating amid smoke from the burning town, under the word *sof* (end).

Koslowsky's other contributions to *Felshtin* include calligraphic embellishments in which a historiated initial begins a portion of text; for example, the enlarged letter *fay* (the first letter in the name Felshtin), which opens a narrative

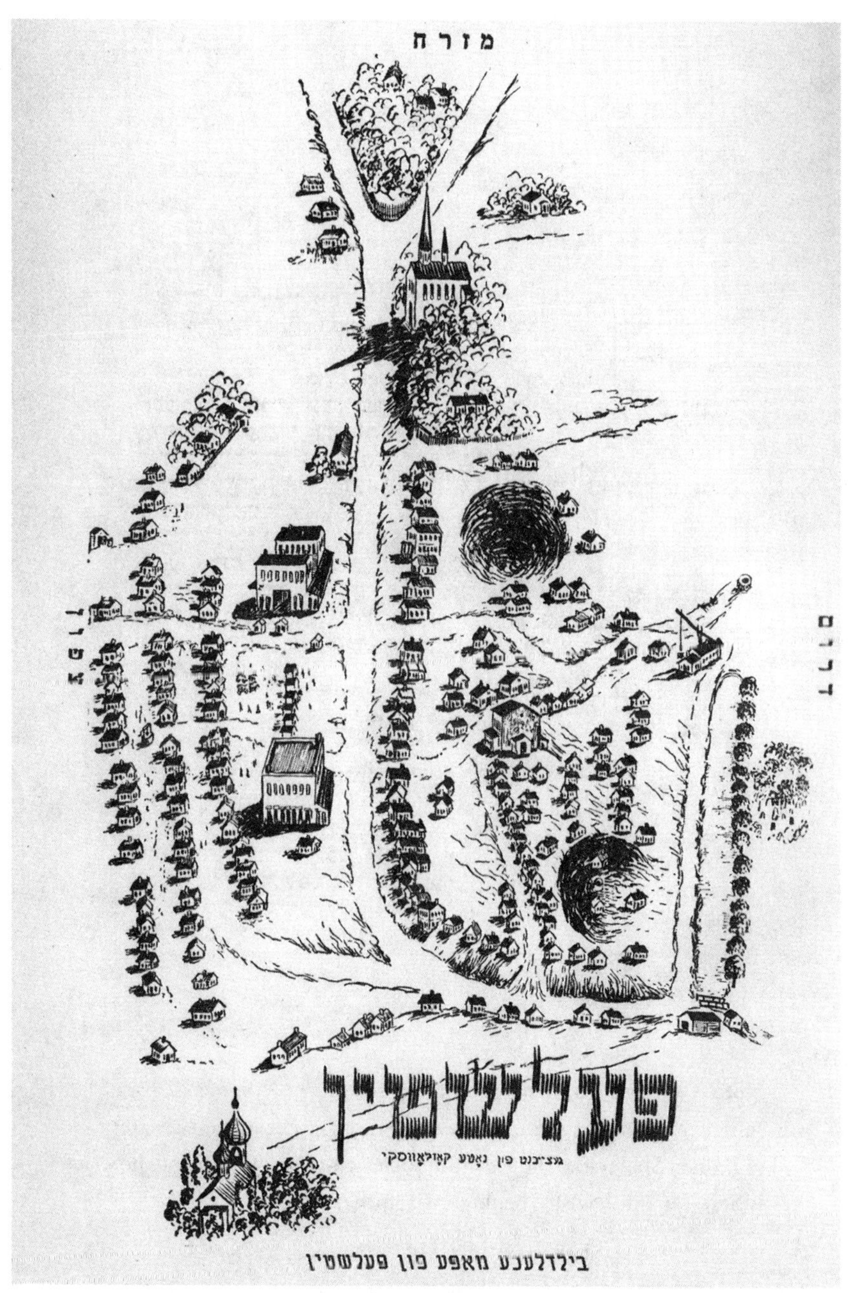

Nota Koslowsky, *Bildliche mapa* [Pictorial map], in *Felshtin: Zamlbukh lekoved tsum ondenk fun di Felshtiner kdoyshim* (1937). Permission courtesy of Sidney Shaievitz, The Felshtin Society. Image courtesy of the Library of the Jewish Theological Seminary.

יונה בוים

פעלשטין

פעלשטין איז א קליין שטעטעלע אין פּראָסקוראָווער אויעזד, פּאָדאָליער גובערניע אוקראַינע, זעהר נאָענט פון די אַמאָליגע עסטרייך-גאַליצישע גרעניצען.

די נאָענטסטע שטעט און שטעטלאַך אַרום פעלשטין זיינען: פּראָסקוראָוו, יאַרמעלינעץ, טשאַרנאָ-אָסטראָוו, שאַריפקע, קוזמין, גריידינג, טאַרנערודע און וואָלאָטשיסק.

די דערמאָנטע שטעטלאַך זיינען מיט פעלשטין, ווי אַ שטוב מיט אַן אַלקער — אינגאַנצען אַן ערך פון צוואַנציג, פינף-און-צוואַנ-ציג וויאָרסט אַוועק.

די שטעטלאַך — פעלשטין איינגעשלאָסען — האָבען דער-האַלטען איינס דאָס אַנדערע ביים לעבען.

די נאָענטסטע דערפער אַרום פעלשטין זיינען: נפתליפקע, חמילפיקע, געלעטעניץ, דאָבראָשטש, דאַניוק, טראָסטינעץ, נאָוואָ-סוויאַט, פּאַריטש, קאַריטנע, מאָסקאַליוּוקע, רייקאָוויץ, מאַלינעטש און נעמיטשענעץ.

די דערמאָנטע דערפער זיינען ניט מעהר ווי דריי ביז פינף וויאָרסט ווייט פון שטאָט. ווי אַ רייף נעמען זיי אַרום דאָס שטע-טעל.

אַרום פעלשטין האָבען זיך אויך געפונען סקיביניעצקי׳ס אַ צענדליג „פולוואַרקעס”.

די גוים פון די דערמאָנטע און פון די איבעריגע, ניט-דער-מאָנטע דערפער, וועלכע צעהלען זיך אין די צענדליגער און רינגלען אַרום פעלשטין, האָבען אַריינגעפירט זייערע פּראָדוקטען אין שטעטעל און פאַרקויפט זיי צו די אידען, און דאָרט איינגעקויפט אַלץ, וואָס זיי האָבען באַדאַרפט.

257

Nota Koslowsky, historiated initial, in *Felshtin: Zamlbukh lekoved tsum ondenk fun di Felshtiner kdoyshim* (1937). Permission courtesy of Sidney Shaievitz, The Felshtin Society. Image courtesy of the Library of the Jewish Theological Seminary.

about the town, is set like a building amid other miniature houses. This technique, associated with Hebrew illuminated manuscripts, elevates its subject and the meaning of Felshtin's past for readers. Overall, and despite the gruesome skull-and-crossbones flourishes, the naïve, almost childlike quality of Koslowsky's work in this book is strongly at odds with the volume's traumatic

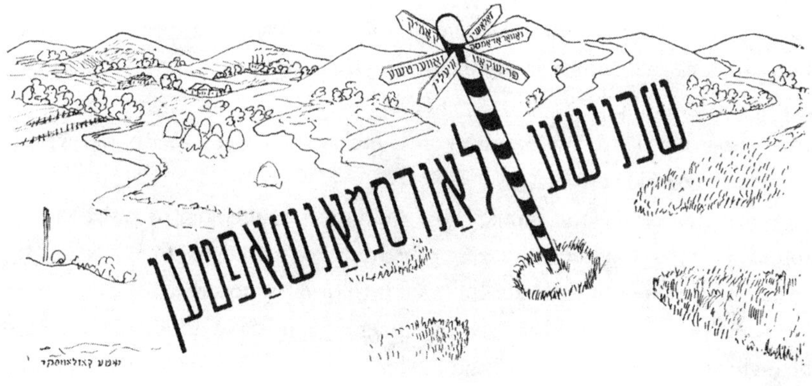

Nota Koslowsky, local *landmanschaftn,* in *Tshenstokhover yidn* (1947). Courtesy of the Library of the Jewish Theological Seminary.

content (section 1, beginning on page 26, is titled "The Slaughter") and commemorative function. This tension between image and text resists the conventional view that visual material in the memorial books complements the textual narrative. In the specific case of *Felshtin,* with its 748-page length (673 pages of tightly spaced Yiddish plus a 26-page English section followed by a sepia-toned supplement of photographs), the text initially overwhelms; it is only through a closer look that we may attend to the dissonance between its naïve visual dimension and the extensive, detailed narrative of the town's history as well as its destruction.

In addition to *Felshtin,* Koslowsky, a painter and prolific illustrator of children's literature, produced similar kinds of drawings and elements of visual design for at least two other memorial books: *Czenstochover Yidn* (New York, 1947) and *Braynsk* (New York, 1948).[47] The illustrations for *Czenstochover Yidn*—published in an oversized format (twenty-nine centimeters), weighing nearly five pounds, Yiddish text in double columns—are downright whimsical, featuring small stick figures and fanciful flourishes as page headers. While the gap between children's literature and memorial books may seem vast, both genres trade on memory and nostalgia.[48]

Indeed, given their visual resonance with other forms, the images of *Khurban Proskurov* and *Felshtin*—with their resemblance to the art nouveau style associated with Zionism and with children's literature, respectively—overflow the boundaries of the book, reminding viewers of other settings in which that particular style appears. The shared visual language potentially stitches together distinctly different literary or textual traditions, suggesting the emergence of specific visual vocabularies in twentieth-century Jewish cultures.[49] The *yizker* book images share some iconic features with other postwar visual discourse about the Shoah, especially art created by survivors; however, they form a distinct subgroup of this work, given their inclusion in the *yizker* book, with its particular generic conventions.

Some memorial book images even more overtly unsettle or resist the surrounding narrative; these images must be encountered on their own terms. Visual images are immediately and even involuntarily absorbed; one can always look away, but once you have seen an image, the initial emotional response—be it empathy, shock, fear, or disgust—lingers.[50] With this in mind, we can appreciate the power of two different memorial book images that remove the traditional prayer shawl from its usual context. During the war, liturgical objects such as prayer shawls and sacred texts seem to have been special targets of looting.[51] A short narrative from one of the earliest memorial books, *Es shtarbt a shtetl: Megiles Skalat* (Munich, March 1948), describes the varying uses to which these sacred materials were put: "There was a new style of clothing in the villages around Skalat: the black-striped women's skirts sewn from stolen *talaysim* [prayer shawls]. The peasant market, however, suffered a shortage in parchment torn from the Scrolls of the Law, which shoemakers had long since learned to convert into lining and padding for boots and shoes."[52] A few pages before the text, the memorial book features a photo of a girl with her back to the camera, dressed in a shirt or dress made from a prayer shawl, captioned *A kleyd fun a tallis* (clothing from a prayer shawl). The placement of the prayer shawl on the girl's body is both offensive and sensational, and the girl glances surreptitiously over her shoulder, as if to acknowledge her potential complicity in the image's scandalous quality, made all the more palpable by its inclusion in the memorial book.

Another image of a prayer shawl was included in two different memorial books: *El mole rachmim* (God of Mercy), a painting by the Polish artist Bronisław Linke, appears in both *Koretz* (Hebrew/Yiddish, Tel Aviv, 1959) and *Sefer Kosow* (Hebrew/Yiddish, Tel Aviv, 1964), in the latter book with a Hebrew caption and attribution.[53] The fact that both books were published in Tel Aviv suggests that the editors knew one another; both Koretz and Kosow were in western Ukraine. The image's title comes from the prayer traditionally recited in the liturgical memorial service. In this surreal postapocalyptic scene, a lone remaining brick wall appears as a bent, praying figure, wearing the traditional garb of a religious Jew. The leather bands of the phylacteries bind his head and are wound around his arm, and a tattered, bloody prayer shawl covers his

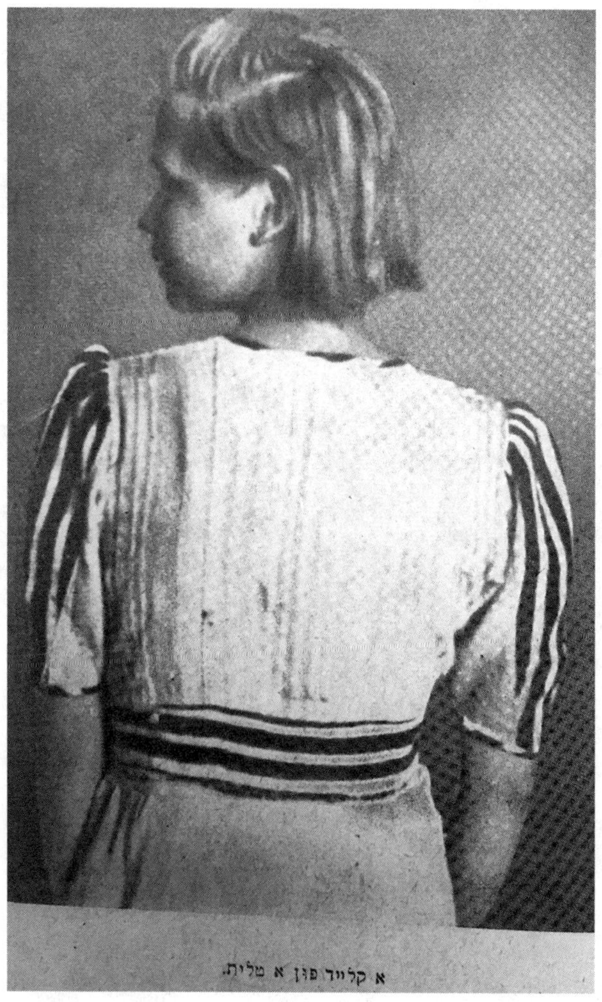

Clothing from a prayer shawl. *Es shtarbt a shtetl: Megiles Skalat* (1948). Permission courtesy of Jonas Weissbrod. Image courtesy of the Library of the Jewish Theological Seminary.

shoulders; face hidden, he presses closed fists to his temples in despair and devotion.[54] In excruciating detail, brick by carefully drawn brick, the figure is surrounded by the smoldering remains of an urban landscape. Even within the morbid array of memorial book illustrations, including cemeteries, skulls, flames, and barbed wire, and graphic photos of life under the Nazi regime, the sheer imaginative expressiveness of this image makes it unique. With the print's title,

El mole rachmim, 1956, watercolor by Bronisław Linke. Image from the collection of the National Museum in Warsaw. Photo Piotr Ligier/NMW.

the image suggests that the Shoah is a direct descendent of earlier scenes of catastrophe in Jewish history.

The original watercolor painting is even more impressive, as is the context in which it first appeared, a volume called *The Stones Shriek* (Warsaw, 1959). A short introduction to Linke's work describes the series of fourteen watercolor paintings and ink drawings as a commemoration of the city's two-stage battle against the brutal Nazi occupation, first in the Jewish Warsaw Ghetto Uprising of April 1943, then in the city-wide Uprising in August 1944. Linke's paintings, some dated as early as 1946, were a reminder that though it might "seem that the ruins of Warsaw ought to be forgotten . . . the need to speak of them still remains."[55] Linke's pictures superimposed swathes of crumbling brick walls and torn metal girders over images of Polish resistance and solidarity—a enormous bruised, raised fist with bloodshot eyes peering out from the wrist; a tall building in tatters bending to comfort a kneeling figure holding a book outside the Pawiak Prison; a collage border of a Polish newspaper pasted next to three figures with barbed wire halos, playing violins; and the striking central image, whose title comes from the Jewish prayer. As part of the original series, the image of a ruined Warsaw cityscape as a weeping, religious Jew embeds a specifically Jewish experience of loss within the wider canvas of the war and its aftermath on Polish soil. It is, in other words, an image of survival, evidence that "Warsaw has risen from the ashes alive."[56]

Detached from the artist's full series, however, the appearance of Linke's picture in two memorial books takes on a different meaning.[57] Within the memorial book, with its desire to embody a physical reminder of a space to which readers will never return, the image points to loss and destruction, with some consolation contained in the garments of tradition that cloak what remains. Both Linke's painting and the scandalous photograph from *Megiles Skalat* are "non-Jewish" sources that have been absorbed into the space of the memorial book. While Linke's image may seem more palatable, whether read as an image of resilience or of grief, it still detaches the prayer shawl from its ritualistic context by embedding it within scenes of Polish resistance. The painting and the photograph of the prayer shawl each exemplify how visual elements in memorial books may not only complement the narrative—illustrate or offer tangible examples—but also potentially supplant or even replace it: once glimpsed, they cannot be "unseen," and they thus persist in testifying in a way that words (alone) cannot. Furthermore, the photograph from Skalat makes more expressly visible an underlying feature of Holocaust photographs more generally: they were rarely the work of the Jewish inmates and victims but were produced either by agents of the Nazi regime or the Allied forces.[58] Photographs that were initially intended as documentary—for example, those depicting the "surrender" of Warsaw Ghetto resistance taken by Nazi officers—now appear as "evidence" of something else entirely, implicating the photographer.[59] These questions of agency and of ownership of a particular image or artifact's provenance will also shape our appreciation for one final element of the memorial book's visual architecture: the map.

MAPPING AS MEMORY AND RESISTANCE

> More delicate than the historians' are the map-makers' colors.
> —Elizabeth Bishop, "The Map" (1946)

Memorial books usually contain some sort of map of the town they commemorate. These maps, which complement the books' other visual elements and "constitute a veritable architecture of memory," are largely hand-drawn and encompass a range of styles and content: some maps exude cartographic confidence, appearing to be professionally drafted, with a legend and measured, proportional lines indicating streets, structures, and property relations, while others are more freehand, featuring whimsical, even childish detail; most seem to have been prepared especially for the memorial books.[60]

For example, the map of Berezne displays the energy and spontaneity of a sketch made on the back of a napkin, while the lyrical sketches of Bzehezhin and the cut-and-paste collage work on Rembertov, though still hand-drawn, seem to have taken more time and thought. The map of Belchatow mimics the appearance of a true map, but its lines are redrawn throughout as railway tracks or barbed wire (both equally chilling). The maps contain information relating to the physical man-made or natural features of the town and its surroundings as well as the social, political, and economic relationships that shaped the community. Some maps are attributed to a specific author; others remain anonymous creations. All of them appear to be shaped by an urge to re-create, on paper and in readers' minds, the town's landscape and infrastructure. Temporally speaking, the maps largely appear to capture the institutions and patterns of prewar life; however, many are also overlaid with the border of the wartime ghetto, sometimes depicted with barbed wire (Belchatow) or simply by a darker, thicker line (Krinik).[61] Iconic representations of the ghetto demonstrate how these maps also narrate temporal conditions; the map of Dokszyce, whose ghetto boundaries appear as a thick dotted line, contains the following note above its legend: "All details—except for the ghetto boundaries—are from 50 years ago."[62] The map, published in Tel Aviv in 1970, is dated July 1969, which suggests that

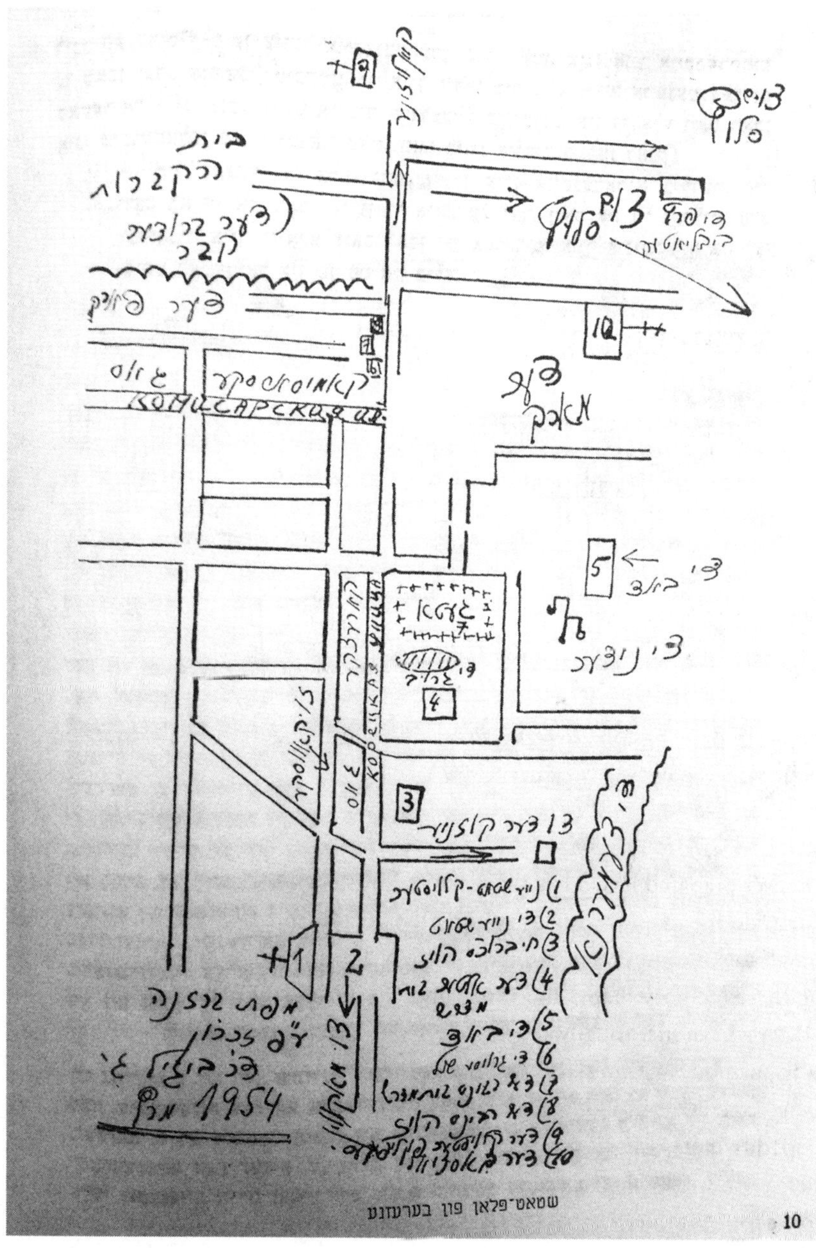

Hand-drawn "city plan," in *Mayne shtetel Berezne* (1954). Courtesy of the Library of the Jewish Theological Seminary.

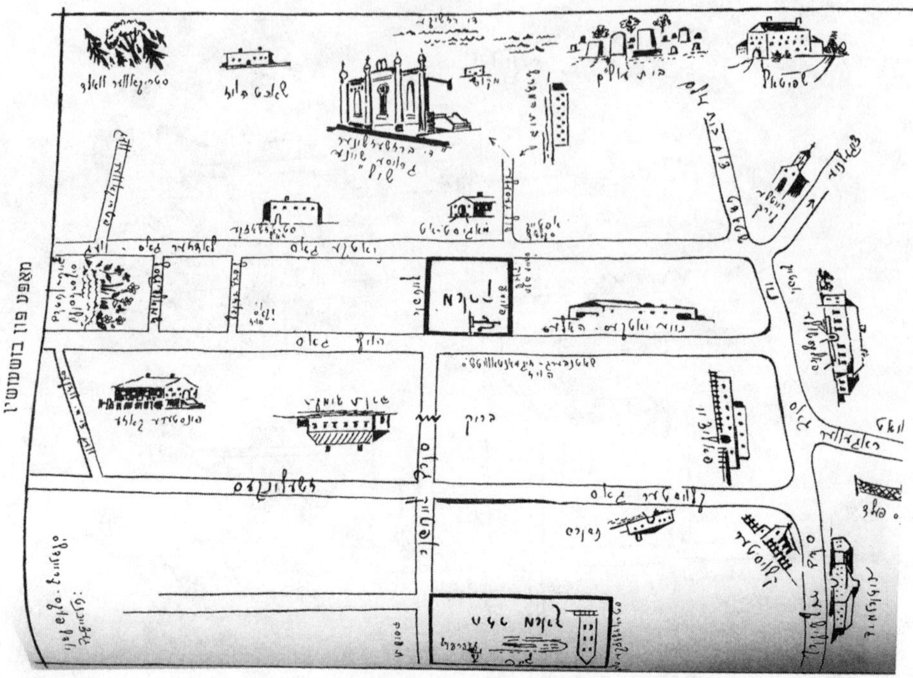

Map with drawings, in *Bzehzhin yizker-bukh* (1951). Courtesy of the Library of the Jewish Theological Seminary.

whoever prepared it had left the town as early as 1919. These temporal markers, alongside the map's relatively minimalist detail and spare line—noted as "not drawn to scale"—offer a telling glimpse of the challenges involved in producing these memory maps, and their difference from conventional maps.

Maps have historically been understood as instruments of power, specifically in modern times and in relation to the evolution of the nation-state. They concretize in iconographic form those landscapes that are themselves shaped by networks of power among various groups in a given setting.[63] Furthermore, maps played an essential role in the process of postwar reparations; for example, Leora Auslander explores archival material—maps, lists, descriptions of household possessions and property—included with French Jewish claims to recover property looted and stolen during the war.[64] These maps possessed a pragmatic function and were framed as demands for compensation; they also expressed an affective connection to home and the past. In contrast, the memorial books maps don't generally possess any pragmatic function; that is, they are not interested in reparations, or even in conveying

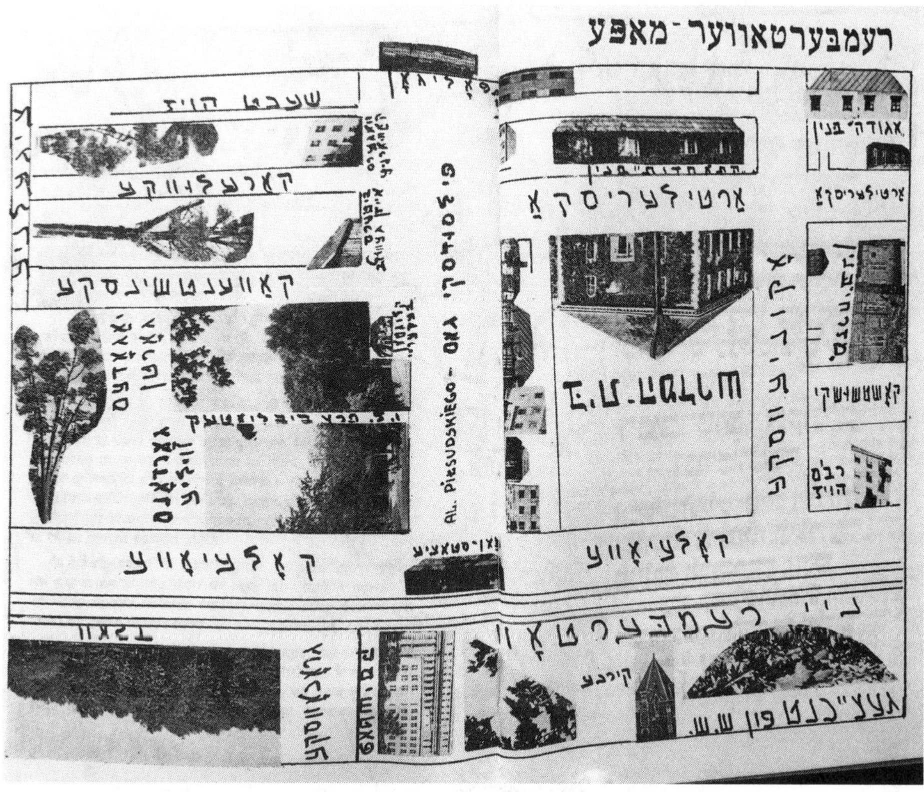

Map with illustrations, in *Sefer zikaron le-keholot Rembertow, Okuniew, Milosna* (1974). Courtesy of the Library of the Jewish Theological Seminary.

practical information. They are, indeed, primarily concerned with memory work. Of course, it is conceivable that a town's descendents might use a memorial book map to imagine, or even visit, the physical contours of places they had never been, but the maps were not primarily intended for informational purposes. Rather, they are evidence of what was, and as such, they constitute a form of testimony. Their specific details as well as their formal representational features were presumably chosen and created by the mapmaker, whose name they often bear, sometimes with the caveat that it has been "sketched from memory." Though not exactly private maps, they are unmistakably the work of an individual whose connection to the town is personal and direct. As such, public or communal sites such as marketplaces, houses of worship, schools, and civic institutions are complemented by places marked for their particular meaning to the mapmaker. For example, on a relatively simple map of Krinik produced in Uruguay in 1948, we find

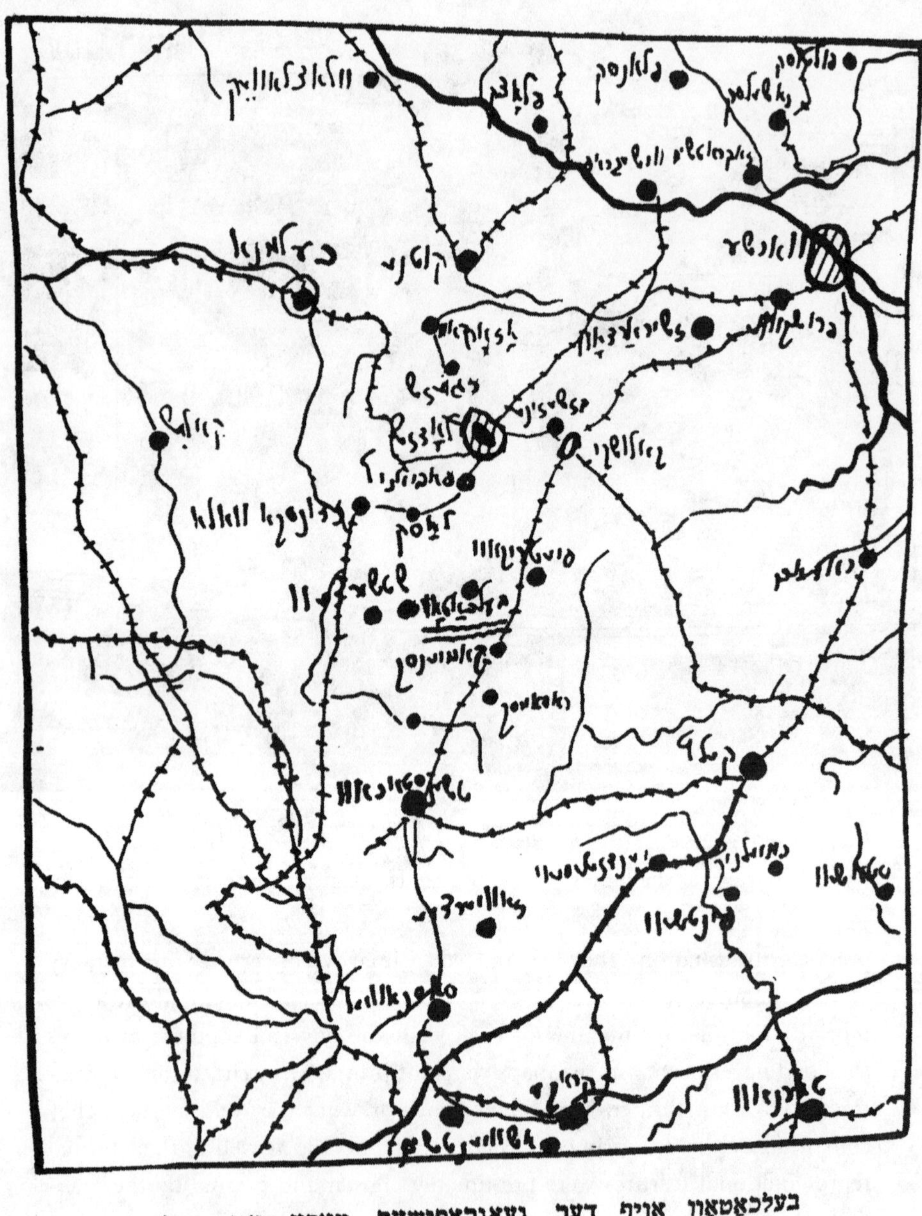

"Geographic map" of town with barbed wire, in *Belchatow yizker-bukh* (1951). Courtesy of the Library of the Jewish Theological Seminary.

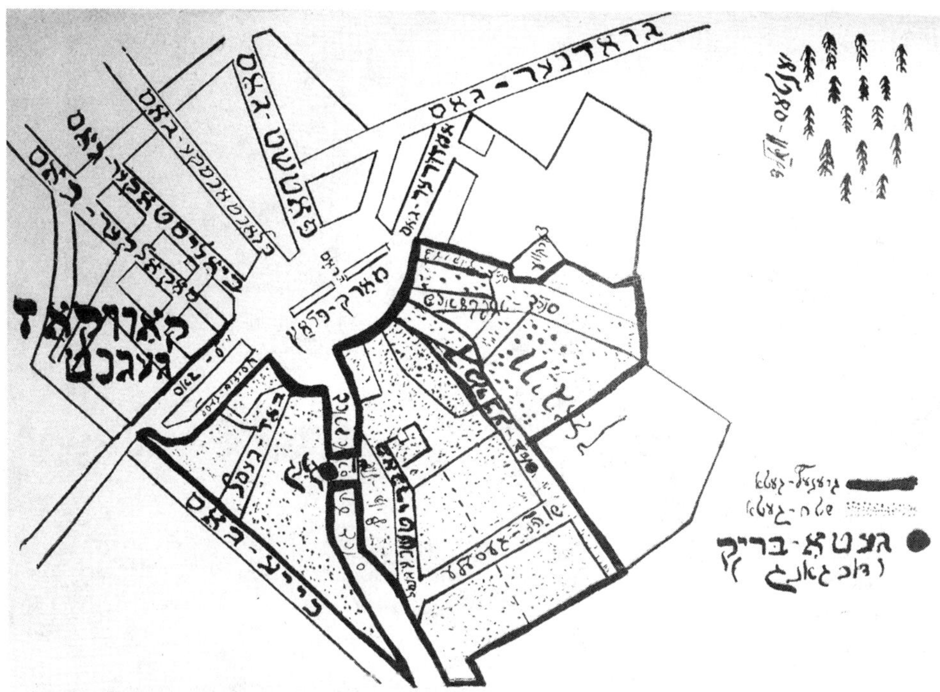

Yentes vald in Krinik, in *Krinik in khurban: Memuarn* (1948). Courtesy of the Library of the Jewish Theological Seminary.

on the margins of a somewhat claustrophobic rendering of the town and the ghetto wall a spot called *yentes vald* (gossips' forest), as we imagine it was known to the locals.

With rare exceptions, the mapmaker's own home is not marked. The map of Voyslavitz contains a legend with names referring to over sixty private homes in addition to civic and commercial sites, including the municipal park, the synagogue, a commemorative statue in honor of someone named Kushtoysku, and "Christian stores"—but withholds the name of the mapmaker.[65] However, the map of Zborow which was prepared by Michael Furman, includes a reference to "My parents' house—Furman" within its legend. This map also designates sites within the ghetto such as the "Ghetto Fighters Bunker" and small hiding places marked with the names of specific families scattered across the town as well as three different kinds of cemeteries (Jewish, Polish, and Ukrainian) and a "mass grave from the first pogrom": this is a map of resistance. It asserts a kind of retroactive ownership over the space of the town within the conditions of military occupation.

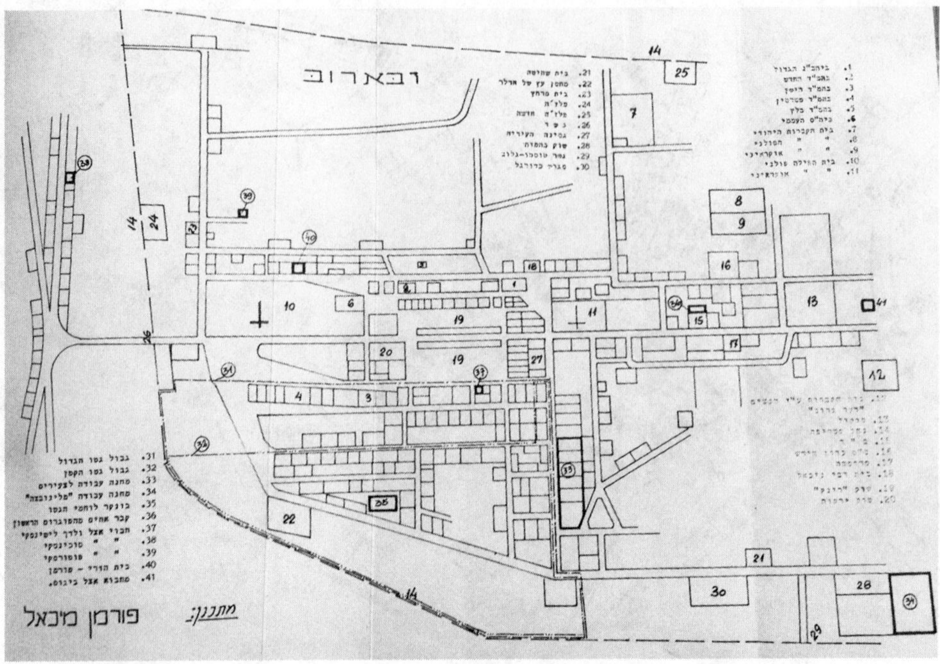

The mapmaker's parents' house, in *Sefer zikaron le-kehilat Zborow* (1975). Courtesy of the Library of the Jewish Theological Seminary.

The Felshstin book's map-cum-illustration is another example of mapping as ownership. In discussing this picture, David Roskies notes: "Remarkably, included are a Roman Catholic church on the top with its tall spires and an Eastern Orthodox church on the bottom, with its onion-shaped domes. This is accurate; there was not a shtetl that did not have at least two churches, but Jewish memory often omits mention of the churches."[66] Roskies's remarks here recall Dan Miron's influential argument regarding the depiction of eastern European shtetl life in classical Yiddish fiction as "an exclusively Jewish enclave, an unalloyed entity . . . a tiny Jewish island in a vast non-Jewish sea."[67] If, as Roskies claims, memorial books are a "species of fiction," the status of "Jewish space" in these maps is more complex than their narrative precursors; the maps display a remarkably varied and independent sense of what must be remembered. Jewish institutions such as the synagogue, bathhouse, and study house are marked cheek by jowl with churches, schools, and civic landmarks. Cemeteries are also indicated by both religious and ethnic affiliation. Rather than depicting the space of the town as an "exclusively Jewish enclave," these maps highlight potential networks of mundane commercial, social, and cultural exchange, all framed under the aegis of Jewish collective memory.

In addition to the maps' visual repertoire, language is an essential component of their ability to frame the past. The maps considered here were annotated in Yiddish, Hebrew, Polish, and German. While this linguistic component shapes their substantive meaning, language is not an entirely stable indicator. Though for some readers, Yiddish may produce a sense of home, within maps produced relatively soon after the war, Polish—and even German—are also languages of memory: Polish is included in both an elegant map containing detailed generic conventions—in *Pinkas Krzemienca* (1954)—and a roughly drawn sketch "from memory" in *Sefer Rypin* (1962).[68] A detailed map of Otwock's three linked ghettos appears entirely in German in a 1948 volume published in a displaced persons camp in the American Zone of Germany.[69] The Hebrew maps—some produced as early as the 1950s—raise a number of questions; while one can imagine the existence of prewar maps of local entities in Yiddish, these Hebrew maps seem possible only as post-destruction artifacts (the existence of prewar European Hebrew culture notwithstanding). Perhaps a response to the social prejudice against Yiddish in Israel during these years, they may also represent an attempt to communicate with a younger generation of descendents who did not speak Yiddish.

Many of these maps depict places that no longer exist. By "places" I mean not only a town's recognizable geographic features and built structures but also the broader, and deeper, terrains of social, political, and cultural relationships, of networks of power, commerce, and—above all—the confluence and reification of all these in the memory of the mapmaker. Historically, maps have often been produced by the powerful; indeed, these memorial book maps refuse to "mask the interests that bring them into being."[70] They may not be the work of victors, but they make painfully, visibly clear the brutal effects of power—and how it may be resisted. Their varied and enduring presence anchors the memorial books in the very spaces they seek to retrieve.

THE HOLOCAUST AND MATERIAL OBJECTS

We have seen how materiality matters for prewar writing in a variety of genres, including poetry, little magazines, and novels. The example of memorial books demonstrates how writing could be reimagined in material terms in the face of physical destruction and change. I noted above that this discussion of the memorial books forms the "spine" of my study. I want to flesh out this idea and its significance in relation to contemporary trends in intellectual work about the Jewish genocide and its meaning as a historical event. Objects and their fate are at the heart of recent scholarship about the Holocaust and other recent traumatic events.[71] As human voices dwindle, even as the record of them expands and multiplies, objects simply endure: housed in museums and archives, passed down through families, or "upcycled" in flea markets across eastern Europe. The status of these things is both contextual and contested: one person's trash is another's exhibit-worthy artifact.[72] Yet these objects left behind, the detritus as well as the personal possessions—clothing, bedding, dishes, cutlery, pots and pans, furniture, toys—all items that potentially bear the shape of the body or evidence traces of use and wear—demand our attention.

While scholarship and public discourse have turned a spotlight on luxury items such as jewelry and the fine arts, the pillaging and looting of everyday items during the war was quite extensive. Martin Dean's vivid account details how the Shoah's physical destruction of people and places also entailed a massive redistribution of the objects of domestic life: as the Germans moved through Jewish areas, towns, and neighborhoods, household items such as dishes, linens, clothing, books, and furniture were collected and sent back to Berlin.[73] Local populations, former neighbors of the deported or murdered Jews, also benefited; Dean quotes a diary from the Netherlands referencing local activities after the town's Jews had been deported: "I and Truus went over to some Jewish homes, but there was little to get—all the essentials had gone, including underwear and linen. The next-door neighbors had got there first; all I could find was a few trifles and Truus got a pedal car and some other toys."[74] Likewise, mass graves were not exempt from the general tendency: "Perpetrators collected wedding rings and even clothing from the victims, with the more precious objects tallied and sent to Berlin."[75] This "stuff" is now scattered across Europe, perhaps especially in Poland because of its large prewar Jewish population.

Interest in the war's material traces has spurred "the forensic turn," in which objects are animated in order to allow the dead to speak.[76] However, despite our current era's seemingly intractable distance from these events, we can appreciate the poignant value of these material possessions. An awareness of the war's material toll is also implicit in the contemporaneous record: two poems written in the ghettos of Vilna and Warsaw—in more or less the same historical moment—take as their point of departure and poetic focus the fate of objects—specifically, personal possessions—within the space of the ghetto and beyond.[77] Abraham Sutzkever's "A Cartload of Shoes" (Yiddish, 1943) and Władysław Szlengel's "Things" (Polish, 1942?) trace the objects' movement: their passage from place to place and evolving ownership, their physical deterioration, their utility as well as their worth.[78] Sutzkever and Szlengel were both connected to prominent wartime activity devoted to the production and preservation of Jewish archives, projects that were themselves cognate enterprises of the memorial books: Sutzkever was part of the Vilna Ghetto's "Paper Brigade," which rescued rare books and manuscripts from YIVO and other institutions during and after the war, and Szlengel's Polish-language manuscripts became part of the Warsaw Ghetto's *Oyneg Shabes* archives. The poems themselves function as artifacts, even relics: both produced in hidden or covert settings within the ghetto, they are appreciated for their poetic power as well as the resonant circumstances of their material production.

Abraham Sutzkever (1913–2010) was a central figure in the *Yung Vilne* literary group before the war, and his charismatic presence shaped cultural life in the Vilna Ghetto. During the war, he was active with the partisans and part of the Paper Brigade.[79] Sutzkever's poem turns on a single horrifyingly intimate detail: the speaker's imagined discovery of his mother's shoes amid a "heap" of shoes being readied for transport from the Vilna Ghetto to Berlin:

The wheels are turning, turning,
What are they bringing there?
They are bringing *me* a cartload
Of quivering footwear.

A cartload like a wedding
In the evening glow;
The shoes—a full heap [*kupe*], dancing
Like people at a ball.[80]

The term used to describe the cart full of shoes—a pile or heap—*kupe*—reverberates for Yiddish readers, echoing as it does Perets Markish's well-known poem "Di kupe" (1921), written in the wake of pogroms in Ukraine.[81] While Markish's poem opens with a disturbing image of corpses laid out in the marketplace, Sutzkever's evocation of violence is muted, even displaced, despite the ghoulish images of the "quivering" footwear and dancing shoes. The ballad form, together with the folk presence of the cart and collective celebrations (a wedding? a holiday?), sets up the narrator's chilling moment of recognition:

I know those shoes at a glance
And look at them with dread.
. . . .
I need not ask whose,
But my heart is rent:
Oh, tell me shoes the truth,
Where were the feet sent?

Among the children's worn out boots
My mother's shoes so fair!
Sabbath was the only day
She donned this footwear.

The poem's roaming delineation of types of shoes from different kinds of people finally comes to rest on a particular pair that the poetic speaker imagines as having belonged to his mother. The poem's curatorial gaze—the focus on a single meaningful artifact within a collection—is disrupted by the emotional connection between the poet and his mother's shoes. For the contemporary reader, Sutzkever's poem anticipates how shoes will become a paradigmatic material rendering of the Holocaust's brute magnitude of loss; hundreds of pairs of shoes sourced from the camps have their own exhibit spaces at both the Auschwitz Museum and in the United States Holocaust Memorial Museum, and sixty pairs of cast-iron shoes are the subject of The Shoes on the Danube Promenade (2005), a memorial site in Budapest. Shoes are among the most intimate of personal possessions, taking on the specific contours of the owner's body in a way that garments in general do not. They were key to survival in the camps, and their very ubiquity makes them a special instance of what museum scholars call "difficult" objects—that is, artifacts that "position their viewers in relation to violence and suffering of 'others' distant in time, place, or experience."[82] Their resonance as perhaps the single most "difficult" object in Holocaust memory is underscored in the enormous exhibit *Auschwitz: Not Long Ago. Not Far Away,* which highlighted the display of shoes in no fewer than three prominent points: a single women's dress shoe "found in the warehouses of Auschwitz after the war," prisoners' clogs from the camp, and a single child's shoe with its sock tucked in, likely left in a dressing room near the crematorium.[83]

Unlike the laser focus on a pair of shoes, the subject of Władysław Szlengel's "Things"—a poem written in the Warsaw Ghetto and found after the war in a manuscript hidden in a table about to be used for firewood—is a broad array of personal possessions and their fate.[84] The author called his work "document-poems," and indeed they are remarkable for their ability to exist simultaneously as both an artifact and a record of their own disappearance. The poem is conceived as both testimony and a tangible form of evidence, a concreteness vividly rendered in "Things," with its attention to physical layout and the increasingly self-possessed agency of its objects:

From Hoza Street and Marszalkowska
carts were moving, Jewish carts:
    furniture, tables and chairs,

suitcase, bundles
and chests, boxes and bedding,
suits and portraits,
pots, linen and wall hangings
cherry brandy, big jars and little jars,
glasses, tea pots and sliver—
books, knickknacks and everything
go from Hoza Street to Sliska.
. . . .
And from Sliska Street to Niska everything
All over again went moving:
furniture, tables and chairs,
suitcase and bundles,
and pots—gents that's it.
Now there is no carpet,
of silverware not a sign.[85]

Szlengel's objects dwindle as they move from the well-furnished locations of Hoda and Marszalkowska to the more modest rooms in Niska and the ghetto, and from there to Ostrowska, the Umschlagplatz, central site of deportations, and finally the "black rails" to Treblinka. At first, the physical shape of the poem suggests a tension or relationship between the different geographic locations—set flush left—and the narrowing list of possessions—indented to the right.[86] However, the sections listing possessions become shorter and shorter until the afterlife of the objects eventually reappears as a steady stream of belongings, set flush left, handled by "Aryans," who close the windows and tidy up.

From the Umschlagplatz across the city
all the way to Marszalkowska,
life, Jewish life, is growing
in houses that are empty.
In abandoned apartments
abandoned bundles,
suits and down covers
and plates and chairs.
. . . .
Ownerless things lie around,
a dead apartment stands waiting
until new people
populate the rooms: Aryans—
they will close the open windows,
begin a carefree life

and make these beds,
these Jewish eiderdowns
and wash the shirt,
put the books on a shelf and empty
the coffee from the glass,
together they will finish the hand of bridge.

Ultimately, however, the things have a kind of agency; they refuse to stay put:

all the Jewish things will come out
from chests and houses.
And they will run out through the windows
walk down the streets
until they meet on the roads,
on the black rails.
All the tables and chairs
and suitcases, bundles
the suits and jars
and silverware and teapots
will leave, and disappear.

The disappearance of both Jews and their stuff seems absolute; however, the poem's final lines describe an unused poison pill, tangible evidence—"*corpus delecti*"—of the enormous crime of the ghetto. The poem thus concludes with a nod toward human action: the process of justice, the possibility of revenge—or of suicide.

Although the manuscript of Szlengel's poem resides in Warsaw's Jewish Historical Institute archives, along with the milk cans in which it was buried and then retrieved, its sentiments endure in spectral fashion at POLIN: The Museum of the History of Polish Jews, built in Warsaw on the remains of the ghetto. In an interview published in conjunction with the museum's founding, Hanna Nowak-Radziejowska—a resident of Muranów, where the museum is located—relates how in 2006, during its construction, large ditches were opened. As she passed by these ditches on her way to work, she "realized she lived and walked on a cemetery. . . . She found [a fragment of] porcelain at the intersection of Nowolipki and Jana Pawla II streets. On her way home from work, Hanna would lower herself into the ditches and look around. . . . Between burnt bricks, she often found remains of everyday life. . . . At the time, the Museum of the History of Polish Jews had started collecting Jewish memorabilia. Hanna decided that the museum was an appropriate place for the items she had found." Her donated bits of porcelain were "one of the first gifts received by the newly

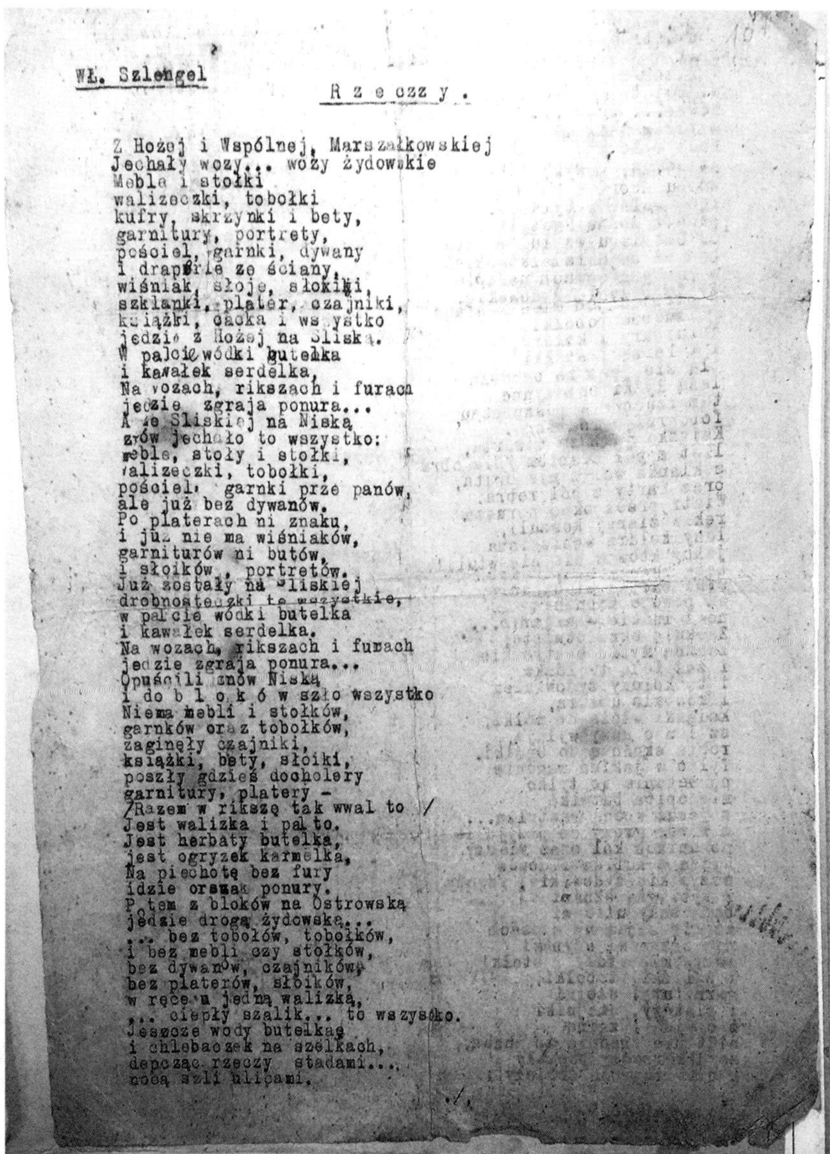

Wł. Szlengel

R z e c z y .

Z Hożej i Wspólnej, Marszałkowskiej
Jechały wozy... wozy żydowskie
Meble i stołki
walizeczki, tobołki
kufry, skrzynki i bety,
garnitury, portrety,
pościel, garnki, dywany
i draperie ze ściany,
wiśniak, słoje, słoiki,
szklanki, platér, czajniki,
książki, cacka i wszystko
jedzie z Hożej na Śliską.
W palcie wódki butelka
i kawałek serdelka,
Na wozach, rikszach i furach
jedzie zgraja ponura...
A ze Śliskiej na Niską
znów jechało to wszystko:
meble, stoły i stołki,
walizeczki, tobołki,
pościel, garnki prze panów,
ale już bez dywanów.
Po platerach ni znaku,
i już nie ma wiśniaków,
garniturów ni butów,
i słoików , portretów.
Już zostały na Śliskiej
~~drobnosteczki te wszystkie,~~
w palcie wódki butelka
i kawałek serdelka.
Na wozach, rikszach i furach
jedzie zgraja ponura...
Opuścili znów Niską
i do b l o k ó w szło wszystko
Niema mebli i stołków,
garnków oraz tobołków,
zaginęły czajniki,
książki, bety, słoiki,
poszły gdzieś docholery
garnitury, platery -
/Razem w rikszę tak wwal to /
Jest walizka i palto.
Jest herbaty butelka,
jest ogryzek karmelka,
Na piechotę bez fury
idzie orszak ponury.
Potem z bloków na Ostrowską
jedzie drogą żydowską...
... bez tobołów, tobołków,
i bez mebli czy stołków,
bez dywanów, czajników,
bez platerów, słoików,
w ręce a jedną walizką,
... ciepły szalik... to wszysko.
Jeszcze wody butelkę
i chlebaczek na szelkach,
depcząc rzeczy stadami...
nocą szli ulicami.

Władysław Szlengel, page from "Things" (Polish, 1942?). From the collections of the E. Ringelblum Jewish Historical Institute, Warsaw created institution."[87] These fragments are perhaps macabre souvenirs, demanding a fuller narrative of their provenance; they also conjure, as a fetish, the warmth of their owner's hand.

Sutzkever himself wrote of the endurance of things, and even of the necessity of text becoming object, in one of his most powerful poems, "The Lead Plates at the Romm Press" (September 12, 1943); the speaker imagines breaking into Vilna's legendary Romm publishing house, stealing the plates used to print their famous edition of the Talmud, and melting the lead down into bullets for the resistance.[88]

> Arrayed at night, like fingers stretched through bars
> To clutch the lit air of freedom,
> We made for the press plates, to seize
> The lead plates at the Rom printing works.
> We were dreamers, we had to be soldiers,
> And melt down, for our bullets, the spirit of the lead.[89]

This "dream" describes how texts become objects, how words are alchemically transfigured into another kind of substance entirely, one whose material efficacy is more immediate, though it's the poem itself that endures. The distance between Charles Reznikoff's rhapsodic devotion to the press as an industrious vehicle for individual self-invention and Sutzkever's fantasy of a collective act that will refashion sacred text into a physical object is one measure of modern Jewish literature's evolving relation to materiality and its limits.

THE AFTERLIVES OF MEMORIAL BOOKS IN LITERATURE AND ART

Memorial books as a transnational literary genre have an afterlife in myriad fictional and nonfiction works, such as Eva Hoffman's *Shtetl: The Life and Death of a Small Town and the World of Polish Jews* (1997), which surveys the history of the town of Bransk as a lens through which to view Polish-Jewish relations, and Nicole Krauss's novel *The History of Love* (2005), in which lost manuscripts circulate in both their original and translation as talismans, ostensibly preserving the memories, and even the lives, of their owners. Daniel Mendelsohn's epic memoir qua family history, *The Lost: A Search for Six of Six Million* (2006), may be understood as a kind of postmodern memorial book; it is a pastiche of the memorial book's hallmark features—local history, maps, photographs as artifacts, what Mendelsohn calls "keepsakes," first-person testimonials, lists and statistics about people, places, occupations—all blended with the author's own "literary" readings of the book of Genesis and the detective fiction–like narrative of his search for information about his family's fate, what happened to "six of six million." *They Called Me Mayer July: Painted Memories of a Jewish Childhood in Poland before the Holocaust,* coauthored by the anthropologist and museum studies scholar Barbara Kirshenblatt-Gimblett with her father Mayer Kirshenblatt, makes a powerful case for the redemptive power of the memory of one particular village. The authors are careful to note the work's essentially autobiographical nature, and the nearly two hundred paintings and accompanying narratives were produced decades after Kirshenblatt left his hometown of Apt.[90] However, the book's physical size, as well as its immersive depiction of Apt's material reality, recalls the memorial book's commitment to the concrete lived experience and history of a single town.

Frank Stella's mixed-media work *Polish Villages* (1972) was inspired by a 1959 volume called *Wooden Synagogues,* a collection of shtetl photographs by Szymon Zajczyk, a Polish art historian with ties to the constructivist school who was killed in 1942.[91] Zajczyk's work feels almost like that of a latter-day An-sky, with one essential difference: according to Mark Godfrey, "The photographer pictured the synagogues in the recently developed visual language of contemporary art."[92] Stella seems to have reacted to this aspect of the photographs, more so, initially, than the fact that they depicted a now-destroyed world. His response to the book, given to him while he was recuperating from surgery, inspired a years-long project: the series of strange and demanding works in *Polish Villages* combines wood, canvas, felt, and paint to create large, abstract, mostly flat objects whose strong verticals and dramatic diagonals recall the distinct design and sloping roofs of eastern European wooden synagogues. Each painting bears the single-word title of a town's name, often in a series, for example, *Felsztyn I, II,* and *III.* Unlike the synagogues in Jewish urban communities, often designed with the neighboring grandeur of churches and/or mosques in mind, these wooden synagogues were built, used, and beloved by their native communities, treated as an authentic form of Jewish "folk art." Stella's works are, in a sense, the *yizker* books of synagogues.

In addition to the visual resemblance, Godfrey describes other meaningful connections between Stella's work and the memory of these synagogues, connections that underscore the centrality of materiality to memory: "The *Polish Villages* recalled the mode of production that characterized synagogue building: the creation of a unique, handmade, crafted structure."[93] Stella's paintings have a kind of violence about them, as if they are in smashed pieces. They resemble material objects that have been broken, and this brokenness constitutes their form. What was incipient in Bergelson's *The End of Everything,* with its bleak depiction of the shtetl as an anxious, vulnerable object, and more express in the *yizker* book's repeated insistence on the book as a memorial object, reaches one kind of conclusion in the work of this non-Jewish American minimalist: Stella's *Polish Villages* connects "the memory of the destruction of constructivism to the memory of the destruction of the Wooden Synagogues."[94] At the same time, it also highlights the possibility of a new language of objecthood for Jewish cultural expression.

The memorial books themselves survive online, both in the digitized versions sponsored by Amherst's Yiddish Book Center and on virtual platforms such as the Yizker Book Project—a website devoted to translating the books and documenting the communities they describe as part of a broader project of Jewish genealogy.[95] However, where might the material spirit, if not the letter, of the memorial book endure? Beyond the "afterlives," what generic settings might support and prolong this preoccupation with materiality?

Chapter 5 From *Maus* to *The Rabbi's Cat:* The Jewish Graphic Novel

BETWEEN LANGUAGE AND GENRE, FROM COMICS TO GRAPHIC NARRATIVE

Graphic novels have a paradoxical relationship to the idea of the book: on the one hand, a kind of respect, bordering on reverence, for the book's power and meaning as a material object; on the other hand, an exuberant, almost heretical, devotion to deconstructing its more normative forms. Graphic novels, with their attention to the alphabet's physical form and the deliberate and ornate juxtaposition of text and image, resemble premodern sacred forms such as the scroll and illuminated manuscripts. In this chapter I examine a paradigmatic cohort of graphic novels from different geographic and linguistic locations. Chosen in part for their centrality to the field, these books demonstrate how Jewish sensitivity to the image may be brought into conversation with the specific language of comics.

Will Eisner coined the term *graphic novel* with the publication of *Contract with God* (1978), a memoirist account of his childhood neighborhood.[1] The term was essentially a marketing category, utilized because—according to popular accounts—Eisner felt that comics weren't sufficiently respected as an art form by the institutions of the publishing world.[2] The problem of definition haunts the study of graphic novels; they upset formal boundaries, exploiting the tentative divide between image and text. In addition, graphic novels are long-form descendents of comic books and cartoons, historically denigrated genres. Both of these attributes—a determined mixed-media mode and a link with what Neil Gaiman has called the "gutter medium" of comics—have shaped critical discussion of the graphic novel, so much so that almost any critical inquiry into their meaning begins, as mine does, with a pre-inquiry into what exactly they are.[3] Gaiman's term playfully captures, and elevates, the formal uniqueness of comics—the white space between the panels is referred to as the "gutter"—as well as their historical status as a genre of dubious repute. Referencing the challenge of definition, comics scholar Thierry Groensteen cautions that "so great is the diversity of what has been claimed as comics . . . it has become almost impossible to retain any definitive criteria that is universally held to be true." Indeed, he concludes that the difficulty of definition pertains to other art as well; while especially the case for modern forms such as film, the challenge of definition also holds for any genre that has evolved over a long period during which its traditional norms may have been "smashed . . . into pieces."[4] The malleability of genre—its tendency to respond and evolve over time—constitutes one of its enduring features. Perhaps graphic novels are simply the latest example of an art form that foregrounds its own instability; however, they are distinguished from other genres discussed in this study by their insistence on the necessity of both image and text as a distinct, "blended" language in its own right.[5] I distinguish here between "comics" as a medium or language and "graphic novels" as a genre: a long, book-bound, narrative form of comics.[6] Graphic novels achieve their effects through the distinctive language of comics in panels and pages that are combined sequentially to tell a story.[7] A reading of a short strip by Art Spiegelman, author of the influential *Maus: A Survivor's Tale* (1986), will provide a brief introduction to how the language and grammar of comics operate.

Spiegelman is an eloquent theorist of his own work and the materiality of comics more broadly. In a retrospective cartoon "Eye Ball," he explores the familial dynamic that shaped his work as a cartoonist.[8] The young Art watches his father pack a suitcase, though he would prefer to be reading a comic book called *Tubby*.[9] His father's packing skills, honed during the "many times [he] had to run with only what [he could] carry," involve cramming maximal content into a relatively small space. In the final frame, Spiegelman's character dons a Tubby mask to announce: "This was the best advice I've ever gotten as a cartoonist!" This final bit of text, as well as a comment in the first panel, is drawn in a speech bubble *without* a "tail" to indicate that this view evolved after the

Art Spiegelman, "Eye Ball, Rego Park, nyc. ca. 1960," reprinted in *Breakdowns: Portrait of the Artist as a Young %@*!* (2008).

depicted conversation with his father and is addressed directly to the contemporary reader. The strip is placed in a specific location and time ("Rego Park, nyc. ca. 1960"), and the naked eyeball is traversed by both baseball stitching and squiggly lines indicating age and imperfections: what the eye sees and suffers, the stress on the eye. We catch a glimpse, tucked into the upper right corner of most of the panels, of a framed photo of Richieu Spiegelman, the author's brother, who died as a toddler during the war and thus experienced neither comics nor baseball. The specifics of the Spiegelman family—Jewish immigrants in the United States, the fraught relationship between father and son, how the experience of the Shoah shapes even a relatively mundane activity like packing a suitcase, and how Art ultimately mines that trauma for his work—are all recalled here as integral elements of the artist's childhood. The strip also underlines Spiegelman's formal method as an artist: the economy of means, the meticulous planning and staging of the comics panel. Every square inch is utilized for a specific purpose and functions in concert with the whole. This principle of thrift extends to the "packing" of multiple time frames within a single set of juxtaposed panels—Richieu's truncated childhood during the war, the author's own childhood around 1960, and the contemporary moment of his work as a cartoonist.

Spiegelman's "Eye Ball" foregrounds the comics panel as an object inside which other objects are contained, some of them hidden ("small things in the shoes"); these must be, literally, unpacked to be read. This central compositional axiom is illustrated through the particularity of the suitcase—a ubiquitous item whose storage and mobility grant it abundant symbolic significance. Spiegelman's work also exemplifies how the historically low or popular language of comics may forward a complex meditation on grand themes. His approach—especially the adroit manipulation of text and image to produce a narrative, and attention to comics as a material artifact grounded in time and space—has been so thoroughly absorbed into the field that it now seems almost natural, a default mode for long narrative comics dealing with history and trauma.

Spiegelman's economy of means relies on a set of formal devices that "break down" a particular narrative into its salient, constituent parts—moments depicted through specific iconic details that in sequential juxtaposition, and in sum, deliver a narrative. His early comics appeared in a single volume called *Breakdowns,* an homage to this important inheritance of the cartooning tradition. In the words of comics historian Robert Harvey, "Narrative breakdown is to a comic strip what time is to life."[10] "Breakdowns" shape the reader's experience, helping her or him to identify and interpret meaningful details within a single panel as well as the significance of sequence from panel to panel. A "disciplined" reader will encounter panels in sequence, or an entire page of comics, and productively wander among them, decoding and interpreting their relationship.[11] This discipline moves graphic narratives as a genre, and comics as a language, more fully into the domain of reader reception. Joseph Witek suggests these forms constitute a genre precisely because they are *read* in a certain way: opposed to essentialist definitions, "'comicsness' might usefully be reconceptualized from being an immutable attribute of texts to being considered as a *historically contingent and evolving set of reading protocols* that are applied to texts, that to be a comic text means to be *read* as a comic" (emphasis added).[12] Genre's historical contingency, its productive instability as an analytical category, may also account for the contentiousness of these debates over what precisely constitutes comics.[13]

Indeed, W. J. T. Mitchell reminds us that the text-image divide has always been ideologically driven.[14] Moreover, while authors may deploy text and image as co-narrative devices, manipulating the features and proportions of visual and textual information on any given page, readers are the ultimate arbiters, absorbing this distinctive system of codes for themselves. Certain features such as color or a larger frame breaking the grid may strongly draw the eye; in contradistinction, some readers may first quickly scan all the text and then integrate the visual material. In any case, the experience of reading a graphic novel is both a dedicated intellectual analysis and an affective, even sensual, absorption of the work at hand.[15] Comics as a medium palpably exploit the ostensible distinctions between image and text while building on their intertwined relationship; image and text together propel the narrative forward. Furthermore, text may also use its iconic features, such as the size, shape, and font of letters, while images may create temporal transitions through layout, sequence, and juxtaposition.[16] Above all, there remain the predilections and experience of the individual reader. Therefore, Mitchell's observation may be tempered, it seems to me wisely, with this observation by another leading theorist, Charles Hatfield: "While the word/image dichotomy may be false or oversimple, learned assumptions about these different codes—written and pictorial—still exert a strong centripetal pull on the reading experience. We continue to distinguish between the function of words and the function of images, despite the fact that comics continually work to destabilize this very distinction. This tension between codes is fundamental to the art form."[17]

These material affordances of comics are profoundly evident in the long-form narrative genre of the graphic novel—what Spiegelman called comics that "needed a bookmark"—whose sheer size allows for an immersive, affective depiction of history.[18] The space of the page becomes an expressive container of time: the reader's dynamic absorption of frame, panel, and page potentially mimics his or her actual experience of the past, its lingering sensual traces in our memory, recalling Faulkner's maxim: "The past is never dead. It's not even past." This material fusion of space and narrative makes the graphic novel a compelling genre for writing about the past: the complex language of comics allows for multiple, even competing, perspectives as well as a densely layered sense of how history is remembered in the present.[19]

TRAUMA AND HISTORY

Each of the graphic novels discussed in this section addresses a different historical period and is set in a distinct "imagined space." By "imagined space" I refer to geographic details of place and landscape as well as the material and concrete features of the comics page.[20] For Spiegelman, comics "are about time being made manifest spatially, in that you've got all these different chunks of time—each box being a different moment of time—and you see them all at once. As a result you're always, in comics, being made aware of different times inhabiting the same space."[21] This spatial and visual simultaneity of past and present is a hallmark of Spiegelman's work and, as Hillary Chute has shown, part of how comics succeed in creating an especially effective grammar for the transmission of historical trauma.[22]

A page from *Maus I: A Survivor's Tale: My Father Bleeds History* sets the tools and tone for the entire project.[23] After interviewing his survivor father Vladek, Art then creates a visual record of his father's oral testimony; the text here alternates between narration in block text and direct dialogue in speech bubbles;

Art interviewing Vladek. Art Spiegelman, *Maus I: A Survivor's Tale: My Father Bleeds History* (1986).

material artifacts from the past (the tattooed concentration camp number on Vladek's arm, a picture of Art's dead brother) literally frame Art's present. When grasping the page as a whole, as a tabular grid rather than as a sequence of panels, the reader observes Vladek's body broken apart by gutters over several panels.[24] This, it seems to me, is a visual rendering of what it means to "bleed history"; as Vladek pedals, he tells his story and the stationary bike's front tire spins and spins, offering a kind of periscope back in time, a cameo framing the young Vladek: "I was in textiles . . . I didn't make much, but always I could make a living." The page delicately manages iconic elements and episodes from the past, demonstrating their effect and meaning in the space of the present.

Hatfield argues that the relation between page and panel creates a tension between what he calls "surface v. sequence."[25] This relation between individual panels and the page constitutes a fundamental element of the language of comics: we are asked to read for sequence or narrativity as well as surface design. This dual action also frames the graphic novel's status as both something you read and something you hold; of course, all books may be both read and held, but the made quality of the graphic novel, its attention to design and craft, heightens its ability to be both "experience" and "material object."[26] This duality allows for comics' unique deployment of narrative and space. Spiegelman describes this quality in architectural terms, directing our attention to the resemblance between a building's façade and the tabular grid of the comics page: "My dictionary defines COMIC STRIP as 'a narrative series of cartoons.' A NARRATIVE is defined as 'a story.' Most definitions of STORY leave me cold. Except the one that says: 'A complete horizontal division of a building [From Medieval Latin HISTORIA . . . a row of windows with pictures on them].'"[27]

The link between architecture and narrative is made explicit in a page from *Maus I,* in which a young Vladek returns home to his family after his release early in the war from a POW camp for Poles.[28] The windowpanes' slanting grid, through which we glimpse a large family dinner, alludes to the grid of panels below it; likewise, the neat white gutters separating a series of family members echo the black lead windowpanes above. The consonance between architecture and narrative, between *story* and *story,* is clear. Bracketing the entire page on the upper-left and lower-right-hand corners, Art's father Vladek pedals his story in the present; above, he refers to his tightly framed self in the context of the scene ("When first I came home it looked exactly so as before I went away") and below, he looks *back* on the scene, retrospectively, in gutter-less shaded hatching ("Herman and Hela . . . were visiting the N.Y. world's fair when the war came. This saved them").

Architecture meets narrative. Art Spiegelman, *Maus I: A Survivor's Tale: My Father Bleeds History* (1986).

Spiegelman was not the first comics artist to capitalize on the form's elastic relation to time and space, but the influence of *Maus*—an ambitious, long-form comic treating a distinctly adult theme—has shaped the emergence of the graphic novel as a preeminent genre of historical trauma. Rutu Modan's *Haneches* (The Property), published simultaneously in Hebrew and English editions in 2013, is in some ways a descendent of *Maus,* but it is also distinctly of its own time—the work of an auteur, a unique comics hand. In 1995, Modan became a founding member of the Israeli comics collective Actus Tragicus, whose English-language publications were influenced by the high quality and production values associated with both the American alternative scene and European comics.[29] Modan has said that her work is always rooted in some aspect of reality, and her success on an international scale—works published with Drawn & Quarterly, a high-profile comics imprint, appearances and prizes in France and the United States—as well as her ongoing teaching at the Bezalel Academy of Arts and Design in Jerusalem, have made her a major force in comics.[30]

Like *Maus, The Property* adopts a cross-generational frame to explore history and the Holocaust. Both books are "roots" projects: at the center of each is a relationship between and a parent or grandparent and a child, each of whom seeks to discover something about the past—something hidden, personal, and idiosyncratic. Art presses his father Vladek to tell him about the war because he wants to understand his mother's suicide and how it has shaped him as a person, husband, father, and artist, while Mica's story is more episodic: a trip back to Warsaw to recover details about the family property exposes details about her grandmother's past, her own father's paternity, and her relationship, as a secular Israeli Jew, to the war, the Shoah, and the Ghetto Uprising. Both books feature an investigative search for answers that defy or complicate normative narratives about the past. In *The Property,* Mica travels from Tel Aviv to Warsaw with her grandmother Regina (this is Regina's first time back in Poland since 1938) in order to recover the apartment—the property—belonging to Regina's family before the war. The book's relatively happy ending—a "meet cute" between Mica and Tomascz, a young Polish comics artist in Warsaw—is worlds away from the painful, tentative closure at the end of *Maus,* a difference that may point to the gap between second- and third-generation work about the Shoah.[31] In addition, Modan's matrilineal formation offers a gentle rebuke to the Art-Vladek dyad in *Maus,* where women as potential witnesses don't have a lot of credibility: they are either dead (Art's mother) or depicted as conniving and interfering (Vladek's second wife). Yet, like *Maus,* Modan's book also draws inventively on comics' accommodation of time and space.

Rutu Modan, Ghosts of the Warsaw Ghetto. *The Property* (2013). Copyright Rutu Modan. Used with permission from Drawn & Quarterly.

The past's enduring presence shapes Mica's encounter with Warsaw and its present-day cityscape. In a street scene set in the remains of the Jewish ghetto, individual panels along the top of the page suggest old photographs in an album; descending downward, speech bubbles reflect the conversation of the two figures in the present, on the sidewalk below; their placement also suggests voices of the past emerging from the sepia-colored windowpanes—an allusion to the link between space, narrative, and memory so crucial in Spiegelman's work, and reminiscent of his connection between "story" and "story."[32] This recovery project also characterizes the grandmother's relationship to the city of her childhood.

On pages 48–49, as Regina travels through Warsaw, the frame of each panel blends with the taxicab window, through which readers glimpse a palimpsestic memory; again, sepia is used to indicate space in the past, specifically Regina's childhood memories; at the entryway to her old apartment building, the names have all changed from Jewish to Polish. Rather than introduce speech or narration, the relative lack of text on these pages allows the images and their sequencing to communicate what Ariel Kahn refers to as Modan's "bravura use of silent pages or panels, which amplify the emotional subtext of the narrative."[33] This practice also enables a more immersive, reader-centered experience, in which Regina's interiority—what she chooses to reveal and conceal about "the property"—is more felt than dictated; the sequencing as Regina enters her building also suggests that she is walking back into the past.

While searching for clues about her grandmother's property, Mica meets Tomascz, a charming young Polish tour guide, who invites her over for pierogis and romance. Tomascz is also a comics artist, and as Mica pages through his sketches, we see that his realistic drawings are stylistically quite distinct from Modan's *ligne claire* (clear line) style.[34] Tomascz's ambition—he wants to create no less than the Polish *Persepolis*—is a reference to comics' ability to tackle "serious" historical topics.[35] Tomascz's version of the past, however, is substantively different from that of Mica; the Polish narrative of heroism, what he calls the Warsaw Uprising, is frankly juxtaposed with what Mica refers to as the Ghetto Uprising. This relative equity of viewpoints, so powerfully enabled by the multi-modal comics space, is a central attribute of Modan's work; in an interview with Joe Sacco, she describes this feature in relation to her first graphic novel, *Exit Wounds* (2007), whose narrative is set amid political violence in Israel during the early 2000s: "In *Exit Wounds*, I tried to suggest that if we drop the victim role, if we try to stop calculating who did what to whom first, stop waiting for closure, for 'justice to be done' . . . we might find a way to live happily ever after."[36] In a later interview, the author makes an even more explicit comparison: "Nowadays Israelis and Germans share, more or less the same narrative

Rutu Modan, Comics and/as history. *The Property* (2013). Copyright Rutu Modan. Used with permission from Drawn & Quarterly.

about what happened during WW2. The Poles and the Jews, on the other hand, have a very different story about the past. The Jews feel they were betrayed by the Poles, while the Poles don't think they were responsible whatsoever for the events. More than that, the Poles see themselves as the number one victim of the war, and they do have some points, I admit. But it is difficult to make peace when you cannot accept the other side of the story. In a way it is similar to the problem Israelis and Palestinians have with one another."[37]

This sense of competing narratives reaches an apex in a full page toward the end of the book, a "masterpiece of tragic-comic staging" that directly imagines the confrontation between these two different versions of history, Polish and Jewish.[38] The *el male rachamim*—traditional prayer for the dead—is chanted in a cemetery on Zaduszki—the Polish All Souls' Day.[39] The juxtaposition of

Rutu Modan, *El male rachamim. The Property* (2013). Copyright Rutu Modan. Used with permission from Drawn & Quarterly.

the Hebrew liturgical text of memory and the densely crowded cemetery in the background alludes to the thickness of historical space in contemporary Warsaw, most of which was rebuilt after the war. The "property" at the heart of this book is therefore not merely a piece of real estate but rather ownership of the past—a diverse set of accounts consisting of both collective and personal attachments. Some readers may hear an echo of another historical quarrel over property—the Israeli-Palestinian conflict. Here, as in *Exit Wounds,* the narrative depicts the effects of political conflict in oblique fashion; dispossession and disenfranchisement are connected across disparate groups in Israeli society, including Palestinians, women, and migrant workers.

The gap between past and present shapes the narrative in both *Maus* and *The Property;* and we have seen how the language of comics allows for a distinctive rendering of memory's allusive thickness. But what about those projects that do not hinge on memory—the express framing of the past via a present-day interlocutor—but are, instead, long-form comics narratives set in the past? What do they add to our appreciation of history? How might they supplement, or even challenge, received ideas about the past and its representation? Joannn Sfar's *The Rabbi's Cat* and Leela Corman's *Unterzakhn* are both historical graphic novels—that is, they use the comics' long form to present a tale set in the past. Elements of both stories complicate normative histories—of Jewish-Arab relations in prewar Algeria in Sfar's work and of twentieth-century Jewish life on the Lower East Side in Corman's. The vocabulary of comics, with their emphasis on juxtaposition and multiple perspectives, accommodates, even demands, this kind of nuance and revision, this undoing of history.

Sfar's multivolume project, *The Rabbi's Cat,* set in Algiers in the 1930s, features a cat who gains the power of speech by killing and eating a parrot.[40] Sfar's story thus upsets the basic divide between human and animal, and eventually disrupts a whole series of dichotomies—including that between East (Algeria) and West (France), Jew and Arab, rational and mystical thought and, of course—because we are reading a graphic novel—between text and image. Unlike the irregular panel layout of both *Maus* and *The Property,* Sfar's fantastical tale is delivered within a relatively orderly grid: while the past may be an arena of ongoing negotiation among diverse groups, motives, and affiliations, the page's neat grid remains consistent and unbroken throughout, therefore staging this negotiation through a kind of formal parity—two across, three down, page after page. At the same time, the book's narrative arc systematically *undoes* fundamental binary distinctions, with the cat himself, and his polemical—even heretical—views, as the main figure of disruption. When his special powers are revealed, the cat refuses to admit that he ate the parrot; concerned for his lack

An argument about God. Joann Sfar, *The Rabbi's Cat* (2005).

of a moral conscience as well for his Jewish identity, the rabbi sets out to educate the cat, bringing him to *his* rabbi for advice.

The cat wishes to become bar mitzvah, a liturgical rite of passage customarily undergone upon reaching the age of thirteen. The handwritten script text at the top of each panel relays the cat's partially omniscient narration: note the visual play of silhouette and background as the cat argues with the rabbi's rabbi over the depiction of God in visual form and the elevation of the linguistic or—as vividly illustrated in the panel—the oral; rather than deciding the argument in favor of one medium over the other, their debate about word and image seems rather to be an argument *for* the unique power of comics, of *picture* and *word* together. Leah Hochman notes that this "verbal, visual volleying for meaning" amounts to a deeply theological discussion, one in which the "idea of God" is allowed to fill the very determined absence of divine form.[41]

As the cat's education evolves, the book launches a direct assault on Western thought's reductive reasoning; the rabbi offers a critique of allegory and symbols, privileging "Jewish teaching" which, he claims, proceeds by analogy. The arbitrariness of language itself is addressed in this scene: the governing body of French Jewry has summoned the rabbi to take a dictation test demonstrating his mastery of French. The tables have turned; the cat now coaches the rabbi in calligraphy (how writing looks), dictation (how it sounds), and, of course, spelling rules; the cat's conclusion deftly captures the entangled quality of prewar Jewish life: "And to lead prayer in Hebrew for Jews who speak Arabic, they want you to write in French. So i say they're nuts."

In the urban space of Algiers, the natives—Jews and Muslims alike—are prohibited from certain spaces.[42] But in the unmonitored space of the great out-

Language and identity. Joann Sfar, *The Rabbi's Cat* (2005).

Urban space. Joann Sfar, *The Rabbi's Cat* (2005).

Language in the great outdoors. Joann Sfar, *The Rabbi's Cat* (2005).

doors, they find positive common ground: during their visit to the Sfar family ancestral tomb, the rabbi and his cat meet a Muslim pilgrim and his donkey, and they realize they share the same destination, a common language, and potentially much more. This moment unfolds in nature's ostensibly pristine, mystical space, as opposed to the urban colonial sphere, tainted by the Western desire to separate and categorize. The relative nostalgia of this depiction belies the fact that urban Algerian Jews were largely part of the colonial elite, closer to the French in some respects than their Muslim neighbors. (One wonders if

Street education. Leela Corman, *Unterzakhn* (2012).

this minor historical revision is somehow related to Sfar's own family situation: a French Jew of both Sephardic and Ashkenazi descent, Sfar has written another series of equally fabulous graphic novels that explore eastern European culture, *Klezmer: Tales of the Wild East.*) Sfar's expressive style embeds a unique story of a feline and his humans within a richly detailed, even familiar, historical setting in a way that gently skewers reader assumptions about the past.

Like *The Rabbi's Cat,* Leela Corman's *Unterzakhn* is a historical graphic novel; it traces the fortunes of twin sisters Esther and Fanya, born on the Lower East Side in the early twentieth century. Neither sister receives a formal education; instead, they remain home to perform housework and help with their mother's lingerie shop—hence the book's title, which means "underthings" in Yiddish. Indeed, both Esther and Fanya are schooled on New York's "mean streets"; each girl absorbs a different set of lessons: Esther begins work in a brothel and eventually ends up on the stage; Fanya learns to read from a "lady doctor" and becomes a pioneering advocate for birth control and legal abortion, in the manner of Margaret Sanger.[43] Within *Unterzakhn,* the street is a site of exposure and education, offering a different version of Jewish immigrant acculturation, one especially attuned to women's experience, men's and women's bodies, and the commercial sphere. The formal properties of comics allow for a nuanced depiction of the space of the street—a vibrant rendering of history from down under; an intimate, detailed depiction of how knowledge is transmitted through human interactions on sidewalks and in alleyways. Unlike in *The Rabbi's Cat,* where the female protagonist, the rabbi's daughter Zlabya, is largely confined to the indoor spaces of her home in Tangiers and that of her betrothed in Paris, girls and women in Corman's work move relatively freely in and out of public and private spaces, mapping networks of women across the stages and ballrooms of Second Avenue and into the delivery room.

The title references not only the mother's store but also the girls' unsentimental education as well as the historically derisive view of comics more broadly—often censored and considered a debased cultural form, bound up in the sensational and lurid, the "graphic" in the graphic novel. As Tahneer Oksman notes, "Through its focus on the vernacular, on everyday encounters with oral and visual forms of knowledge, Corman's graphic novel . . . reflects

"Underthings." Leela Corman, *Unterzakhn* (2012).

how comics can emphasize aspects of those experiences that have yet to be fully explored."[44] Corman's book thus reveals what has been left out of normative historiographic accounts, elevating both women's experience and comics as legitimate vehicles of history.[45]

It is by now a commonplace of comics scholarship to note that Superman and his justice-seeking friends were created by young Jewish immigrants, themselves feeling as if they had fallen to earth from another planet, anxious about their ability to "pass" as Americans.[46] This more recent raft of Jewish graphic narratives—represented in this chapter by Spiegelman, Modan, Sfar, and Corman—are, in one sense, the postmodern progeny of that prewar sensibility; their work resists simplistic narratives of good and evil, instead plumbing the messy contradictions at the heart of historical narratives, giving us a more complex sense of the past and its meaning today. We have seen thus far two distinct examples of how graphic novels address history: the *Maus-Property* model, in which memory—what Spiegelman calls "the retrieval of memory, and ultimately, the creation of memory"—is foregrounded, and *The Rabbi's Cat* and *Unterzakhn,* in which a historical narrative is itself front and center.[47] All of these works rely on the unique ability of comics to manipulate time and space—from panel to page and across an entire book.

In order to argue for the uniqueness of comics as a vehicle of history through imagined space, I confess to having set up "normative" historiography as a bit of straw figure. Of course any historical account worth its salt will account for the kind of multiple narratives described in this chapter. However, the language of comics provides a unique opportunity for historical discourse. How else to account for the oversized presence of history, and specifically historical trauma, as a key theme in contemporary graphic narratives? In *Why Comics: From Underground to Everywhere* (2017), Hillary Chute offers a panoramic view of themes driving the creation of comics in recent decades; the chapters are organized around questions: why superheroes? why punk? why girls? why war? why queer? and so on. I would add to this list why Jews? Indeed, a comparative reading of work published in the United States, Israel, and France illuminates the degree to which the genre's typical features have emerged, in part, from a specifically *Jewish* preoccupation with material and historical rupture. This sense of rupture, of the past's fundamental distance, may be related to the "two-ness" of history depicted in historical graphic novels by Jewish authors. Furthermore, the deep structure of comics—their play of absence and presence across empty gutters and between teeming panels—alludes to the very structure of memory, how it conjures the past in the terms of the present. This is not to claim a unique or proprietary relation to these ideas on the part of Jewish graphic novels. But they can be identified as salient, distinguishing features of work by major artists—Spiegelman and Modan, especially—whose influence on the field at large is undeniable.

Witness the extraordinary example of Nora Krug's *Belonging: A German Reckons with History and Home* (2018). Krug's book maps the author's relationship to her German roots, specifically the wartime activities of her parents' families. Moving gracefully between her current home in the United States and the material and social landscapes of her German childhood, Krug's work evokes the investigatory impulse propelling both *Maus* and *The Property*. Furthermore, her desire to plumb the chasm between the present and the murky terrain of the past recalls the primal impulse driving *Maus* as well as other works of Holocaust literature, including the postmodern experimentation of novels such as Nicole Krauss's *The History of Love* and nonfiction such as Daniel Mendelsohn's *The Lost*. The author is well aware that she could uncover potentially damning aspects of her family's behavior, even complicity with the Nazi regime, and indeed some Krug family secrets emerge toward the end of the book, although other issues remain obscure. *Belonging* draws on photographs, archival documentation, and a keen sense of how cultural identity is yoked to both language and material objects to create a wholly unique work—something between a graphic novel, detective fiction, and a scrapbook. Krug frames some of her chapters as ethnographic "Field Notes"; others describe "Things German" and flea market finds. Most disturbing, perhaps, is the generic resemblance between Krug's book—the work of a non-Jewish German inquiring into her family's actions during the war—and the hybrid features of the *yizker* book. The focus on micro-history, including important local events and personalities, supplemented with family trees, maps, photographs, found objects, and personal testimony, underscores how material artifacts, including photographs and archival scraps of paper, "become openings for living stories, refashioning evidence of lives lived before one's own."[48]

WHY JEWS? MATERIALITY AND THE SACRED

Considering the question "Why Jews?" in relation to graphic narratives raises two related issues: the particular attitudes or dispositions within Judaic tradition toward image and text, and the question of the sacred. Regarding the former, I refer not only to the Second Commandment prohibition on sculptural representations of the divine but also to something more general about how images operate, especially their potential to insult or offend.[49] In a 2014 interview, when asked specifically about his early work in a comics anthology called *Outrageous*

Tales from the Old Testament (1987), the great fantasy writer Neil Gaiman notes: "Every culture has its own way of interacting with the image."[50] His comment alludes to a normative suspicion of images within Judaic tradition, an issue emerging from *Outrageous Tales,* where often profane illustrations accompanied biblical stories. More generally, however, as Gaiman explains, we are likely to be offended by images because, relative to text, they are more easily absorbed; that is—to use Gaiman's example—for a reader to be offended by a novel like D. H. Lawrence's *Lady Chatterly's Lover,* she or he actually has to spend time and energy reading it. Images, on the other hand, demand no such investment: they are more readily absorbed, less avoidable, and, once viewed, cannot be "unseen." Minimally, we might ask how this potentially transgressive nature of images somehow figures within Jewish graphic novels. This question suggests that the image-text debate in *The Rabbi's Cat,* whether God is either picture or word, might be understood as a specifically *Jewish* intervention. At issue here is less the direct representation or depiction of Jews and more the idea of Jewishness as an interpretive mode. Jewishness potentially allows for a greater sensitivity to certain kinds of images and to certain image-text combinations. This quality seems especially relevant for projects like Gaiman's biblical work or other long-form comics that adapt or engage a traditionally sacred text.[51]

Beyond comics' ability to offend, the particular material affordances of the graphic novel as a genre—its mix of text and image—suggest new ways of approaching the sacred. Indeed, for the editors of *Comics and Sacred Texts,* the boundary-busting juxtaposition of text and image is precisely what makes "the graphic form . . . ideally suited to reveal how the sacred appears in uncanny places." With their inventive play of text, image, and layout, "graphic narratives can inform how readers imagine and reconstruct the sacred as a material, visual experience."[52] The link between materiality and sacredness is supported by the graphic novel's "writerly" qualities; according to Roland Barthes, "writerly" texts demand a co-construction of meaning on the part of readers, a process that foregrounds the crafted quality of the work before them. The microactivity of bridging across gutters between panels in sequence further amplifies these features; graphic narratives with an explicitly Jewish focus provide a unique opportunity to examine how the relation between sacredness and the book might unfold in a modern, material idiom.

J. T. Waldman's *Megillat Esther* (2005) presents the biblical book of Esther in its entirety, in both its original Hebrew and English translation. In addition, the author includes interpretative side narratives based on midrashic sources as well as bibliographic information about these sources and the various visual styles and codes that inform the dazzling, intricate illustrations. Narrating the

A "writerly" text. J. T. Waldman, *Megillat Esther* (2005). Courtesy of the artist.

dramatic victory of Persian Jewry over the machinations of the archvillain Haman, the book of Esther itself occupies a distinct position within the corpus of ancient works of classical Judaic tradition: God's name does not appear in the text, thus potentially reducing its status as a sacred object; it is associated with the carnivalesque holiday of Purim; and it is a dramatic tale of ethnic, gendered power relations—all these factors have made the book of Esther the subject of elaborate, often expensively produced illuminated scrolls and other editions.[53] These features make Waldman's *Megillat Esther* a kind of test case for Jewish graphic narrative engagement with materiality and the sacred. The book deploys some of the key features of graphic novels discussed in this chapter: the co-work of text and image; the tension between page and panel and between surface and sequence; the deliberate play of font as an iconic device. However, though Waldman's work displays an occasional trace of an underlying grid, most pages present a more singular use of space: ornate drawings occupying an entire page, text crisscrossing the page on a diagonal, human forms and text bubbles leaking over gutters and page margins. All of this makes for a kind of slow reading, contributing to a sharpened consciousness of the reading experience and the materiality of this "writerly" text.

In *Megillat Esther,* the iconic qualities of text and typography are heightened through the presence of two different alphabets throughout, each read in the opposite direction. Needless to say, the eyes are quite busy! Beyond the calligraphic project, the text's iconic features are driven by Hebrew's status as a sacred language in the biblical domain. (This is quite different from *The Property*'s play with spoken language, including Hebrew and Polish, where the alphabet's iconographic features are related to composition and communication.) Waldman's visual intertexts, documented in the bibliography as well as a companion website, constitute a catalogue of visual styles available throughout history for Jewish artists, some of which we have observed in this study's other generic categories. For example, *Megillat Esther*'s prologue recalls both the art nouveau work of Ephraim Lillien and Franz Masereel's expressionist woodcuts. Other pages allude to well-known art by figures such as Frieda Kahlo and even pop art by Lichtenstein and Warhol, work whose trajectory was itself shaped by the emergence of comics forms.[54]

The central intertext is, of course, the illuminated manuscript, historically a rich source within Jewish tradition and specifically for the book of Esther. In a recent prodigiously illustrated volume, scholars praise Waldman's *Megillat Esther,* noting that the "distance between the exquisitely painted and gilded manuscripts of the Middle Ages and the intense, fiery, passionate universe of the frames of the graphic novel" is actually not so great: "examining Waldman's work closely, one finds that both in graphic skill and in the learning of text, midrash, and context that constantly bubbles restlessly to the surface, its function is startlingly analogous to that of medieval manuscripts, interpreting, contextualizing, linking the rabbinic past with the present via an engagement with art and iconography as exegesis. Waldman's iconography does not merely illustrate text and exegesis, it becomes powerful exegesis in and of itself."[55] Waldman himself seems to view his work as a kind of modern midrash, and this

Scrolls unwinding. J. T. Waldman, *Megillat Esther* (2005). Courtesy of the artist.

observation brings us closer to the ways in which his text might approach the sacred and participate in an exegetical tradition.

The physical engagement with the language of the text—the stylized Hebrew alongside a generally more austere English—peaks during a key moment in the plot: on page 92, as King Ahashverus tosses and turns in the night and the fate of Persian Jewry hangs in the balance, the intertwined fortunes of

The artist's "hand." J. T. Waldman, *Megillat Esther* (2005). Courtesy of the artist.

Haman and the Jews reverse, or "turn over," and readers are forced to turn the book upside down in order to continue reading; the action mimics the story's famous reversal of fortunes, reminds us that the book is an object, and alludes to the story's origins as a scroll. A series of drawings toward the end of *Megillat Esther* illustrates Esther's decree establishing the rituals of Purim; the text notes, "And it was written in the book" above a brief set of panels across the bottom of the page depicting the unraveling of a scroll. Drawings of hands reading and writing, themselves a kind of visual pun on the special pointer (a *yad*, or "hand") used to follow the Torah's scroll's densely scripted text, amplify readers' awareness of the premodern origins of Waldman's text.[56]

Noting the material affordances of genre throughout this study has allowed for a different way of tracking literary history: from lyric poetry's creative engagement with the material core of language and the little magazines' exuberant take on image-text relations to the novel's preoccupation with a rapidly changing material landscape and the memorial book's staging of itself as a substitute for that very landscape to the graphic novel—a decidedly postwar invention—which ironically retains, in Benjaminian terms, the "aura" of its original production, bearing as it does the singular physical traces of the author's hand. Indeed, though subsequently mass-produced and widely circulated, the graphic novel begins as a unique artifact, produced by the auteur in the language of comics. This singularity resembles—and may even serve as a replacement for—the sacred.[57] Of course, not all singular objects are sacred. However, given its particular connection to the tradition of illuminated scrolls, Waldman's work demonstrates how some trace of the sacred may linger in ostensibly secular literary forms. Recalling the anxiety over the commodification of writing in early twentieth-century modernist work by Hebrew and Yiddish novelists and editors of little magazines, we may observe how postmodern genres such as the graphic novel and the artist's book—the subject of chapter 6—invent new methods for elevating the status of the book, both as a cultural form and as a material object in its own right.

Chapter 6 On the Seam: Artists' Books and the Unmaking of the Book

Everything in the world exists only to end up in a book.
—Stéphane Mallarmé, "The Book, Spiritual Instrument" (1897)

In the old art the writer writes texts.
In the new art the writer makes books.
—Ulises Carrión, "The New Art of Making Books" (1980)

Books are things that hold things.
—Adrian Piper, *Book Was There: Reading in Electronic Times* (2012)

Of all the genres discussed in this study, the artist's book might most prompt a raised eyebrow regarding its origins or species. As I have argued throughout, the capaciousness of any genre allows for an elastic sense of what constitutes its exemplary instances. However, before we ask, "What is an artist's book?" we might pose another, more fundamental question: "What is a book?" A few possible responses have emerged thus far—most notably in relation to the *yizker* books, where the book is conceived as a memorial object, and the little magazines, which are conceived as objects of art. Both genres maintain the traditional structure of the codex—multiple pages contained between a back and front cover—which is "read" by a person holding it in his or her hands, and flipping through its constituent parts. (This fundamental experience is what many virtual or digital platforms attempt to mimic.) Anticipated audience and readership also shape our sense of what constitutes a book—for example, the intended audience of the *yizker* book, the descendents of the town, or the network inscribed by the circulation of the little magazine. These essential parameters of bookishness, and the material limits thereof, form the basis of what we anticipate when encountering a book. Nevertheless, scholarship on the history of the book describes the tremendous variety of forms that have been used to record, convey, and absorb information, tracing the evolution of said forms through different stages of production and readership. Historians of the book embed its emergence as material form in specific networks of social and economic relations. Robert Darnton introduced the influential model of the "communications circuit," which traces the book as an object through six key stations: author, publisher, printer, distributor, bookseller, and reader.[1] Roger Chartier reminds us that "reading is not uniquely an abstract operation of the intellect: it brings the body into play, it is inscribed in a space and a relationship with oneself or with others."[2] These "communities of readers" are not the endpoint of a book's communicative circuit but also inflect and shape the book's meaning, with special attention to its material form. Books exist to be read, and they have historically set the parameters of their own consumption; their evolving form has determined how we read, and how we treat and handle them as objects.

In addition to these questions of material format and reception, other factors come into play when considering the status of Jewish book forms in the wake of material disruption. Throughout this study, I have been interested in how secular literary genres are produced in relation to those religious forms against which they ostensibly rebelled. What happens when those earlier forms appear to be entirely emptied out, even violently so, when "the Book" and its authority seem irredeemably lost? No twentieth-century figure has more assiduously and provocatively explored this condition than the Egyptian-born French Jewish writer Edmond Jabès, whose work is animated by the experience of wandering, trauma, and rupture as well as a persistent engagement with the idea of "the Book" in the wake of the Shoah. Jabès's multivolume project delineates a metaphysical conception of "the Book" alongside select portions of Judaic heritage, all refracted through a poetic sensibility shaped by juxtaposition, dialogue, and tautology. Offering neither a clear linear frame nor easy resolution of vexing philosophical dilemmas, "the Book" for Jabès is at once a repository of tradition and a way out of the ostensible confines of that tradition. It is both a dwelling that offers comfort and shelter and a model for a more productive form of exile. A brief foray into Jabès's postwar conception of the book will help foreground some of the issues that Jewish book artists have addressed in the years since.

At the very beginning of Jabès's *The Book of Questions* (1963), a conversation titled "At the Threshold of the Book" tests the limits of rabbinic "privileged readers" with an enigmatic series of questions and answers between two voices, one of which identifies himself as "the keeper of the house":

> "Who are you?"
> "I am the keeper of the house."
> "Where do you come from?"
> "I have wandered."
> "Is Yukel your friend?"
> "I am like Yukel."
> "What is your lot?"
> "To open the book."
> "Are you in the book?"
> "My place is at the threshold."
> "What have you tried to learn?
> "I sometimes stop on the road to the sources and question the signs, the world of my ancestors."[3]

Yukel, Sarah, Yaël, Elya, and Aely serve as a kind of paradigmatic family of postwar wandering Jews; these names also serve as titles of Jabès's expanding series of volumes. The poetic speaker's location is simultaneously at the heart of and adjacent to Judaic sources; these texts are approached and handled, physically as well as cognitively, with wonder and respect on the most granular of levels: page, syllable, letter. This process—what Rosmarie Waldrop aptly describes as a kind of "structural indirection," with "multiple gradual approaches to 'the book' through ground after ground, gateway after gateway, threshold after threshold, door after door"—is also an encounter with a certain kind of space.[4]

> "You are a Jew, and you talk like one."
>
> "The four letters JUIF which designate my origin are your four fingers. You can use your thumb to crush me."
>
> "You are a Jew, and you talk like one. But I am cold. It is dark. Let me come into the house."
>
> "There is a lamp on my table. And the house is in the book."[5]

In an essay on Jabès, Jacques Derrida describes *The Book of Questions* as "one long metonymy, the situation of the Jew becomes exemplary of the situation of the poet."[6] The book itself in Jabès's work becomes a cipher for a complex range of mediations in which writing and language struggle to name an absent, yet vividly imagined, wholeness: "Any book is but a dim likeness of the lost book."[7] Jabès's work repeatedly links this rupture to postwar Jewish experiences, in named and unnamed settings. For example, an apocryphal story about someone named Nathan Seichell and the violence that ensues following his disappearance concludes with this warning, which also contains a kernel of promise: "Every Jew drags behind himself a scrap of the ghetto, a scrap of rescued land where he takes refuge when alarmed."[8] More broadly, the speaker reflects: "I have spoken of the difficulty of being Jewish, which is the same as the difficulty of writing, because Judaism and writing are one and the same waiting, one and the same hope, and one and the same wearing down."[9]

Writing—and more concretely the form of the book—becomes a kind of evolving tether on which the shifting, indeterminate voice of Jabès's speaker turns. Jewish writing throughout the twentieth century is preoccupied with this simultaneous sense of invention and collapse, of constructing and deconstructing the book, the canon, the nation, the self:

> Have you seen how a word is born and dies? . . .
> Have you seen how a book is made and unmade?[10]

What does it mean for a book to be "unmade"? Being unmade is not the same as physical destruction, the fate of so many Jewish books in the twentieth century. A book's "unmaking" involves some other kind of activity, one in which the book is disassembled and readers come to appreciate its constituent parts. One might conclude that the unmaking of a book is in fact its demise. But Jabès's voluminous project—seventeen books between 1943 to 1985—also intimates a spiraling sense of what might endure: "Tomorrow is another moment of the book to be deciphered."[11]

Artists' books demonstrate how a book may be productively unmade. As a genre, the artist's book shares with the book as a historical form an essential quality: one's relationship to it is shaped by its material features—its paper, binding, size, weight, and shape. Emerging in the 1960s and 1970s in the United States and Europe in relation to both contemporary art institutions and political activism, the artist's book resembles, in some respects, the modernist experimentation of the little magazines. Its status as a made object also ties it to older iterations of the book, especially the scroll or early codex produced on vellum or parchment, whose material presence implied some kind of value—whether economic or religious (or both). However, the artist's book, more than both its modern and its premodern predecessors, most concretely and persistently demands attention to the book qua book. In considering the plethora of examples falling under this term—the multitudes of style, format, cost, theme, materials, circulation, and so on—we may keep our eye on this key material affordance or feature: whatever other features it may or may not possess, an artist's book must always, in some fashion, interrogate its properties as a book.[12] This interrogation can take many forms, some more explicit than others: some artists' books challenge, or even resist, the very practice of reading—becoming almost an "anti-book" in the process.

Take, for example, the related domain of "book art"—objects of art created out of actual books. Doug Beube's elaborate books use *rimonim* ("pomegranate"-shaped knobs) or other decorative forms from Torah scrolls to create elevated, "sacrosanct" objects.[13] In *Fallen Borders,* the artist physically altered pages to suggest "a clash between nations": "In the second to last chapter entitled, 'Atlas of Bible Lands,' using the tip of a small belt sander I erode the paper alluding to climate change that is drastically altering our planet. The pages with reproductions and maps result in an overlay of faux languages of both Arabic and Hebrew. There's a synthesis, a place together, between the diacritic vowels, the dots and consonant pointing, of the 'Tashkeel' in Arabic and in Hebrew, 'Nikud.' Fallen Borders can be read from back to front as in reading Arabic and Hebrew."[14]

Beube's work exemplifies what Richard Kostelanetz describes as an important, though not absolute, prerogative of the artist's book: "Most books are primarily about something outside themselves; most book art books are primarily about themselves."[15] Along this slippery continuum of self-reference, artists' books are less dramatic than Beube's aggressive intervention, offering instead slightly amended book forms in the service of a particular narrative and/or set of images.

Artists' books may also exploit those forms considered to be universal formats of the book (the trajectory from tablet through papyrus and scroll to codex and on to screen). The codex, in particular, is a major target of formal experimentation in contemporary artists' books. In order to appreciate this critical engagement, let's first note the features of a typical encounter with the codex. Even before opening it, readers know a lot about a book in codex form due to its paratextual features: publication details as well as the identity of the author are featured on the front and back covers; images on the covers may also convey details about the content; material features such as quality of paper and print indicate the intended audience. Sequence is essential to the experience of the codex: readers know how to access (that is, open and close) the book and, therefore, also know where the book starts and ends. As a genre, the artist's book upends these qualities, often through play or parody. The relative linearity of narrative may be productively upset, as may expectations regarding the page's normative attributes, including margins, typeface, and the like. The use of non-standard bindings, different types of paper (with varying degrees of opaqueness, different textures) and sequences of folds or openings—all of these features potentially disrupt the codex's sequential form as well as readers' normative expectations.

However, while the innovation of the artist's book often begins with the codex, it certainly does not end there; as Johanna Drucker notes, the artist's book is a "highly mutable form, one which cannot be definitively pinned down by its formal characteristics." The artist's book is indebted in its origins to conceptual art's focus on the object, such that it is sometimes easier to say what it is not rather than what it is.[16] Indeed, in what Ulises Carrión called "the new art" of making books, "every book requires a different reading."[17] Some artists' books hearken back to older forms in their use of rare materials and handmade features; these, often published in limited editions, possess a kind of aura, which translates in the marketplace as price or inclusion in an archival collection. Artists' books may be a product of either traditional techniques or cutting-edge technology. In either case, with this attention to itself as book qua object, the artist's book as a genre addresses the means of its own production. Whether a true "democratic multiple," an inexpensively mass-produced artifact intended for wide distribution; a limited edition produced in a numbered sequence with high-quality materials, an extension of brick-and-mortar gatekeeping institutions such as the art museum or gallery; or a one-off, that is, a singular, "auratic" object that challenges the holder to encounter it as a book-object in three-dimensional fashion—all address the status of the book as an object in a commodified aesthetic domain.

For the examples discussed in this chapter, the particular trajectory of the book in Jewish cultures shapes these "investigations of the book as a form through an examination of its material, thematic, and formal properties."[18] Given the centrality of the text within Judaic tradition, it is not surprising to find many Jewish artists working with this genre. At least one prominent book artist (Doug Beube) explicitly references the idea of the Jews as a "people of the book" in explaining their work, suggesting that he views his attention to the book qua object as connected to some ahistorical form of Jewishness.[19] While we might intuit this connection more directly in work like *Fallen Borders,* Beube seems to suggest a general principle: not an engagement with religious or spiritual motifs per se, but an awareness, more implicit than expressed, of the historical background of this particular relationship. Noting this affinity, the Library of Congress has published an illustrated catalogue of its Hebrew and Yiddish artists' books, organizing its holdings temporally and by theme and author, from the Bible to present-day work.[20] Here, I organize the discussion in relation to my broader concern with materiality: each artist's book discussed references or revisits specific material matters from earlier chapters. Beyond engagements such as the linkage of image and text, or attention to things and objecthood, the artist's book also foregrounds the presence of the sacred within an ostensibly secular form. Ultimately, and regardless of its particular form or subject matter, the artist's book is that secular genre in which a trace of sacred aura most enduringly abides.

Jewish book artists like Lynne Avadenka seem aware of the book's material, sacred features; many of her books directly engage canonical works from antiquity and modern Hebrew literature, including biblical texts such as the book of Lamentations, medieval Hebrew poetry, and works by Amos Oz, Yehuda Amichai, and Dan Pagis.[21] In *By a Thread* (2006, in an edition of three hundred copies), two figures from classical storytelling—the biblical Queen Esther

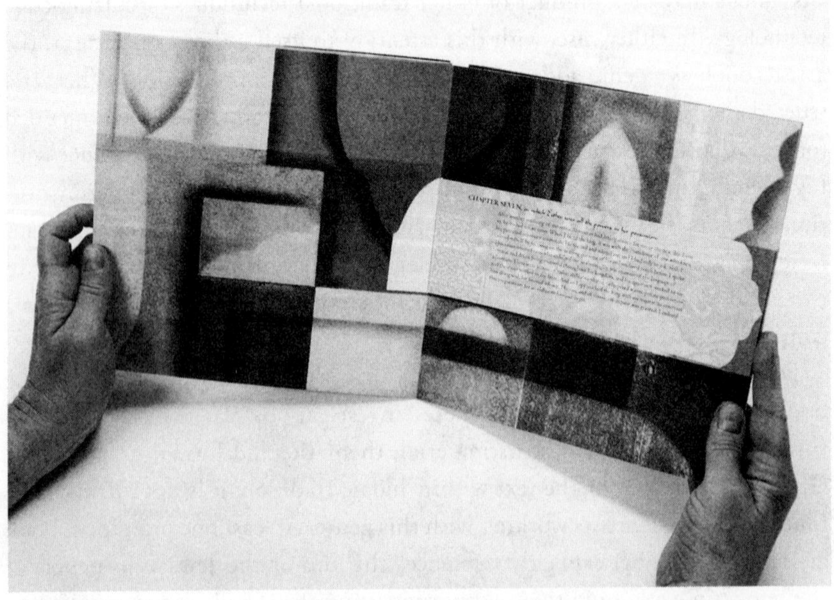

By a Thread (2006), artist's book courtesy of Lynne Avadenka. Color offset lithography, die-cutting. Photograph by R. H. Hensleigh.

By a Thread (2006), artist's book courtesy of Lynne Avadenka. Color offset lithography, die-cutting. Photograph by R. H. Hensleigh.

and Scheherazade of *A Thousand and One Nights*—speak directly to each other in short "chapters"; the intricate folding book opens to reveal arches and ornate script, challenging the form of the codex and also recalling the tradition of the scroll.

The illustrations, drawing on motifs from architecture and the natural world typical of Islamic mosaic art, fill the entire page, over which is laid a shorter, tab-like page containing the text; both sets of pages unfold and open like the petals of a flower, creating a dual motion that mirrors the conversational structure. The two figures share their stories "over centuries," providing perspectives that depart from and even challenge the more well-known details of their narratives. For example, Esther begins to enjoy the luxuries of palace life and gradually learns to use her position as queen to cultivate advantage and power: "Here's what men forget about women wearing the veil: we can see them and they can't read us."[22] Like J. T. Waldman's *Megillat Esther,* the book's form literalizes the story's "reversal" of fortunes: in order to read Scheherazade's story, readers must turn the book around and upside down, creating a cyclical narrative movement that is reiterated, with an explanatory comment by the author, at the conclusion of Scheherazade's tale, leading back to Esther once again:

> No historical thread connects Esther and Scheherazade, though it should be simple enough to find one: two women from ancient Persia, both second wives of brutish, brutal kings, both aided in their acts of courage by trusted family companions. . . . When was the link between them broken? What have we lost because of this break? To console ourselves, we invent our own story, one of connections between two women, Jewish and Muslim, and while historians are dismissive, it is this connection between these women that leads to . . . [flip page] stories that lead to stories, there is no end to the stories, and so we turn to [flip page]

The book's cyclical form mirrors the historical connection between the two women and their stories.[23] The privileging of women's voices and experience in *By a Thread* exemplifies a significant trend within the American scene, notable as early as the emergence of artists' books and other alternative print and visual cultural forms in the 1970s. Indeed, "the book" became a locus of practice for women artists interested in critiquing patriarchal institutions. In her introduction to a catalogue of artists' books from the National Museum of Women in the Arts, Drucker explores why women have been so central in the production of book arts: "To find the reasons why women artists are drawn to the book form—a complex format that is difficult to exhibit and laborious to produce—one must consider the power of books to confer authority upon their makers. The cultural icon of a book remains a potent sign, even in this era of new technology.

At the same time, the experience of making and reading books occurs in a private and meditative space, amounting to immersion in a virtual world. For the woman artist, the paradoxical private-public nature of books serves dual desires—for self-protection and recognition, for the preservation of modesty and the display of competence."[24]

This idea of bookmaking as a public-private discourse lurks within the peekaboo format of Avadenka's *By a Thread,* where Queen Esther and Schcherazade and their stories are simultaneously visible and hidden. Furthermore, the notion of the thread as both physically and metaphorically binding reminds us how "the activities associated with bookmaking are socially coded in a positive way as feminine"—specifically, the material acts of cutting fabric or paper and sewing, pasting, and creating objects such as clothing, scrapbooks, or other crafted items.[25] The sewn "seam" of the book—invisible to the eye but essential to narration and form—marks the boundary between public and private, between ancient oral traditions and their modern material incarnations.

We may also note the particular presence of Jewish women artists, such as Drucker herself, who created a work called *The Word Made Flesh* (1996). The archivist-librarian-editor Judith Hoffberg—a major figure in feminist print culture, including artists' books and the alternative press—curated the pioneering exhibit *Women of the Book: Jewish Artists, Jewish Themes* (2001), featuring books by ninety artists from all over the world on themes such as biblical motifs, the Holocaust, family relations, and the liturgical centrality of the book in religious practice. In her introduction to the exhibition catalogue, Hoffberg noted that "there was something in the air among Jewish women artists, . . . although closeted or segregated as 'the other,' they had much to say via their bookworks."[26] Given the symbolic authority of the book within traditional Jewish culture, it might not come as a surprise that it becomes a target for Jewish women artists. Hoffberg's volume contains a dazzling and imaginative array of themes and materials: books that engage family trauma and sacred texts, books that draw on historical memory and first-person testimony, books combining archival and personal photographs with found objects, books influenced by traditional Judaic paper arts such as the *ketuba* (wedding contract) and calligraphy, books made of vellum and sealed in boxes, damaged books, accordion books, books covered with beads, thread, fabric, wire, gold leaf, clay, and even hair and teeth.

One of the collection's most confounding books, whose image is featured on the catalogue cover, is Tatana Kellner's *B11226: Fifty Years of Silence,* a disturbing and moving tribute to the author's parents that details their experiences during the war.[27] The work was originally produced in two copies, one for the

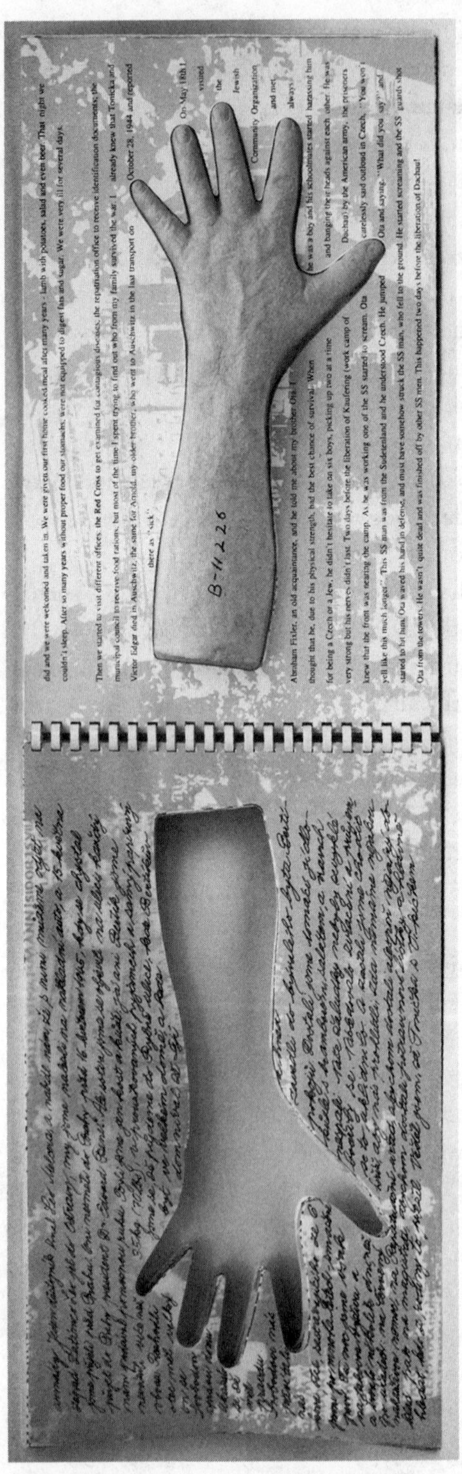

Tatana Kellner, *B11226: Fifty Years of Silence, Eugene Kellner's Story* (1992). Handmade cast paper. Silkscreen, die cut. Spiral bound codex. Issued in a wooden box (36 × 58 × 8 cm.). 81 pages. Edition: 50. Women's Studio Workshop, 1992.

mother's story and one for the father's. An edition of fifty copies of the father's book was published by the Women's Studio Workshop in 1992. The book begins with the author's own introduction to her father's story: "I have known since I was a child that my parents were concentration camp survivors, since both of them had a number tattooed on their left arm. I used to spend a long time studying their tattoos, wondering what it must have been like. My mother never talked about her experiences. My father only talked about it when he was scolding us, especially about eating everything on our plates."[28] Her parents eventually agreed to write down their memories in Czech, and the book presents their handwritten testimony facing a typescript translation. Created around this testimony and personal photographs of the author and her family as well as photos taken by the author during visits to the camps, the book is anchored by a full-size plaster of paris arm, painted in flesh tone and marked with the father's concentration camp number. The arm cuts through each page, interrupting Kellner's father's detailed narrative of his experiences in Terezin and Auschwitz. In macabre fashion, the writing on the skin recalls parchment, making the book a kind of sacred testimonial.

Kellner's book also functions as a sculptural form that concretizes a metaphorical aspect of reading. On each page, the arm leaves or creates a hole across the middle, suggesting permanent damage, especially when it literally tears apart photographs of the author's family. The hole stymies the linearity of the codex, intruding upon each page, disrupting readerly satisfaction. Reading requires recognizing the arm as a marker of absence. In addition to the emotional, often graphic, detail, the text of the story seems to function in almost decorative fashion, like "an element of pictorial composition" or "simply as the grid on which an abstract design is enmeshed or from which a pattern is elicited."[29] As the book's final page is turned, the surrounding case of the arm is fully revealed within the space of the back inside cover; this cover also features a number corresponding to the book's edition—a paratextual detail that grotesquely echoes the tattooed number on the father's arm.

The absolute uniqueness of the cast as a physical, almost totemic, marker of the father's story is supported by some of the book's other materials. The handwritten Czech is printed on translucent paper, with photographs visible from the other side, an effect suggesting the layering of language implicit in both translation and cross-generational transmission of memory. The book's cover consists of a close-up image of the Holocaust memorial wall at the Pinkas Synagogue in Prague printed on reflective hardboard. One of the oldest of its kind in Europe, the memorial's original design dates from 1954–59, and the handwritten names on the wall commemorate victims of the Holocaust from Bohemia

Tatana Kellner, *B11226: Fifty Years of Silence, Eugene Kellner's Story* (1992). Handmade cast paper. Silkscreen, die cut. Spiral bound codex. Issued in a wooden box (36 × 58 × 8 cm.). 81 pages. Edition: 50. Women's Studio Workshop, 1992.

and Moravia—"an epitaph for those who have no grave."[30] The reflective effect implicates the reader, and the image of names carved on stone recalls not only a cemetery but also the memorial work of *yizker* books, themselves conceived as objects of memory.

Finally, Kellner's book, with its cast of the father's tattooed arm, is encased in a wooden crate, reminiscent of a ceremonial or ritual box, even a coffin, or perhaps a boxcar. Handling it, opening and closing it, in order to retrieve the father's story requires concerted, coordinated effort, further enhancing our experience of the book as an object. Kellner's work, in which "materiality is content, content is materiality," thus exemplifies what "emerges from interactions between physical properties and a work's artistic strategies."[31] Artists' books make concrete the productive, dialectical relationship between materiality and content. This relationship too is a kind of connective, even generative, seam.

Another kind of seam shapes the production of artists' books at the Jerusalem Print Workshop (JPW), a workspace, gallery, and archive located in Jerusalem's Musrara neighborhood. The area is also known in reference to the Hebrew term for "seam" (*tefer*), used colloquially to refer to the former border or Green Armistice Line—*kav ha-tefer*—that once divided Jerusalem into a Jordanian east and an Israeli west.[32] I build on the significance of the seam for artists' books and the specific social meaning emerging from artists' books created by women to further embed this material term from bookmaking within the social and political terrain of a particular city. If Jerusalem's "seam" still stretches like a spine across the city's topography, what does it mean to produce books—objects with seams—in this place? What kinds of materials may be bound together, and what refuses to be joined?

The neighborhood of Musrara has been both a target of military conquest and a site of socioeconomic upheaval and gentrification. Besides the Jerusalem Print Workshop, Musrara is home to the Museum on the Seam: Socio-Political Contemporary Art Museum (MOTS). The museum, located in a neoclassical structure built in 1932 by the Palestinian architect Adoni Baramki, later served as an Israeli military outpost near the Mandelbaum Gate.[33] A third site in Musrara—*Ha-mifal* (the Factory)—is a community arts space, created and maintained by the activist art collective Bayit Rek (Empty House); it is located in a nineteenth century structure formerly owned by a Christian Arab family forced to abandon the house during the war in 1948. All three art institutions—the Jerusalem Print Workshop, the Museum on the Seam, and the Factory—are embedded in the city's entangled narratives of ownership and displacement, housed as they are in preexisting structures whose very presence constitutes an argument.[34] These "micro" art spaces—supported by municipal and private funding, sourced locally and abroad—potentially counter the city's historical meta-narratives with local stories of collaboration and creation. They address both details of the immediate conflict *and* the broad relation between culture and its host communities, thereby illuminating how place, politics, and art interact within Jerusalem's contested multi-ethnic urban sphere.

Since 1974, the workshop has hosted Israel's leading artists, practitioners, and curators as well as faculty and students from the Bezalel Academy of Arts and Design. A far cry from the olive wood frames and books produced by Agnon's fictional Bloykoff and real-life early twentieth-century artisans in the city, the workshop began to produce artists' books in the 1980s. Many of these books feature the work of a single living artist alongside that of a well-known Hebrew poet and utilize a variety of materials and formats, including woodcuts, letterpress, polymer prints, Japanese silk, goat skin, and vellum bindings, even a metal box to contain the finished product.[35] These efforts attest to the sheer variety of visual material in artists' books—abstraction, photographs, color, drawings, prints—and force readers to appreciate the book in relation to its physical facts as well as our normative assumptions of what constitutes a book.

A series produced over a number of years at the JPW, *Etchings for Poems: Nine Albums of Etchings and Poems* (1989), offers miniature variations on a single comparative method: treat a poem as an object and create visual art, as well as a material artifact, to complement it. For each book, a contemporary artist engages the work of a central Israeli poet, living or dead. The books are largely uniform in style and material, each containing a series of etchings and poems screen-printed on thick, cream-colored paper and attractively nestled in an obeche wooden box that resembles a jewelry chest. The format is also usually the same—consisting of pages with a simple center fold, with poem and print each on its own side; some tentatively exploit the codex form, using triple or accordion folds or allowing text to leak or spill onto the image's page. Curator Irena Gordon evokes the talismanic quality of the project thus: "page after page of visual image and poetic image that fit into the palm of your hand and whose presence is complex: a personal notebook, a charm, a piece of jewelry, a prayer book."[36] Likewise, Gideon Ofrat refers to the tomblike quality of the project: "The poem's body lies as in a grave—in the box, covered in a silk-paper shroud, united with its glorious monument, the work of art."[37] We encounter these as objects of art in private, archival, museum, or library settings. These often confounding artifacts don't appear to want to be read in any regular sense of the activity. They prompt readers to consider how books might become permanent presences in our lives, at once inscrutable and familiar.

Moshe Gershuni's monumental homage to this poem-image exercise—*Thirteen Etchings for Poems by H. N. Bialik* (1987)—offers an opportunity to revisit Bialik's work as a key locus of materiality in Jewish literary history; Gershuni's project also recalls the work of expressionist prints in little magazines and the notion of the book as a potentially sacred object.[38] A towering figure in Israeli art from the 1970s until his death in 2017, Gershuni was one of the first Israeli artists to consistently incorporate themes such as the Holocaust, traditional Jewish liturgy, and Yiddish texts. Gershuni's provocative conceptual work subverted social and political norms and elevated art's concrete, material dimension.

Gershuni's oversized book of etchings and poems is luxuriously produced on Arches paper and enclosed in a cardboard box. The poems themselves are

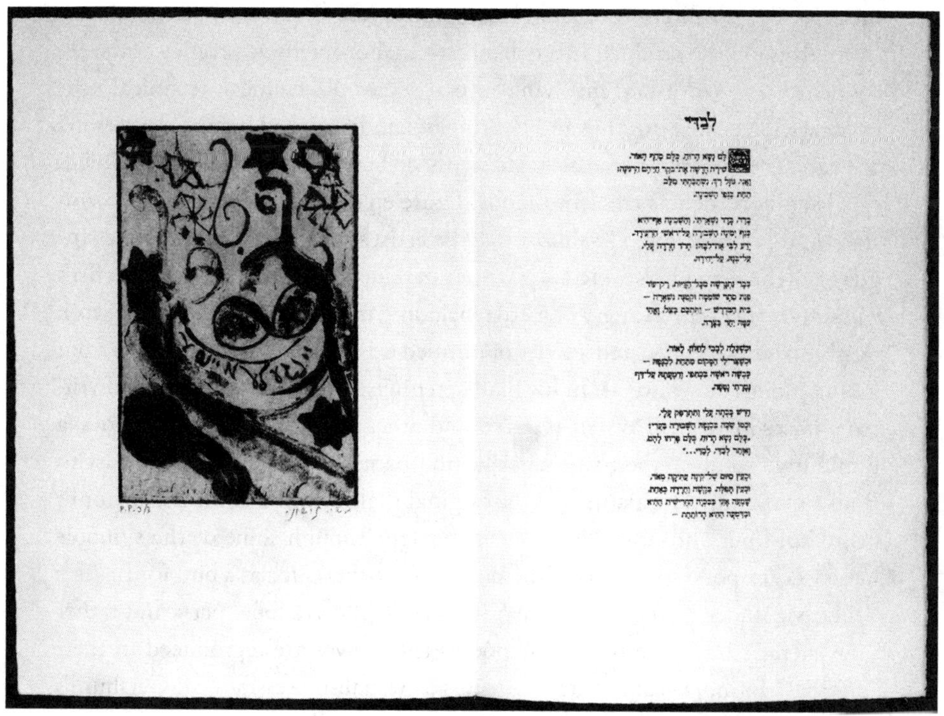

Moshe Gershuni, *Levadi,* in *Thirteen Etchings for Poems by H. N. Bialik* (1987). 13 etchings and 13 poems in screen printing on 240-gram Arches paper in a cardboard box. Etching, aquatint, dry-point, soft-ground, electric pencil, and sugar-lift. Cardboard box: Yehuda Miklaf. Page size: 37 × 26.5 cm. Edition: 50. Jerusalem Print Workshop, 1987.

silk-screened facsimile reproductions of an edition of Bialik's poetry published in Berlin in 1923 by the artist and printmaker Josef Budko. Considered a masterpiece of early modern Hebrew culture and Jewish bookmaking, that landmark edition of the poet's work emerged from the same milieu that produced little magazines such as *Milgroym/Rimon.* Budko meticulously designed each and every aspect of the edition, including the binding, font style and size, and page layout. In consultation with the poet, he produced a unique illuminated letter for each poem as well as a series of miniature prints that complement the poems and narrate three life stages—child, youth, young adult—throughout Bialik's work.[39]

According to curator Edna Moshenson, the meeting between Gershuni's work and Bialik's poetry was "inevitable," following a period in which the artist increasingly engaged canonical or popular works from Zionist culture, modern Hebrew literature, and traditional Judaic literature.[40] The etchings themselves are the products of a collaborative labor-intensive practice at the Jerusalem Print Workshop involving several stages of chemical, technical processes with repeated printing and layering of hand-sketched images. The results are dark and moody: large, abstract swirls of black and gray laid over archetypal symbols such as crescent moons, figure eights, eternity symbols, Jewish stars, and Hebrew letters—almost like the artist's own mythical symbolic language.[41] These symbols were an essential development throughout the artist's work in the 1980s in a variety of media including massive canvases, smaller work on glass and rice paper, and a series of untitled ceramics featuring excerpts from Psalms alongside swastikas. In his Bialik etchings, Gershuni includes handwritten phrases in Yiddish as well as letters and other words in Hebrew: my boys, a diminutive form of the name Yitsḥak, the name of the poet. In contrast to Budko's contained miniatures in the original Bialik edition of 1923, Gershuni's prints spill out and nearly fill the entire page. Though some of the symbols loosely correspond to images or themes in the poems (such as a bird for Bialik's "Take Me under Your Wing"), the prints aren't "illustrations" per se but rather idiosyncratic interpretations. The poems themselves are reproduced in their "original" form, co-equal with the prints as visual impressions. In Gershuni's revision of Budko's impression of Bialik, the poet finally gets his wish: the poem becomes an object.

Gershuni's work also includes Bialik's "Unter di grinike beymelech" (Under the Green Trees), published in Yiddish (1903) and later in Hebrew (1930).[42] The poem does not appear in the 1923 volume of Bialik's work, and Gershuni's inclusion of it here, in his own handwriting, feels like a deliberate intervention, a challenge to the normative aversion to traditional Jewish religious culture within

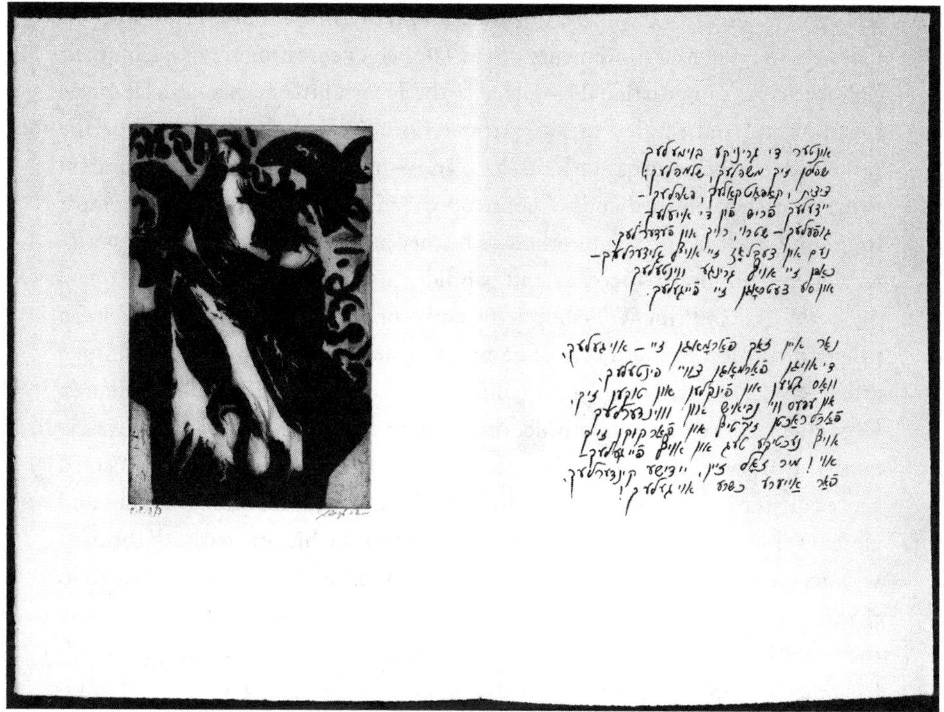

Moshe Gershuni, *Unter di grinike beymelekh,* in *Thirteen Etchings for Poems by H. N. Bialik* (1987). 13 etchings and 13 poems in screen printing on 240-gram Arches paper in a cardboard box. Etching, aquatint, dry-point, soft-ground, electric pencil, and sugar-lift. Cardboard box: Yehuda Miklaf. Page size: 37 × 26.5 cm. Edition: 50. Jerusalem Print Workshop, 1987.

the ostensibly secular world of Israeli art.[43] Gershuni situates himself as a Jewish artist in relation to the diverse materials of his European past: the intimate quality of the handwritten Yiddish seems to interrupt the carefully wrought fonts and embellished letters of the Berlin edition; using his own handwriting for the Yiddish brings the language into the present, making it less a stylized object from the past. With his expressive hand, Gershuni's work pays homage to Yiddish as a visual language, a dynamic cultural form, as against the dominant view of Yiddish within secular Israeli culture as irredeemably "exilic" and defunct. Indeed, the Berlin edition was produced in an era in which Yiddish enjoyed a kind of vibrant, affective pliability that Hebrew was just beginning to develop as a literary vernacular. Furthermore, the iconic use of Hebrew letters and phrases suggests a mythical quality, despite the language's ostensibly secularized status as the speech of state and daily life. From a historical perspective, the material movements of the languages seem to mirror each other: Yiddish was the international language of the Jewish little magazine, a language that traveled and reveled in its "extraterritoriality"; at the other end of the century, Hebrew "returns" to Jerusalem, and—in the location of the Jerusalem Print Workshop, in the hands of contemporary Israeli Jewish artists—attempts to ground itself in the neighborhood's history and current moment, the entire web of contemporary discourse and conflict.

The Jerusalem Print Workshop is, by any economic or aesthetic yardstick, an unqualified success: it is a hive of constant creative activity, publishing unique artists' books as well as museum-quality prints using many different techniques. Regardless of the political, ethnic, or sectarian strife outside, artists arrive everyday, work steadily through the morning hours in a set of messy, connected spaces on the second floor, eat an informally prepared communal lunch, and close up shop by 3 p.m. Considered in relation to the historic basin to the east, with its plethora of religious shrines and other sites, and the major museums to the west, the Israel Museum and Yad Vashem: The Holocaust History Museum, the Jerusalem Print Workshop and Musrara's other art institutions seem to offer something different—a sense of art as active and ongoing, embedded in local networks of exchange and community. They serve as what urban planner Maria-Rosario Jackson has called "cultural kitchens," sites that encourage a participatory "cultural vitality" driven by the city's inherent diversity.[44] Furthermore, given their location "on the seam," the JPW, the Museum on the Seam, and the Factory could offer art practices that would help unpack the city's competing historical narratives. In order to do this, however, they would need to more expressly thematize their former lives as Palestinian homes and incorporate this history into their current institutional practices. For now, they largely reproduce the spatial patterns of power that have shaped Jerusalem's urban sphere over the past half century or so. Despite the genuine creative energies, the quality, and the sheer quantity of art produced and exhibited, they do not fully integrate the story of the place into their work.

And what about the books? What do the artists' books have to say about any of this? Not so much. Between Jabès's utopian, diasporic refrain—"The house is in the book"—and the lived politics of contemporary Jerusalem exists a chasm that many artists' books seem to observe at a relative distance. Andi Arnovitz's *Living Borders* (2015) is a notable exception.

An American-born multimedia artist based in Jerusalem, Arnovitz has said that religion, gender, and politics meet in her work.[45] According to art historian David Sperber, Arnovitz is preoccupied with "categories, delineations, borders

Andi Arnovitz, *Living Borders* (2015). Courtesy of the artist. Hand-cut digital prints of artist's drawings. Bound, embossed, and assembled by hand. Photograph: Yaacov Fish.

Andi Arnovitz, *Four Poems of Esther Raab* (2019). Courtesy of the artist. Hand-pulled etchings, silk-screened text, hand-made linen box and book covers. Photograph: Yaacov Fish.

and separations, pervasive subjects in Israeli art."[46] Furthermore, as Sperber notes, Arnovitz's affiliation as modern Orthodox puts her and her work somewhat adjacent to the largely secular Israeli art world. Like other religious feminist artists, her artistic practice engages politics from the location of faith, sometimes drawing on textiles and items of clothing to suggest the female body in relation to both place and conflict. Some of Arnovitz's work seems driven by the idea of *tikkun olam,* or "repairing the world," a notion embedded in mystical philosophy that also undergirds contemporary social justice movements. This act of metaphysical repair is enacted on a micro level in the space of the artist's book, where disparate materials are yoked together. *Living Borders,* a tunnel book whose layered cut-paper panels create an illusion of depth and perspective, is bound in rust-red canvas with a short text in Hebrew, English, and Arabic. The pages feature ink drawings of an archetypal Israeli urban landscape with various architectural details. Slicing through the center of the book and receding into its center is a "living border" (the Hebrew term for a hedge is "living fence") created from the colorful *chatzav*—flowering sea squill—referenced in the Talmud as a plant indicating territorial distinctions among the biblical tribes of Israel. Arnovitz calls the desire to replace the separation barrier along the Green Line with a hedge of flowers "sheer fantasy" and "an artistic folly but not without historic precedent."[47] The whimsical use of flowers to mark a border reminds this reader how thick plantings of prickly pear cactus were typically used to demarcate Palestinian agricultural space.

Arnovitz's work also capitalizes on the link between bookmaking's materiality and traditional notions of "women's work," connecting these practices to what the artist identifies as the fundamental gestures of Jewish ritual observance—"motions of wrapping, binding, wrapping and tying."[48] Her book of Esther Raab's poetry formally resembles other Jerusalem Print Workshop volumes in boxes and is also similar in its attention to material detail that engages the poetry's thematic thrust. In this case, Raab the landscape poet finds her latter-day match in Arnovitz's soft-ground etchings of plants sourced from the artist's own garden and neighborhood. The etchings are printed on the reverse side of four poems chosen by the artist for their connection to landscape and aging. According to the artist, the soft ochre-colored paper and linen box with its wood hinges mimic the "finished" quality of crafted objects, providing what she calls "a very coherent female sensibility."[49]

We conclude our discussion of artists' books with the monumental example of Harold Schimmel's *Ha-sifriya* (The Library, 1999), a collection of poetry and

כי בכל זאת
זה היה ביאליק דברי
ביסטריצקי לחברתו בפנת

גן בקפה פטר
היא החזיקה בקבוקון של
קוניאק בתיקה שהוציאה

ומזגה קמעה בכוס
תה הסופר . בין כל
הענגונים חדשים כישנים

ביאליק עם איזוריה
של הצירת היפה בבריכה
הכחולה ללא שם

בסוף שמתחת לשערי
אורה סמוך הספרות של
מספר שלפון ישן

712082 והשם נרדה
מכסים ניר לבן של
מעבר יבוק . ספר

הישר ברפוס צפון
אפריקאי ליד כבר אינני
מזהה האורם האדם

ט

Harold Schimmel, *The Library* (1999). Offset print in Drogolin font on 140-gram Hadar paper. Photographs printed on 80-gram Chromecut paper. Bibliographic edition printed on 160-gram Arches paper in edition of 18 copies, like the number of "chapters" in Harold Schimmel's Library. Photographs by Avigail Schimmel, printed by the artist. Special edition is numbered and signed by both artists. Ra'anana: Even Hoshen, 1999.

photographs created by the poet and his daughter Avigail Schimmel. Produced at the Even Hoshen fine press in a bibliographic edition of eighteen copies, *The Library* presents eighteen poems facing eighteen color photographs of the poet's library, translating an important number within Jewish tradition into the book's structural design. (Using the numerical value of its letters, the Hebrew word for life—*chai*—equals the number 18.) The library itself as well as the poems and photos documenting it indeed tell the story of Schimmel's life, tracing significant personal relationships and cultural and geographic topography. The poems are digressive and associative, commenting on books in relation to the author's life and their acquisition over several decades, beginning with the author's arrival in Israel as a new immigrant. The critic Shahar Bram views the book in expressly autobiographical terms: Schimmel's library is "a metonymy for its owner and a metaphor for culture and civilization, with flexible borders that every reader and every writer shapes anew, and, as such, it is also a metaphor for a way of life and a way of constructing identity." The photos too are "self-portraits of a tradition and synecdochic portrait of the ideal library."[50]

The photos are exquisitely printed large-format close-ups of different shelves from the author's library, each packed with books and other personal possessions; each photo's frame is dictated by the length of the shelves it depicts. On the shelves in between the books: drawings, knick-knacks, miniature reproductions of artwork, photographs, a couple of old stereo speakers. Paging through Schimmel's *The Library,* readers encounter the book itself as a space as well as a crafted object that is exchanged as a purchase, loan, or gift. The book's large nonstandard size (nine by twelve inches) allows for a minimalist layout of both photographs and poems, which float within the expanse of cream-colored pages. The poems are spare, spilling down the page in measured triplets. This relatively open architecture of the page is at odds with the photographs' dense clutter. The color photographs are pasted onto each page (even in the "regular edition"), not reproduced on the page itself, amplifying the photograph's quality as a material artifact and heightening the sense of the book as a container of things, gathered and set aside from the world.

The poems reference the multiple languages of books whose titles and authors are clearly visible on their spines and span centuries and continents: major works from classical antiquity and the Judaic tradition, the work of medieval and modern Hebrew and Yiddish poetry, Anglo-American poetry (especially Pound but also Frank O'Hara and John Ashbery) sit next to American pop icons (Bruce Springsteen, from the poet's native New Jersey). All these are the poet's heritage. Likewise, a shelf full of blank spines allows for musing and speculation regarding their contents or language.[51] The photographs also jog the poet's memory: the poems mention poet-peers as well as editors, the literary magazines and publishing houses that hosted their work, and personal anecdotes about where a book was purchased or who gave it to him, including one book with his wife's phone number scrawled inside and another containing letters from an archive. The juxtaposition of personal connections enables a long view of Hebrew poetry: for example, the Hebrew poet Dan Pagis and Haim Shirman, editor of a popular edition of medieval Hebrew poets (a set that once sold in the thousands), are joined via the physical fact of the book, which Pagis gifted to Schimmel. This too is a kind of memorial, as the audience for these medieval metaphysical poems has dwindled.

The book's first poem seems triggered by the photography facing it:

He raised his
Chin and pointed to "the Greeks"
Arranged in a row on

A shelf they are a part
Of literature that is the spine
Of the library.

These Greek volumes also contain:

remnants of words and parts
of letters that equal in value the writing
on a page on

its side in Greece exists
and sometimes from there taken and to here
copied in the rhythm of the line [*mishkal ha-shura*].[52]

The Greek volumes are the "spine" (*amud ha-shidra*) of the library, concretely in their location on the shelves and metaphysically as a measure against which other texts and literary traditions are measured; and the poet tests the line's meter, literally its "weight": *mishkal ha-shura.* Other poems also appear to capitalize on the idea of the page as a foundation; *amud* means "page" and "column," both in print and as an architectural term. When the reader learns in poem 8 that the stereo speakers act as a base, we therefore understand this to mean a physical base or bookend as well as how music may act as the foundation of literature and other art forms, represented in this poem through collections by David Hockney and R. B. Kitaj. All that's missing in the poem is an explicit mention of *bayit,* the Hebrew word for both "stanza" and "home," but the photographs themselves seem to mimic the steady building of that house, with the squat solidity of their shelves, filled to bursting with books, or in the likewise crammed quality of the photographs. This relative efficiency recalls the economy of form crucial to the work of a poet whose presence goes unremarked here but whose ghost nonetheless hovers throughout *The Library:* Charles Reznikoff. In an interview with Charles Bernstein and Ariel Resnikoff (a relative of the poet) about his work as a translator, Schimmel describes his initial exposure to American modernist poetry: as a young immigrant in Jerusalem, he would visit the university library at Givat Ram and take out books by Reznikoff, Zukofsky, and Oppen: "Ariel's uncle would send every book to the

National Library in Jerusalem because that's what a good New York Jew should do, he should have his books in Jerusalem. And so there were first editions. . . . [George] Oppen did the same."[53] Schimmel's poems mimic the concrete spare lyrics of the American Jewish Objectivists. If we recall that Reznikoff's poetic principles were shaped, in part, by his view of Hebrew as a material artifact, we may appreciate Schimmel's work, underlined by the physical circulation of Reznikoff's books from New York to Jerusalem, as a kind of metaphysical exercise, a translation of Objectivist poetics back into the spare materiality of the Hebrew that inspired it.

In *The Library,* certain books become touchstones for a material unfolding of literary history—"books cover books / you knew that was the nature of things." The "new and old Agnons" sit a shelf or two away from what appears to be a kind of ur-text of Jewish bookish materiality: the Romm Talmud: "My father used to say that the brothers / And widow Romm offered / A complete set of [their] Mishnah / to anyone who found a mistake in the Gemara."[54] Above all, and perhaps not surprisingly, there are numerous references to Bialik and his work, including this:

> And after all
> That was Bialik the words
> Of Bistrizki to his friend on the corner
>
> Of the park in café Peter
> She held a little bottle of
> Old cognac that she took out
>
> And poured a bit into a cup
> Writer's tea—among all
> The new and old Agnons.[55]

Ultimately, instead of standing "before the bookcase," this poem invites readers in, asking them to get up close and peruse the shelves, pull up a chair and browse through the poet's own journey among cultures and traditions. Schimmel's work realizes the proposition of Bialik's poem, in which books are literalized as objects.

Ironically, however, Uri Nissan Gnessin's melancholy modernist novella *Sideways* (1905), does not appear on its side:

> Not on its side
> *Sideways* a volume Brenner edited
> After Uri Nissan

Was no longer. Inside it
I pasted letters and poems of
Them both that I found in the basement

Of the Writers House Archive named after
Tchernichovsky and photocopied
. . . .

A young adult book
By the poet Regelson with

Woodcuts by the dancer
Amos Chetz. *Zisha Landau*
Feierberg Sutskever Shriftn.[56]

The poem's elegiac conclusion, in which the names of authors appear as book titles, recalls the tactile, memorial quality of Bialik's *gvilim* (scrolls), even the folios of Soyer's *The Lover of Books.* Ultimately, it seems to me, Schimmel's poem offers a gentle rebuke to Benjamin's dismissal of the library's "mild boredom of order."[57] The ruminative, associative order offered by the poet in conversation with his daughter's work is itself a form of solace, in the sense that all poetry presents a challenge to absence.

Scholars have made an impassioned case for the artist's book as a specifically twentieth-century form: though related to other modern and postmodern forms that probe the text-image divide, it fundamentally recasts the relation between art and the world, raising questions about the very definition and categorization of the book as an object as well as its proper "native" environment: museum, library, archives, coffee shop?[58] However, even granting the form's ostensible uniqueness, its material features seem to exist more on a continuum with other genres discussed in this book rather than constituting a radical break from them. Features of the artist's book are implicit in other genres; the artist's book incorporates other material features discussed in this study and amplifies their significance, allowing readers to appreciate the ways in which literary texts may engage in, and become, material forms.

With the artist's book as a genre we arrive at a kind of apotheosis of the material translation of the sacred to the secular: uniquely haptic forms such as the scroll and the codex as well as tactile features such as calligraphy and the texture of paper are transformed to create objects that draw in readers to the concrete materiality of their features, but also disturb our sense of what books can be. This shift from sacred to secular seems related to the general movement from text to object, what literary historian Leah Price describes as the passage from "Bible" to "bible."[59] This process has been characterized as one of diminishment, what Charles Taylor critiques as the "subtraction theory" of secularism, where secularism equals religion minus the sacred. But this claim only works in the absence of materiality and the fullness of the sensorium, the part of the brain that experiences or comprehends a work in its sensual entirety. The embodied qualities of those genres discussed in this study—the plasticity of poetic language; the mobile circulation and concrete design of the little magazines; the novel's elaborate motivation of objects and possessions; the *yizker* book's monumental quality as a memorial object; the graphic novel's play of image and text in the service of history; the artist's book's stubborn retention of aura and the sacred in a secular age—demand an attention to literary history's material unfolding. This unfolding begins, in one sense, with the dual material registers of Bialik and Tchernichovsky—the petrification of Judaic tradition, the poet left holding the broken beads, the straddling of sacred and profane traditions, and a desire to claim ownership of both. However, as readers and scholars encountering their work at a remove, a century or so later—standing in its presence, so to speak—we bring an awareness of how manifestations of the material persist, shaping postmodern cultural forms and their descendents. What does materiality even mean in a post-book era, when the digital domain threatens to supplant our most mundane and tangible experience—the brittle page, the crumbling spine? Viewed up close on a touch screen and given the appropriate platform or interface, we might even interact with the page with some tactility—not quite Bialik and his scrolls, but maybe as close as we can get? Ultimately, an attention to how materiality has mattered historically for literary forms makes us better readers of our own more and less material worlds.

Notes

INTRODUCTION

1. Talia Rappaport, "Recycling and Repurposing, Art and Belief," in *Life* (1995).
2. David Sperber, "Israeli Art Discourse and the Jewish Voice," *Images* 4 (2011): 109–31. For Jano's work in relation to religion and the secular specifically, see David Sperber, *Fringes: Jewish Art as an Israeli Periphery* [Hebrew] (Jerusalem: Bar Ilan University, 2010), 37–39.
3. Y. Ch. Brenner, "Atsabim" [Nerves], *Shalechet* (Lvov,1911).
4. Modern Jewish literary history has typically been told as a history of languages, as in Hana Wirth-Nesher's *Call It English: The Languages of Jewish American Literature* (Princeton: Princeton University Press, 2006), or a history of places, as in Sidra DeKoven Ezrahi's *Booking Passage: Exile and Homecoming in the Modern Jewish Imagination* (Berkeley: University of California, 2000). Both approaches have shaped the field's focus on the relation between Jewish writing and the nation.
5. Anita Norich and Joshua Miller, *Languages of Modern Jewish Cultures: Comparative Perspectives* (Ann Arbor: University of Michigan Press, 2016), 3.
6. Amaranth Borsuk, *The Book* (Cambridge, MA: MIT Press, 2018), 1.
7. See Robert Darnton, "What Is the History of Books?" *Daedalus* 111:3 (Summer 1982): 65–83, for a relatively pithy review of his general claims and method; Roger Chartier, "Laborers and Voyagers: From the Text to the Reader," *Diacritics* 22:2 (Summer 1992): 49–61; and Roger Chartier, *The Order of Books: Readers, Authors and Libraries in Europe*

between the Fourteenth and Eighteenth Centuries (Philadelphia: University of Pennsylvania Press, 1994. Excerpts from these and other related critical sources on the topic are collected in *The Broadview Reader in Book History,* ed. Michelle Levy and Tom Mole (Tonawanda, NY: Broadview, 2015).

8. Chartier, "Laborers and Voyagers," 53. For related scholarship on Hebrew books, see *History of the Early Printed Hebrew Book,* Penn Libraries, accessed June 30, 2021, https://guides.library.upenn.edu/earlyprintedhebrewbook; and Zeev Gries, *The Book in the Jewish World, 1700–1900* (Portland, OR: Littman Library of Jewish Civilization, 2007).
9. Caroline Levine, *Forms: Whole, Rhythm, Hierarchy, Network* (Princeton: Princeton University Press, 2015), 9.
10. Levine, *Forms,* 10.
11. On genre as performance, see Jacques Derrida, "The Law of Genre," trans. Avital Ronell, in *Acts of Literature,* ed. Derek Attridge (New York: Routledge, 1992), 221–52. For a review of the extensive critical scholarship, see John Frow, *Genre* (New York: Routledge, 2015); and Wai-Chee Dimmock, "Genres as Fields of Knowledge," *PMLA* 122:5 (October 2007): 1377–88, and this entire special issue edited by Dimmock, "Remapping Genre."
12. I am not interested in the accuracy or veracity of arguments about Jewish "aniconism." Rather, following the groundbreaking work of Kalman Bland, I appreciate how claims regarding Jewish antipathy for certain kinds of visual expression were used to promote the emergence of Jewish secular forms (for example, Martin Buber's programmatic writing about Jewish art in the 1920s in the Berlin journal *Ost und West*). See Kalman Bland, *The Artless Jew: Medieval and Modern Affirmations of the Visual* (Princeton: Princeton University Press, 2001).
13. See Bill Brown, *A Sense of Things: The Object Matter of American Literature* (Chicago: University of Chicago Press, 2003); W. J. T. Mitchell, *Picture Theory: Essays on Verbal and Visual Representation* (Chicago: University of Chicago Press, 1994); and Sherry Turkle, *Evocative Objects: Things We Think With* (Cambridge, MA: MIT Press, 2007).
14. I use the term *transnational* in the broadest sense possible, as in Jahan Ramazani, *A Transnational Poetics* (Chicago: University of Chicago Press, 1994), x: "poetic connection and dialogue across political and geographic borders and even hemispheres."
15. Leora Auslander, "Beyond Words," *American Historical Review* 110:4 (October 2005): 1015–45; and Ken Kulton Fromm, *Material Culture and Jewish Thought in America* (Bloomington: Indiana University Press, 2010).
16. For context and analysis of Taylor's influential and massive tome *A Secular Age* (Cambridge, MA: Harvard University Press, 2007), see Michael Warner and Jonathan VanAntwerpen, eds., *Varieties of Secularism in a Secular Age: Essays on Charles Taylor's "A Secular Age"* (Cambridge, MA: Harvard University Press, 2013). From the editors' introduction: "The secular is never just the absence of religion, or its privatization, or its waning. It is a cumulatively and dialectically achieved condition." (25).
17. Charles Taylor, "Two Theories of Modernity," *Hastings Center Report* 25:2 (March–April, 1995): 29. Taylor references Pierre Bourdieu's notion of *habitus* when describing social space and unnamed "contemporary French writers" as the source for the *l'imaginaire social.*

18. Henri Lefebvre's tripartite model of space includes one domain specifically tagged as the space of cultural and aesthetic production. See Lefrebvre, *The Production of Space* (Cambridge, MA: Blackwell, 1991). For a study of spatial critical theory in relation to Jewish cultures, see Barbara Mann, *Space and Place in Jewish Studies* (New Brunswick: Rutgers University Press, 2012).
19. Scholars have described the historical conditions in which secularism emerged from Christianity, and replicated its supersessionist structure of grace as a progressive narrative of reason. In this regard, Amnon Raz-Krakotzkin argues that Jews represent a kind of "rupture" or stumbling block: much as they "refused" that narrative of grace, so they resisted the Enlightenment narrative of reason. See his "Secularism, the Christian Ambivalence towards the Jews, and the Notion of Exile," in *Secularism in Question: Jews and Judaism in Modern Times,* ed. Ari Joscowitz and Ethan B. Katz (Philadelphia: University of Pennsylvania Press, 2015), 276–98.
20. From *The Book of Resemblances* (1976), in Edmond Jabès, "At the Threshold of the Book," in *From the Book to the Book: An Edmond Jabès Reader,* trans. Rosmarie Waldrop (Hanover, NH: University of New England Press, 1991), 156.
21. See Avner Holtzman, *Aesthetics and National Revival: Hebrew Literature against the Visual* [Hebrew] (Haifa: Zmora Bitan/Haifa University Press, 1999); and Barbara Mann, "Visions of Jewish Modernism," *Modernism/modernity* 13:4 (2006): 673–99.
22. Saul Tchernichovsky, "Before a Statue of Apollo," in *Shirim* [Poems], vol. 1 (Tel Aviv; Dvir, 1966), 86. Originally published in his *Ḥezyonot ve-manginot,* vol. 2 (Warsaw: Tushia, 1902). Translation from Eisig Silberschlag, *Saul Tchernichovksy: Poet of Revolt* (Ithaca: Cornell University Press, 1968), 97–98.
23. "Apollo Belvedere," Wikipedia, accessed July 4, 2021, https://en.wikipedia.org/wiki/Apollo_Belvedere.
24. Yaakov Shavit, "Tchernichovsky Facing the Statue of Apollo" [Hebrew], *Ha-aretz,* August 7, 2009.
25. We might note here that Tchernichovsky almost certainly knew Shelley's "Ozymandias" (1818), a poem also preoccupied with the passing of civilizations. (He translated Shelley's "The Cloud" earlier in that same decade, around 1894.) The conclusion of "Facing a Statue of Apollo" evokes a desert world including an enormous immobilized deity that recalls the "colossal wreck" of Shelley's poem.
26. Holtzman, *Aesthetics and National Revival,* 138.
27. See Lital Levy and Allison Schachter, "Jewish Literature/World Literature: Between the Local and the Transnational," *PMLA* 130:1 (2015): 92–109.
28. On Bialik's dexterity with prosody, and the relation between ideology and Hebrew poetics, see Vered Karti Shemtov, *Changing Rhythms: Towards a Theory of Prosody in Cultural Context* [Hebrew] (Jerusalem: Bar Ilan University Press, 2012).
29. Ch. N. Bialik, *Collected Poems* (Dvir: Tel Aviv, 2004). Translation by the author.
30. Dan Miron, *Bo 'ah, lailah: Hasifrut haivrit ben higayon leihigayon bemifneh hame 'ah haesrim: iyunim biyetsirot Ḥ. N. Bialik uM. Y. Berditchevski* (Tel Aviv: Dvir, 1987), 160.
31. Among the voluminous scholarship on early modern Jewish print culture, see the short but valuable critical intervention by Yaacob Dwek, "What Is a Jewish Book?" *AJS Review* 34:2 (2010): 367–75. On the Talmud in particular, see Marvin J. Heller, "Earliest Printings of the Talmud," in *Printing the Talmud: From Bomberg to Schottenstein,* ed.

Sharon Liberman Mintz and Gabriel Goldstein (New York: Yeshiva University Museum, 2005), 61–79.

32. A similar attention to the letter as such shapes Bialik's prose memoir of his childhood, *Safiah* (1925), where he recalls learning the alphabet and its sounds.
33. I will return to Latour in chapter 3. For an overview of his relevant influence, see Graham Harman, "Demodernizing the Humanities with Latour, *New Literary History* 47:2–3 (Spring/Summer 2016): 249–74.
34. Claude Lévi-Strauss coined the phrase "good to think with" in 1962 in relation to animals in his *Totemism,* trans. Rodney Needham (London: Merlin, 1991), 89.
35. Walter Benjamin, "Unpacking My Library: A Talk about Book Collecting" (1931), in *Illuminations: Essays and Reflections* (New York: Schocken, 1969), 67.
36. Claire Cavanaugh, *Osip Mandelstam and the Modernist Creation of Tradition* (Princeton: Princeton University Press, 1994), 112, 114.
37. It is as if, in Claire Cavanaugh's moving phrasing, "his Jewish past followed him into the non-Jewish 'home and family' he attempted to construct for himself in Russian and European literature." Cavanaugh, *Osip Mandelstam,* 106.
38. *The Noise of Time,* ed. and trans. Clarence Brown (New York: Penguin, 1993), 77.
39. "Morning of Acmeism," in *The Complete Critical Prose,* ed. Jane Gray Harris (Dana Point, CA: Ardis, 1997), 40–43.
40. "The Bookcase," in *The Noise of Time,* 78–79.
41. "The Judaic Chaos," in *The Noise of Time,* 84–85.
42. For details on the Soyer brothers and their place in American Jewish painting, see Norman L. Kleeblatt and Susan Chevlowe, eds., *Painting a Place in America: Jewish Artists in America, 1900–1945* (New York: Jewish Museum, 1991).

CHAPTER 1. JEWISH IMAGISM

1. Virginia Woolf, *Mr. Bennett and Mrs. Brown* (London: Hogarth, 1924), 4.
2. "Introspectivism" (manifesto of 1919), trans. Anita Norich, in Benjamin Harshav and Barbara Harshav, *American Yiddish Poetry* (Berkeley: University of California Press, 1986), 775–78.
3. "Introspectivism," 780. This defensive tone may be understood as a response to the fact that, historically, Yiddish was viewed as connected to the "feminine" sphere, while Hebrew was associated with the largely masculine world of traditional religious study. Despite Hebrew's liturgical and historical cachet, Yiddish writing was in some sense, and in part due to its vernacular roots, more suitable for the production of secular literary forms.
4. "Introspectivism," 777.
5. "Introspectivism," 782–83.
6. "Introspectivism," 778.
7. "Introspectivism," 775.
8. "Introspectivism," 775, 783.
9. In a 1926 letter to Franz Rosenzweig, Scholem refers, with some trepidation, to the "abyss" created through the "actualization" of Hebrew; its use as a vernacular language and the consequent loss of sacredness may end, Scholem warns, with a kind of apocalyptic

eruption. Gershom Scholem, "On Our Language: A Confession," *History & Memory* 2:2 (Winter 1990): 97–99. Scholem approached with anxiety what poets such as Fogel, and even Bialik, viewed as a creative opportunity.

10. Robert Hass, introduction to Rainer Maria Rilke, *The Selected Poetry of Rainer Maria Rilke,* trans. Stephen Mitchell (New York: Vintage, 1982), xxi.
11. Introduction to Rainer Maria Rilke, *New Poems [1907]*, trans. Edward Snow (New York: North Point, 1984), x.
12. See the excellent discussion of these parallel movements in Elaine Rusinko's "Russian Acmeism and Anglo-American Imagism," *Ulbandus Review* 1:2 (Spring, 1978): 37–49. The phrase "small, dry things" is from T. E. Hulme's "Romanticism and Classicism" (1912), accessed July 15, 2021, https://www.poetryfoundation.org/articles/69477/romanticism-and-classicism.
13. Ezra Pound, "A Retrospect," in *Literary Essays* (New York: New Directions, 1968), 3–4. "A Few Don'ts" first appeared in *Poetry* 1:6 (March 1913).
14. Pound, "A Retrospect."
15. On the historical emergence of Hebrew's sacredness, see David H. Aaron, "Holy Language," in "Critical Terms in Jewish Language Studies," *Frankel Institute Annual* (Ann Arbor: University of Michigan), 2011, 13–15, http://hdl.handle.net/2027/spo.11879367.2011.005.
16. On the meaning of Christian iconography and themes for Hebrew and Yiddish writers in this period, see Matthew Hoffman, *From Rebel to Rabbi: Reclaiming Jesus and the Making of Modern Jewish Culture* (Stanford: Stanford University Press, 2007); and Neta Stahl, *Other and Brother: Jesus in the 20th Century Jewish Literary Landscape* (Oxford: Oxford University Press, 2013).
17. *Albatros* 1 (Warsaw, 1922), 10.
18. Neta Stahl, "'Uri Zvi Before the Cross': The Figure of Jesus in the Poetry of Uri Zvi Greenberg," *Religion & Literature* 40:3 (Autumn 2008): 49–80, here 60.
19. His claim that "the poet is Job" and his poem "Toil" (1927) both appropriate traditional imagery in the service of two "new religions": art and labor.
20. *Hedim* 1:11–12 (1924): 93–95, reprinted in Zohar Shavit, *The Literary Life in Eretz Israel, 1910–1933* [Hebrew] (Tel Aviv: Hakibbutz hameuchad, 1982), 409–10. Translation by the author.
21. "Art un profanatsiye," *Der Inzel* 1 (March 1925): 13–16. Translation by the author.
22. In decrying those strains of modern Hebrew and Yiddish literature that are simply the "old-time allegory" in modern garb, Shlonsky and Ayzland identify a conflict felt by Jewish artists in this period: the opposition between ethics and aestheticism. See Ruth Wisse, "Di Yunge and the Problem of Jewish Aestheticism," *Jewish Social Studies* 38:3–4 (Summer/Fall 1976).
23. The same sentiment appears in another Yiddish article from this period, Perets Markish's "With Closed Eyes," published in the Warsaw journal *Bikher velt* in 1922: "If we remember the prohibition 'Thou shalt not make yourself an image,' we will understand why the image has remained so alien to Jewish art. . . . And indeed why the Imaginist movement, which essentially consists of an image, found expression in Yiddish poetry." Cited in Roy Greenwald, "Pogrom and Avant-Garde: Perets Markish's *Di kupe,*" *Jewish Social Studies* 16:3 (Spring/Summer 2010): 65–84, here 69–70.

24. See David Fogel, *Kol Hashirim* [Collected Poems, 1915–1941], 3rd ed., ed. Dan Pagis (Tel Aviv: Hakibbutz hameuchad, 1975 [1966]); and Fogel, *Le'ever ha-dmama* [Toward Stillness], ed. Aharon Komem (Tel Aviv: Hakibbutz hameuchad, 1983). This chapter also refers to a more recent edition of Fogel's poetry: *Kol Hashirim* [Collected Poems], ed. Aharon Komem (Tel Aviv: Hakibbutz hameuchad, 1998) and to a facsimile edition of *Before the Dark Gate* [Hebrew] (Tel Aviv: Hakibbutz hameuchad, 2010), originally published by Machar in Vienna, 1923. See also the special issue of *Prooftexts* 13:1 (1993), "David Fogel: The Emergence of Hebrew Modernism"; and the comprehensive review of Fogel's critical reception by Dan Miron in "Conditional Love: The Critical Reception of David Fogel's Poetry" [Hebrew], in *Aderet le-Binyamin* [An Overcoat for Benjamin], ed. Ziva Ben-Porat (Tel Aviv: Porter Institute of Poetics and Hakibbutz hameuchad, 1999), 29–98.
25. On the relation between this interiority and Fogel's essential Europeanness, see Robert Alter, "Fogel and the Forging of a Hebrew Self," *Prooftexts* 13:1 (January 1993): 3–13.
26. *Taḥanot Kavot* [Stories, Diary], ed. Menachem Perry (Tel Aviv: Hakibbutz hameuchad, 1990). See also *Viennese Romance* [Hebrew] (Tel Aviv: Am Oved, 2012); Lilach Nethanel, "David Vogel's Lost Hebrew Novel, Viennese Romance," *Prooftexts* 33:3 (September 2013): 307–32.
27. Bialik's assessment is according to Avigdor Ha-meiri, cited in Dan Pagis's introduction to Fogel, *Collected Poems,* 34. Barash is quoted at 37.
28. "Before the Dark Gate," *Hedim* 6 (1923): 66–67, cited in Michael Gluzman, "Deterritorialization and the Politics of Simplicity," in *The Politics of Canonicity: Lines of Resistance in Modernist Hebrew Poetry* (Stanford: Stanford University Press, 2003), 82.
29. Pagis, introduction, 33.
30. The lecture was printed in *Siman Kri'ah* 304 (1974): 387–91, and translated as "Language and Style" by Yael Meroz and Eric Zakim, *Prooftexts* 13:1 (January 1993): 15–20.
31. Fogel, "Language and Style," 18–19.
32. *Takhanot Kavot,* 295.
33. Yael Schwartz, "Flashes of All the Colors" [Hebrew], *Siman Kri'ah* 1 (September 1972): 76–108; and Shimon Sandbank, "George Trakl, David Fogel—And Colors, in *Two Pools in a Wood: Connections and Parallels between Hebrew and European Poetry* (Tel Aviv: Hakibbutz hameuchad, 1976).
34. Fogel mentions Rilke's prose as a model in his 1931 lecture "Language and Style in Our Young Literature." It is likely that the reference is to *The Notebooks of Malte Laurids Brigge* (1910), a book composed under the influence of Rilke's experience of Cézanne.
35. *Letters on Cézanne,* ed. Clara Rilke, trans. Joel Agee (New York: Fromm International, 1985 [1952]), 75. From a letter dated October 21, 1907.
36. On the importance of color in passage and generally in Cézanne's work, see John Elderfield, "The Whole World: Color in Cézanne," *Arts Magazine* 52:8 (April 1978): 148–52.
37. This process and its epistemological implications are eloquently detailed in Maurice Merleau-Ponty, "Cézanne's Doubt," in *Sense and Non-sense,* trans. Hubert and Patricia Dreyfus (Chicago: Northwestern University Press, 1964), 9–25, though the essay does not use the term *passage.*

38. See Gluzman's discussion of Fogel and his reference to modernist painting's critique of the "figure in the field." In Gluzman, "Deterritorialization and the Politics of Simplicity," 94–95.
39. Dan Pagis characterizes the book's overall structure in terms of discrete thematic units relating the poetic speaker's "life in the shadow of death" (introduction, 67). Joseph Frank, *The Idea of Spatial Form* (New Brunswick: Rutgers University Press, 1991 [1945]).
40. David Fogel, *Before the Dark Gate,* 28–30.
41. As Chana Kronfeld notes regarding another poem from this series, "the only direct and unambiguous textual marker in the language of the poem that points to *The Song of Songs* is the word *dodi* ("my beloved"). Kronfeld, *On the Margins of Modernism: Decentering Literary Dynamics* (Berkeley: University of California Press), 99.
42. Throughout this chapter, I will refer to English translations and offer transliteration of certain words from Hebrew and Yiddish, using uppercase and lowercase letters, in order to highlight specific aural and orthographic properties and patterns.
43. See Sandbank, *Two Pools in a Wood,* 71.
44. Kronfeld has demonstrated how this use of shifting tense aspect, due largely to the "incompleteness within the Hebrew syntax of his time," perfectly serves Fogel's creation of an indeterminate state or mood: "a hesitation between impressionist, atmospheric shades of a discrete moment in space and time, and the expressionist, internalized reality of the speaker's state of mind." Kronfeld, *On the Margins of Modernism,* 97–98. See also Gluzman's analysis of this syntactic device in "Deterritorialization and the Politics of Simplicity," 88–92.
45. Sandbank, *Two Pools in a Wood,* 71.
46. Wendy Steiner, *The Colors of Rhetoric: Problems in the Relation between Literature and Painting* (Chicago: University of Chicago Press, 1982), 191.
47. For a discussion of poetry and politics in this period, see Gluzman, "Deterritorialization and the Politics of Simplicity." On the 1920s as a critical period within Hebrew verse, see Uzi Shavit, "The New Hebrew Poetry of the Twenties: Palestine and America," *Prooftexts* 12:3 (September 1992): 213–30. Avraham Ben-Yitzhak's verse provides another important contemporary example of a kindred poetic spirit.
48. In "Gilboa," Sabbath prayers and other textual references replace the particulars of the speaker's immediate environment. Shlonsky, *Poems* [Hebrew], vol. 1 (Tel Aviv: Hakibbutz hameuchad, 1954), 162.
49. Shlonsky, *Poems,* 197.
50. On the multilingual landscape of the Jewish community in Mandate Palestine, see Liora Halperin, *Babel in Zion: Jews, Nationalism and Language Diversity in Palestine, 1920–1948* (New Haven: Yale University Press, 2015). On the relative "nativeness" of Raab's Hebrew, see Adriana Jacobs, "Paris or Jerusalem: The Multilingualism of Esther Raab," *Prooftexts* 26:1–2 (2006): 6–28.
51. Y. Lichtenbaum, "Esther Raab's Poetry," *Moznayim* 2:3 (1930), 40.
52. Roland Barthes, *Empire of Signs* (New York: Hill & Wang, 1983), 74.
53. Raab, "Tel Aviv," in *Kimshonim* (Tel Aviv: Hedim, 1930), 16–17. Translation by author. The first two lines contain intertextual allusions to both Lamentations 1:1 ("How does the city sit solitary") and Isaiah 3:16 ("The daughters of Zion are haughty . . . walking and mincing [*haloch ve-tafof*]").

54. Dan Miron has argued that the poem represents early opposition to Tel Aviv's urbanity, insisting instead on the primacy of contact with the soil in the national revival. Dan Miron, *Founding Mothers, Stepsisters: The Emergence of the First Hebrew Poetesses and Other Essays* (Tel Aviv: Hakibbutz hameuchad, 1991), 193–94.

55. On gender and the land in Raab's work, see Wendy Zierler, "My Mother, My Land," in *And Rachel Stole the Idols: The Emergence of Modern Hebrew Women's Writing* (Detroit: Wayne State University Press, 1994), 127–86; and Hamutal Tsamir, "Gender and Territory Meet: The Case of Esther Raab," in *Beshem hanof: Le'umiyut, migdar vesubyektiviyut bashira hayisre'elit bishnot haḥamishim vehashishim* (Jerusalem and Be'er sheva: Keter and Heksherim Center, Ben-Gurion University Press, 2006), 91–124.

56. Annette Kolodny, *The Land Before Her: Fantasy and Experience of the American Frontiers, 1630–1860* (Chapel Hill: University of North Carolina Press, 1984). In Cézanne's felicitous phrasing: "Landscape reflects itself, humanizes itself, thinks itself in me." "Le paysage se reflete, s'humanise, se pense en moi," in P. M. Doran, ed. *Conversations avec Cézanne* (Paris, 1978), cited in Peter Halter, *The Revolution in the Visual Arts and the Poetry of William Carlos Williams* (New York: Cambridge University Press, 1994), 67.

57. Raab, *Kimshonim,* 20–21.

58. Halter, *The Revolution in the Visual Arts,* 238.

59. See Benjamin Harshav, *The Meaning of Yiddish* (Berkeley: University of California Press, 1990).

60. On Margolin's work, see Avrom Novershtern, "'Who Would Have Believed a Bronze Statue Could Weep': The Poetry of Anna Margolin," *Prooftexts* 10 (1990): 435–67; Kathryn Hellerstein, "From Ikh to Zikh: A Journey from 'I' to 'Self' in Yiddish Poems by Women," in *Gender and Text in Modern Hebrew and Yiddish Literature,* ed. Naomi B. Sokoloff, Anne Lapidus Lerner, and Anita Norich (New York: Jewish Theological Seminary, 1992), 113–43. For a gendered reading of this problematic, see my "Of Madonnas and Magdalenes: Reading Mary in Modernist Hebrew and Women's Poetry," in *Leket: Jiddistik heute | Yiddish Studies Today,* ed. Marion Aptroot, Efrat Gal-Ed, Roland Gruschka, and Simon Neuberg (Düsseldorf: Düsseldorf University Press, 2012), 43–62.

61. I cite here from Margolin's *Lider* (New York: Orium, 1929), 42. Translation by the author. An academic edition of her work is Avrom Novershtern, ed., *Anna Margolin: Poems* (Jerusalem: Magnes, 1991).

62. For a fuller discussion, see Barbara Mann, "Picturing the Poetry of Anna Margolin," *Modern Language Quarterly* 63:4 (December 2002): 501–36.

63. Ruth Wisse, *A Little Love in Big Manhattan* (Cambridge, MA: Harvard University Press, 1988), 7. Wisse also notes that Ayzland—a central Di Yunge poet and critic—was known, and even parodied, for his "excessive use of gilded phrases like 'flaming gold,' 'evening gold,' 'golden dreams'" (15).

64. *Lider,* 63–64.

65. See Benjamin Hrushovski [Harshav], "On Free Rhythms in Modern Yiddish Poetry," in *The Field of Yiddish: Studies in Yiddish Language, Folklore, and Literature,* ed. Uriel Weinreich (New York: Linguistic Circle of New York, 1954), 219–66.

66. "Whither Yiddish Poetry," trans. Anita Norich, in Harshav and Harshav, *American Yiddish Poetry,* 798.

67. I am indebted to Avrom Novershtern's thoughtful selection and editing of Margolin's letters in his "Materials on Her Poetic Personality" [Yiddish], *YIVO Bleter* 1 (1991): 129–72.

68. According to Ayzland, most thought the poem was written by a man. It was not uncommon for male Yiddish poets of the period to publish under female pseudonyms. The poem appeared on January 8, 1921. The reaction is reported in Novershtern, "Materials," 150.

69. In Jewish dietary law, "parve" means neither meat nor dairy; in idiomatic usage—"bland" or "neutral."

70. Novershtern, "Materials," 153.

71. Novershtern, "Materials," 153.

72. Charles Baudelaire, "Richard Wagner and Tannhauser in Paris," in *Selected Writings on Art and Literature,* trans. P. E. Charvet (London: Penguin, 1992), 330.

73. Benjamin Hrushovski [Harshav], "The Main Systems of Hebrew Rhyme from the *Piyut* to the Present Day [Hebrew], *Hasifrut* (1973): 728.

74. Hrushovski [Harshav], "Main Systems of Hebrew Rhyme," 746. Also see the comparison of Cézanne's color modulations to Rilke's use of rhyme in "Rainer Maria Rilke and Paul Cézanne: A Stylistic Comparison," in *Probleme der Komparastik und Interpretation: Festschrift fur Andre von Gronkia zum 65. Gerburstag am 25.5.1977,* ed. Walter H. Sokel et al. (Bonn: Bouvier, 1978): 189–90.

75. Similarly, Roman Jakobson describes a sound's expressive function unfolding over the reading of the poem as both "shadow" and "echo." According to Jakobson, "Sound symbolism is an undeniably objective relation founded on a phenomenal connection between different sensory modes, in particular between the visual and the auditory experience." Jakobson also notes that specific qualities of rhyme vary from language to language. Yiddish's status as a fusion language, and the particular meaning of its Hebraic strand, is one such distinction. Roman Jakobson, "Linguistics and Poetics," in *Language in Literature,* ed. Krystyna Pomorska and Stephen Rudy (Cambridge, MA: Harvard University Press, 1987), 87.

76. Norman Bryson, *Looking at the Overlooked: Four Essays on Still Life Painting* (Cambridge, MA: Harvard University Press, 1990), 9.

77. Bryson, "Still Life and 'Feminine' Space," in *Looking at the Overlooked,* 142.

78. *Lider,* 26.

79. "Whither Yiddish Poetry?" 798.

80. *Lider,* 62. See the discussion of this poem and "She with the cold marble breasts," which appears on the poet's gravestone, in "Picturing the Poetry of Anna Margolin," 505–10.

81. Wisse, *A Little Love in Big Manhattan,* viii–ix.

82. Ruth Whitman, "Charles Reznikoff: A Personal Encounter," in *Charles Reznikoff: Man and Poet,* ed. Milton Hindus (Orono: National Poetry Foundation, University of Maine, 1984), 93.

83. In 1970. Cited in *The Poems of Charles Reznikoff, 1918–1975,* ed. Seamus Cooney (Boston: Godine, 2005), 391.

84. According to Stephen Fredman, "The poet remained haunted throughout his life by a longing for Hebrew." *A Menora for Athena: Charles Reznikoff and the Jewish Dilemmas of Objectivist Poetry* (Chicago: University of Chicago, 2001), 25.

85. Charles Reznikoff, *Jerusalem the Golden* (New York: Objectivist, 1934), 1.
86. Reznikoff, "Hellenist," in *Jerusalem the Golden,* 1.
87. Louis Zukofsky, "Sincerity and Objectification: With Special Reference to the Work of Charles Reznikoff," *Poetry* 37 (1931): 275–76.
88. Written in 1970. Cited in *The Poems of Charles Reznikoff,* 391.
89. Rachel Blau DuPlessis and Peter Quartermain, introduction to *The Objectivist Nexus: Essays in Cultural Poetics,* ed. Rachel Blau DuPlessis, Peter Quartermain, Eric Homberger, Peter Middleton, Burton Hatlen, and Alan Golding (Tuscaloosa: University of Alabama Press, 1999), 15.
90. Reznikoff, *Jerusalem the Golden,* 6.
91. Fredman, *A Menora for Athena,* 30. The conventional scholarly distinction between Reznikoff as a "Hebraic" American poet and his fellow Objectivist Louis Zukofksy as a "Yiddishist" has symbolic value, but the division of linguistic labor doesn't feel quite right. According to Fredman, "Reznikoff seems to have feigned his lack of competence in Yiddish" (24). Zukofsky's often hilarious, scathing, and somewhat self-loathing correspondence with Pound contains a vivid snapshot of what it was like to be a certain kind of Jewish urban poet in the interwar years, including the political and cultural conditions that both enabled and thwarted that experience. For a more recent exploration of the role of Yiddish and language consciousness in American Jewish writing, see Sarah Ponichtera, "Yiddish and the Avant-Garde in American Jewish Poetry" (PhD diss., Columbia University, 2012).
92. On the relationship of Reznikoff's work to Jewish modernity and the cohort of writers surrounding *The Menorah Journal,* see Ranen Omer-Sherman, "Convivencia, Hybridity, and the Jewish Urban Modernist," in *Diaspora and Zionism in Jewish American Literature: Lazarus, Syrkin, Reznikoff and Roth* (Waltham, MA: Brandeis University Press, 2002).
93. DuPlessis and Quartermain, introduction, 7.
94. From a posthumously published essay, "Obiter Dicta" (1977), evidently based on an interview Reznikoff gave in 1969; cited in *The Poems of Charles Reznikoff,* 373.
95. Reznikoff received his law degree from New York University in 1916; the first edition of *Testimony* was published in 1934.
96. Poems numbered 14 and 15 in *A Fifth Group of Verse* (1927), from *The Poems of Charles Reznikoff,* 58. In a moving and insightful reading, Charles Bernstein calls this poem Reznikoff's "most Jabesian moment." See Charles Bernstein, "Reznikoff's Nearness," in DuPlessis and Quartermain, *The Objectivist Nexus,* 210–39, here 226.
97. Fredman, *A Menora for Athena,* 33.
98. Walter Benjamin, "The Task of the Translator," in *Illuminations* (New York: Schocken, 1969 [1923]), 76, 79.
99. Bernstein, "Reznikoff's Nearness," 210–39, here 216. Seriality has a brief but powerful prehistory in American poetry, going back to Emily Dickinson but also the contemporaneous examples of Williams's *Spring and All* and Stein's *Tender Buttons.*
100. Bernstein, "Reznikoff's Nearness," 219. Also note the resemblance between the reception of Fogel's work and that of Reznikoff: "a fragmentary style that annoys and bewilders"; "cumulative effect . . . is promising shavings"; "He is unable to focus . . . apparent incoherence" (Malcolm Cowley); "half-baked, [showing] a lack of development" (223).

101. Bernstein, "Reznikoff's Nearness," 217.
102. Charles Hatlen, "Objectivism in Context: Charles Reznikoff and Jewish American Modernism," *Sagetrieb* 13:1–2 (Spring–Fall 1992): 147–68, here 148.
103. Fredman, *A Menora for Athena,* 41.
104. *The Poems of Charles Reznikoff,* 249.
105. Cited in *The Poems of Charles Reznikoff,* 384.
106. See the evocative discussion of Reznikoff's relation to his family textile business as a model for creation and self-publication in Joshua Logan Wall, "Family Business: Charles Reznikoff in Text and Textile," *Studies in American Jewish Literature* 37:1 (2018): 37–55.
107. Reznikoff, "Early History of a Writer" (1969), in *The Poems of Charles Reznikoff,* 332–33.
108. Reznikoff, "Early History of a Writer," 330.

CHAPTER 2. THE LITTLE MAGAZINE

1. Ryback's work appeared in *Albatros* 3–4 (1923): 6, published in Berlin. Of the journals discussed in this chapter, *Albatros* has the largest physical dimensions: at thirty-six centimeters it is slightly bigger than its closest competitors, *Milgroym* at thirty-one centimeters and *Khalyastre* at twenty-nine.
2. For biographical notes see the following entries in *The YIVO Encyclopedia of Jews in Eastern Europe,* accessed July 6, 2021. "El Lissitzky," https://yivoencyclopedia.org/article.aspx/Lissitzky_El; "Yisakhar Ber Rybak," https://yivoencyclopedia.org/article.aspx/Rybak_Yisakhar_Ber; "Uri Tsvi Greenberg," https://yivoencyclopedia.org/article.aspx/Grinberg_Uri_Tsevi.
3. Originally reported in "Gentiles and Yiddish Literature," *In Zikh* (July 1923), cited in Benjamin Harshav and Barbara Harshav, *American Yiddish Poetry* (Berkeley: University of California Press, 1986), 797.
4. For a discussion of Yiddish little magazines of the interwar period, see Leonard Prager and A. A. Greenbaum, *Yiddish Literary and Linguistic Periodicals and Miscellanies* (Darby, PA: Norwood, 1982).
5. For an engaging and panoramic view of Jewish creativity during this period, see Kenneth Moss, *Jewish Renaissance in the Russian Revolution* (Cambridge, MA: Harvard University Press, 2009).
6. Peter Brooker, "General Introduction: Modernity, Modernisms, Magazines," in *The Oxford Critical and Cultural History of Modernist Magazines,* vol. 3, *Europe 1880–1940,* part 1, ed. Peter Brooker et al. (Oxford: Oxford University Press, 2013), 14.
7. Raymond Williams, *The Sociology of Culture* (New York: Schocken, 1981), 68.
8. Williams, *Sociology of Culture,* 84.
9. See Seth Wolitz, "Khalyastre and Yiddish Modernism in Poland," *Yiddish* 4 (1981): 5–19. Wolitz's work creates admirable order from this tangled collaborative production, offering critical analyses as well as brief biographies of these writers, artists, editors and their journals, and tracing routes of lineage and influence. I am indebted to his decades of research in this area, which has been collected and beautifully illustrated in *Yiddish Modernism: Studies in Twentieth-Century Eastern European Jewish Culture,* ed. Brian Horowitz and Haim A. Gottschalk (Bloomington, IN: Slavica,

2014). Though Wolitz's lines of descent—from *Yung-Yiddish* through *Khalyastre* to *Albatros*—are empirically grounded, the relationships between these journals and their creators feel, in historical retrospect, messier than that.

10. One scholar describes the repeated disbanding of these editorial committees, whose members "quickly went their separate ways, pre-ordained, as it were, by their divergent personalities and longer-term intellectual interests." A. Tilo Alt, "Ambivalence toward Modernism: The Yiddish Avant-Garde and Its Manifestos," *Yiddish* 8 (1991): 52–62, here 52.
11. A French translation of the complete text of both issues appears in Rachel Ertel et al., *Khaliastra: Revue Littéraire Varsovie-Paris, "La Bande"* (Paris: Lachenal & Ritter, 1989).
12. For example, Wolitz notes that Greenberg and Melech Ravitch were from prewar Lemberg and Perets Markish was Ukrainian. New York also hosted a web of little magazines in Yiddish with similarly transplanted immigrant contributors—the modernist journal *Inzikh* and, notably, its predecessor *Shriftn.* However, with the exception of some visual material included in early issues of *Shriftn,* the New York journals are, it must be said, relatively drab, lacking the avant-garde pop of their European contemporaries. Is it possible that, unlike their European comrades—whose manifestos read like declarations of people who feel themselves on the brink of something new and unfamiliar—the United States felt like a more final, stable destination for the newly American Yiddish poets?
13. See discussion in chapter 1 about the Introspectivist manifesto and also Alt, "Ambivalence toward Modernism."
14. Eric Bulson, *Little Magazine, World Form* (New York: Columbia University Press, 2017), 6. See also the "communications circuit" in Robert Darnton, "What Is the History of Books?" *Daedalus* 111:3 (Summer 1982): 65–83.
15. Brooker, "General Introduction: Modernity, Modernisms, Magazines," 17.
16. "General Introduction: Modernity, Modernisms, Magazines," 18.
17. For this general condition and its relevance for my project, see the discussion in chapter 4 on *yizker* books.
18. On the Kultur-Lige, see *The YIVO Encyclopedia of Jews in Eastern Europe*, accessed November 20, 2020, http://www.yivoencyclopedia.org/article.aspx/Kultur-lige; and Hillel Kazovsky, "The Art Section of the 'Kultur-Lige,'" *Jews in Eastern Europe* 3.22 (1993): 5–22.
19. "*Contimporanul* and Its Circle," in Brooker et al., *The Oxford Critical and Cultural History of Modernist Magazines,* vol. 3, part 2, 1166.
20. Images of the journal are available online at *Milgroim, The National Library Newspaper Collection*, accessed July 5, 2021, https://web.nli.org.il/sites/JPress/English/Pages/Milgroim.aspx. See Glenn S. Levine, "Yiddish Publishing in Berlin and the Crisis in Eastern European Culture, 1919–1924," for details about the explosion of Yiddish publications in Berlin between 1922 and 1924, *Leo Baeck Yearbook* 42 (1997): 85–108, and specifically on the advantageous conditions of the German economy, 91–92. Also Leo Fuks and Renate Fuks, "Yiddish Publishing in the Weimar Republic, 1920–1933," *Leo Baeck Yearbook* 33 (1988): 417–34; Francesco Melfi, "A Rhetoric of Image and Word: The Magazine Milgroym/Rimon, 1922–1924 and the Jewish Search for Inclusivity" (PhD diss., Jewish Theological Seminary, 1996); and Naomi Brenner, "*Milgroym* and *Rimon,* Fraternal

Twins," *In geveb,* June 2018, https://ingeveb.org/blog/milgroym-and-rimon-fraternal-twins on the question of the journal's multilingualism.

21. For a detailed and expansively illustrated treatment, see Gil Weissblei, *The Revival of Hebrew Book Art in Weimar Germany* [Hebrew] (Jerusalem: Carmel, 2019).

22. Ruth Wisse, *A Little Love in Big Manhattan* (Cambridge, MA: Harvard University Press, 1988), 42. Wisse mentions another anecdote related by Ignatoff: "when [he] had designed an issue of *Shriftn* containing reproductions of contemporary artwork, he asked the Yunge to devote an evening to gluing them in at the printer's, since he had no more money to pay for the job" (99).

23. Wolitz, "Between Folk and Freedom," *Yiddish* 8 (1991): 26–51, reprinted in Horowitz and Gottschalk, *Yiddish Modernism,* 365–80, here 369. See also Marek Bartelik, *Early Polish Modern Art: Unity in Multiplicity* (Manchester: Manchester University Press, 2005), 154, 156.

24. This difficulty is implicit in the thematic organization of a recent anthology, *Global Modernists on Modernism* (New York: Bloomsbury Academic, 2019): the *Inzikh* manifesto is reprinted in a section called "Modernism of the Ashkenazi Jewish Diaspora," a unique title in a volume where other sections are either geographically or nationally defined.

25. These sentiments characterized expressionist art and literature with its healthy representation of Jewish figures. For example, this laconic historiographic observation from an introduction in *The Oxford Critical and Cultural History of Modernist Magazines:* "Fritz Herzog's study of mainly avant-garde journals was published in 1940. Throughout the volume, every publisher, editor, critic, artist and writer of Jewish descent was identified as such with 'Jude' given after their name" (vol. 3, part 2, 693).

26. Jankel Adler, "Expressionism (Fragments from a Lecture)" in *Between Worlds: A Sourcebook of European Avant-Gardes, 1910–1930,* ed. Timothy O. Benson and Éva Forgács (Cambridge, MA: MIT Press, 2002), 181–82. (Originally published in Polish in *Nasz Kurier,* December 5, 1920.) On Adler's biographical details, see *The YIVO Encyclopedia of Jews in Eastern Europe,* accessed November 20, 2020, https://yivoencyclopedia.org/article.aspx/Adler_Yankl.

27. See Rosa Schapire, "Schmidt-Rottluff's Religious Woodcuts" (1919), excerpted in *German Expressionism: Documents from the End of the Wilhelmine Empire to the Rise of National Socialism,* ed. Rose-Carol Washton Long (Berkeley: University of California Press, 1993), 150.

28. From the inaugural issue of *Ringen* in Warsaw: Henryk Berlewi's "The Struggle for a New Form," *Ringen* 1 (1921). Translation from Benson and Forgács, *Between Worlds,* 182–83, here 182. The Yiddish original in the first issue (31–33) may also be found in Karoliny Szymaniak's marvelous anthology of writing and visual work from this era, *Warszawska awangarda jidysz: Antologa tekstow pod* (Gdańsk, Poland: Słowo/obraz terytoria, 2005), 122–26.

29. Biographical details from the online entry on Berlewi in *The YIVO Encyclopedia of Jews in Eastern Europe,* accessed July 15, 2021, http://www.yivoencyclopedia.org/article.aspx/Berlewi_Henryk.

30. Berlewi's views here were likely shaped by the fact that the *lubok*—a staple of Russian folklore—was promoted as a potential source for Jewish art as early as 1918 by An-ski

and Avram Efros, among others. See Susan Goodman Tumarkin, Ziva Amishai-Maisels, et al., eds., *Russian Jewish Artists in a Century of Change* (Munich: Prestel, 1996).

31. Henryk Berlewi, "Jewish Artists in Contemporary Russian Art," trans. Rachel Field, *In geveb,* February 2018, https://ingeveb.org/texts-and-translations/jewish-artists-in-contemporary-russian-art.
32. Berlewi, "Jewish Artists in Contemporary Russian Art."
33. Franz Kafka, "For a Small Literature: Kafka's Diary Entry for December 25, 1911" and "An Introductory Talk on the Yiddish Language, 1912," in *Reading Kafka: Prague, Politics, and the Fin de Siècle,* ed. Mark Anderson (New York: Schocken, 1989), 259–62.
34. From a review by Yankev Shatzky in the Polish Jewish Warsaw daily paper, *Nasz Kurier* 160 (1922), 3, cited in Karolina Szymaniak, "The Language of Confusion and Dispersion: Perets Markish's Manifestos from the *Khalyastre* Period," in *A Captive of the Dawn: The Life and Work of Peretz Markish (1895–1952),* ed. Joseph Sherman et al. (London: Legenda, 2011), 66–87, here 82.
35. El Lissitzky's "Overcoming Art," *Ringen* 10 (1922): 32–34. Translation from the Polish in Benson and Forgács, *Between Worlds,* 185. This distinction, and especially the privileging of the engineer over the artist seems to anticipate Claude Lévi-Strauss's elevation of the bricoleur, the creative, engineering figure that works with the "material at hand."
36. El Lissitzky, "Overcoming Art," 186. The Yiddish for this is quite precise—*der proup kompanirt nisht, nor konstruirt*—and uses throughout, somewhat bafflingly, the term *proup,* not *proun.*
37. These ideas about the Proun and the figure of the engineer are found elsewhere in the artist's writing; for example "UNOVIS, 1920," written when he was part of the Vitebsk art collective founded by Malevich. Some of Lissitzky's ideas (about Cézanne, form and color, cubism) echo Malevich's writing. See El Lissitzky, "Proun," in *Chagall, Lissitzky, Malevich: The Russian Avant-Garde in Vitebsk, 1918–1922*, ed. Angela Lampe (New York: Prestel, 2018), 234–35, and notes and explanatory material by Angela Lampe; and Jean-Claude Marcade, "UNOVIS in the History of the Russian Avant-Garde," in *Chagall, Lissitzky, Malevich,* 219–23.
38. Perets Markish, "The Aesthetics of Struggle in Modern Poetry," *Ringen* 10 (1922): 35–41. The original Yiddish appears with a Hebrew translation in *Huliyot* 3 (Spring 1996). The manifesto was originally delivered in an apparently electrifying Saturday morning performance, an *Oyneg Shabes,* to an adoring crowd in Warsaw; this event encapsulates the use of a traditional form filled with revolutionary content, intended, no doubt, to shock the genteel sensibilities of bourgeois Jewish Warsaw. Szymaniak appreciatively cites Melech Ravitch's vivid account of this event and the surrounding atmosphere. See "The Language of Confusion and Dispersion," 66–67.
39. Biographical details on Markish from the online entry in *The YIVO Encyclopedia of Jews in Eastern Europe,* accessed November 20, 2020, https://yivoencyclopedia.org/article.aspx/Markish_Perets.
40. Seth Wolitz, "The *Khalyastre* (1918–1925): A Modernist Movement in Poland," *Yiddish* 4:3 (1981): 5–20, here 12.
41. See Szymaniak, "The Language of Confusion and Dispersion," 72–75. On Markish's poetics in relation to the historical tumult of this period, see Amelia M. Glaser, "The

Market Crucified: Peretz Markish's Civil War, 1917–1921," in *Jews and Ukrainians in Russia's Literary Borderlands: From the Shtetl Fair to the Petersburg Shop* (Evanston: Northwestern University Press, 2012), 111–40.

42. Untitled, *Khalyastre* 1 (1922), 2.

43. See the discussion on the "poetic body" in Szymaniak, "The Language of Confusion and Dispersion," 79–81. For Mosse, see his *The Image of Man: The Creation of Modern Masculinity* (New York: Oxford University Press, 1998).

44. Jayne Marek, *Women Editing Modernism: "Little" Magazines and Literary History* (Lexington: University Press of Kentucky, 2015).

45. For details, see Avidov Lipsker, "The Albatrosses of Young Yiddish Poetry: An Idea and Its Visual Realization in Uri Zvi Greenberg's *Albatros*," *Prooftexts* 15:1 (1995): 101.

46. *Albatros* 1 (1922), 10.

47. For details on Shumiatcher and her work, see *Yiddish Leksikon,* accessed August 2, 2021, https://yleksikon.blogspot.com/2019/08/ester-shumyatsher-esther-shumiatcher.html.

48. "Proclamation" [Yiddish], *Albatros* 1:3. Translation from David Roskies in *Prooftexts* 15:1 (1995): 109.

49. "Proclamation," 110.

50. On alphabets and images, see Johanna Drucker, *The Visible Word: Experimental Typography and Modern Art, 1909–1923* (Chicago: University of Chicago Press, 1994); and the discussion in Bulson, *Little Magazine, World Form,* 50–51. "Crimes of typographic disobedience" is quoted in William Owen, *Modern Magazine Design* (New York: Rizzoli, 1991), cited in Bulson, *Little Magazine, World Form,* 50–51.

51. Tristan Tsara, "Manifesto Dada," *Dada,* March 23, 1918, translation in Benson and Forgács, *Between Worlds,* 313.

52. On the different approaches to folk motifs in Hebrew and Yiddish culture during this period, see Zehavit Stern, "The Purim-shpiler and the Melancholy Clown: Folk Performance between Tradition and Modernism in the Work of Avraham Shlonsky and Moyshe Broderzon," *Journal of Jewish Identities* 17:1 (2014): 49–78.

53. Christian Weikop, introduction to Peter Brooker et al., *The Oxford Critical and Cultural History of Modernist Magazines,* vol. 3, part 2, 706.

54. Wolitz, "Between Folk and Freedom," in Horowitz and Gottschalk, *Yiddish Modernism,* 365–80, here 376. Bergelson apparently also complained, in 1919, about the lack of a sophisticated Yiddish readership: see Wolitz, "The Kiev-Grupe (1918–1920) Debate: The Function of Literature?" *Yiddish* 3:3 (1978): 97–106, reprinted in Horowitz and Gottschalk, *Yiddish Modernism,* 355–64.

55. *Khad Gádye*'s merging of Judaic tradition and abstraction has been the subject of scholarship. In addition to sections in the exhibition catalogue *Chagall, Lissitzky, Malevich,* see also the valuable sources included in Alexander Kantsedikas, *El Lissitzky: The Jewish Period* (London: Unicorn, 2017); Alan C. Birnholz, "El Lissitzky and the Jewish Tradition," *Studio International* 186:959 (October 1973): 130–36; and Samuel Spinner, "Reading Jewish," *PMLA* 134:1 (2019): 150–56.

56. Founded by Moyshe Broderzon (1890–1956) and the artists Jankel Adler and Marek Szwarc, with Berlewi also a key figure, *Yung-Yiddish* appeared in six issues (collected and published in three separate volumes) in Lodz in 1919–20.

57. On the shared iconography of *Yung-Yiddish* and *Khalyastre,* and the connections between the Lodz-based group of artists, Jewish figures in Paris such as Chagall and Soutine (*Machmadim*), and Jakob Steinhardt in Berlin *(Die Pathetiker*), see Jerzy Malinowski, "The Yung Yiddish Group and Jewish Modern Art in Poland, 1918–1923," *Polin* 6 (1991): 223–30. For further details on *Yung-Yiddish,* see Gilles Rozier, "Yung-yidish," *The YIVO Encyclopedia of Jews in Eastern Europe,* accessed July 13, 2021, https://yivoencyclopedia.org/article.aspx/Yung-yidish. For a different context, see Lidia Głuchowska, "Poznań and Łódź: National Modernism and the International Avant-Garde: *Zdrój* (1917–1922); *Yung-Yiddish* (1919); and *Tel-Awiw* (1919–1921)," in Brooker et al., *The Oxford Critical and Cultural History of Modernist Magazines,* vol. 3, part 2, 1208–33.
58. See Lissitzky's "The Mohilev Synagogue: Reminiscences" (1923), in Kantsedikas, *El Lissitzky: The Jewish Period,* 148–53. Originally appeared in Yiddish in *Milgroym,* 3 (1923): 8–13. On Ryback and Lissitzky, see Kazovsky, "The Art Section of the *Kultur-Lige*" and also the appendix from Kantsedikas, *El Lissitzky: The Jewish Period* for photographs of the wooden synagogue paintings they might have seen during their 1916 trip.
59. Lissitzky, "The Mohilev Synagogue," 152. Lissitzky was impressed by the "kinship" between the synagogue paintings, regardless of their "authorship," and contemporary art more broadly: "There still remains the question of the national character of these paintings. We leave that to the psychologists and the ethnographers. We want to point out, however, that the kinship of the work, [which is] displayed so generously on the walls and ceilings of the Mohilev synagogue, with the contemporary styles employed by other nations should force us to give serious thought to the matter" (152).
60. According to a 1960 account by Meyer Levin provided on *Marek Scwarc,* accessed January 21, 2019, https://www.marekszwarc.com/texts.html. Another image in this journal by Szwarc is also based on his bronze relief *The Returning Spy.* The bronze relief appeared in *Menorah Journal* 9 (1923): 296.
61. Rudolf Adrian Dietrich, "Geschichte (zur Ausstelung 'Der expressionistische Holzschnitt' bei Goltz in Munchen)," *Die Schone Raritat* 2 (1918–19), excerpted in Washton Long, *German Expressionism,* 140.
62. Gustav Hartlaub, *The New German Print* (1920), *Die neue deutsche Graphik* (Berlin: Erich Reiss Verlag, 1920), cited in Washton Long, *German Expressionism,* 142.
63. Wilhelm Valentiner, "Karl Schmidt-Rottluff," *Der Cicerone* 2 (1920): 467, cited in Washton Long, *German Expressionism,* 140.
64. Hartlaub, *The New German Print,* 142.
65. Hartlaub, *The New German Print,* 143.
66. The poem appears in its entirely in *Yung-Yiddish* 2–3 (1919), with another print by Broyner. On Broderzon and his contemporaries, see Gennady Estraikh, "Yiddish Literary Life in Soviet Moscow, 1918–1924," *Jews in Eastern Europe* 2:42 (Fall 2000): 25–55.
67. This figure recalls Reuven's paintings of Moses from 1923 and his series of woodcuts, *The God-Seekers.* Reuven, in Czernowitz in 1919–21, was influenced by Jakov Steinhardt's woodcuts (Steinhardt later emigrated and became part of Bezalel). These artists, whether they began in Lodz and ended up in Berlin or began in Czernowitz and ended up in Tel Aviv, seem to have all been drinking from the same expressionist-mystical-symbolist trough. See Amitai Mendelsohn, ed., *Prophets and Visionaries: Reuven Rubin's Early Years, 1914–1923* (Jerusalem: Israel Museum, 2006).

68. See the discussion of some of these prints and their folkloric motifs in Lipsker, "The Albatrosses of Young Yiddish Poetry."

69. See Bulson on Dadaism and the grid as a formative shape for little magazines: *Little Magazine, World Form,* 51–58.

70. Bulson, *Little Magazine, World Form,* 52.

71. Bulson, *Little Magazine, World Form,* 14.

72. Brooker et al., *The Oxford Critical and Cultural History of Modernist Magazines,* vol. 3, part 2, 693.

73. Bulson, *Little Magazine, World Form,* 6.

74. Lital Levy and Allison Schachter, "Jewish Literature/World Literature: Between the Local and the Transnational," *PMLA* 130: 1 (2015): 96.

75. Levy and Schachter, "Jewish Literature/World Literature," 93.

76. Bulson describes these geographic limits: "Transatlantic shipping remained expensive for already strapped budgets, and without any editorial offices on the ground, it was a particularly unreliable way to find readers since the distribution itself was so difficult to monitor" (*Little Magazine, World Form,* 16). Though little magazines benefited from some advances of modernity, including printing technologies, "mobility was not one of them. . . . There was never any robust infrastructure in place that would enable the easy transatlantic circulation of any of them. . . . [The situation] was really a more restricted, nationally defined geography of the little magazines where they published. . . . If writers were moving, in other words, the magazines were not" (79). Bulson's idea of "transatlantic immobility" pertains less to Yiddish little magazines, which may have more easily circulated between cities in Europe. Bulson offers an astute critique of Ramazani, who describes transmission or circulation of "texts," but misses the "material processes that would allow for any poem to travel in the first place" (80).

77. Samuel Werses, "Kitve-'et 'ivriyim lesifrut bePolin ben shete milḥamot 'olam," in *Ben shete milḥamot 'olam: Perakim me-ḥaye ha-tarbut shel yehude Polin li-leshonotehem* (Jerusalem: Hebrew University, 1997), 96–127.

78. It is telling, perhaps, that when Bulson discusses this point in his book, his example includes correspondence between Walter Benjamin and Gershom Scholem (*Little Magazine, World Form,* 17).

79. Henryk Berlewi, "The International Exhibit in Dusseldorf" (originally published as "Miedzynarodowa wystawa w Dusseldofie," *Nasz Kurier,* August 2, 1922), in Benson and Forgács, *Between Worlds,* 399. This anthology seems to efface the Jewish connection of some of its sources.

80. Berlewi, "The International Exhibit in Dusseldorf," 397; Hartlaub, "The New German Print," 144.

CHAPTER 3. "GOOD TO THINK WITH"

1. Dovid Bergelson, *Nokh alemen* (Vilna: B. A. Kletskin, 1913), 187; and *The End of Everything,* trans. Joseph Sherman (New Haven: Yale University Press, 2009), 86. For longer quotations, the page number of the Yiddish edition follows the page number of the translation.

2. Eugene Avrutin et al., *Photographing the Jewish Nation: Photographs from S. An-sky's Ethnographic Expeditions* (Waltham, MA: Brandeis University Press/University Press of New England, 2009), 9–10.
3. Avrutin et al., *Photographing the Jewish Nation,* 192.
4. See Valerii Dymshits, "The First Jewish Museum," in Avrutin et al., *Photographing the Jewish Nation,* 189–212.
5. In her reading of the novel, Luisa Banki notes that "the object of mourning for European Jewry in modernity was the imaginary unity of tradition" (106). See Luisa Banki, "Melancholy and Modernity: Dovid Bergelson's *Nokh Alemen," European Journal of Jewish Studies* 4:1 (2010): 91–114.
6. Marx distinguished between the use value of objects (their utility) and their exchange value (their worth in terms of other objects, or their fetishized, imagined form as commodities). For a lucid reading of the fetish in both Marx and Freud, see Tim Dant, "Fetishism and the Social Value of Things," *Sociological Review* 44:3 (1996): 495–516.
7. In the words of Daniel Miller, "The best way to understand, convey and appreciate our humanity is through attention to our fundamental materiality." Daniel Miller, *Stuff* (Cambridge: Polity, 2010), 4.
8. Bill Brown, "The Secret Life of Things (Virginia Woolf and the Matter of Modernism)," *Modernism/modernity* 6:2 (1991): 1–28, here 2.
9. Bill Brown, *A Sense of Things: The Object Matter of American Literature* (Chicago: University of Chicago Press, 2003), 14.
10. "What distinguishes the novel from the story (and from the epic in the narrower sense) is its essential dependence on the book." Walter Benjamin, "The Storyteller," in *Illuminations* (New York: Schocken, 1968), 87.
11. Susan Stewart, *On Longing: Narratives of the Miniature, the Gigantic, the Souvenir and the Collection* (Durham: Duke University Press, 1993), 29.
12. Karl Marx, "The Fetishism of Commodities and the Secrets Thereof," in *Capital* (1867), vol. 1, accessed July 6, 2021, https://www.marxists.org/archive/marx/works/1867-c1/ch01.htm#S4.
13. Benjamin, "The Storyteller," 223.
14. Benjamin, "The Storyteller," 221.
15. Benjamin, "The Storyteller," 224.
16. See Dan Miron, "The Literary Image of the Shtetl," *Jewish Social Studies* 1:3 (Spring 1995): 1–43.
17. From "Mendele Mokher Sefarim" [Hebrew], in *Kol Kitvey D. Frishman* (Warsaw and New York: Hotsa'at Lili Frishman, 1931), 6:74, quoted in Miron, "The Literary Image of the Shtetl," 6.
18. See the essays in Steven K. Katz, ed., *The Shtetl: New Evaluations* (New York: New York University Press, 2007).
19. David Roskies, *Against the Apocalypse: Responses to Catastrophe in Modern Jewish Culture* (Cambridge, MA: Harvard University Press, 1984), 122.
20. For biographical details, see the article on Dovid Bergelson in *The YIVO Encyclopedia of Jews in Eastern Europe,* accessed November 20, 2020, https://yivoencyclopedia.org

/article.aspx/Bergelson_Dovid; and also Sherman's excellent introduction to his translation of *The End of Everything.*

21. Mikhail Krutikov, *Yiddish Fiction and the Crisis of Modernity, 1905–1914* (Stanford: Stanford University Press, 2001), 38.
22. Krutikov, *Yiddish Fiction and the Crisis of Modernity,* 47.
23. This observation and examples from the Soviet critic Yekhezkl Dobroshin in 1947, cited in Krutikov, *Yiddish Fiction and the Crisis of Modernity,* 43–44.
24. Bergelson, *The End of Everything,* 18.
25. Bergelson, *The End of Everything,* 138.
26. For a critical appreciation of the symbolic function of objects in Bergelson's novel, see Daniela Mantovan, "Language and Style in *Nokh Alemen* (1913): Bergelson's Debt to Flaubert," in *David Bergelson: From Modernism to Socialist Realism,* ed. Joseph Sherman and Gennady Estraikh (Leeds: Legenda, 2005), 89–112.
27. Bergelson, *The End of Everything,* 93.
28. Henry James, *The Spoils of Poynton* (New York: Penguin Books, 1987), 81. The comment occurs as it is revealed that Mrs. Gereth has taken "the very best pieces" of her art collection from the family home, which her son is about to inherit with his new wife (whom Mrs. Gereth disapproves of), and installed them in her new house, leaving "the rubbish" behind.
29. Marx, "The Fetishism of Commodities and the Secrets Thereof."
30. Bergelson, *The End of Everything,* 77.
31. Bergelson, *The End of Everything,* 66/166.
32. Bergelson, *The End of Everything,* 67–68/168. The Yiddish term *lebenloser zach* (lifeless thing) is especially resonant.
33. Quoted in Axel Honneth, "Reification: A Recognition-Theoretical View," in *The Tanner Lectures on Human Values* (Berkeley: University of California Press, 2005), 96.
34. "Georg Lukács, Reification and the Consciousness of the Proletariat" (1923), accessed July 6, 2021, https://www.marxists.org/archive/lukacs/works/history/hcc05.htm.
35. Bergelson, *The End of Everything,* 172–73/279.
36. Bergelson, *The End of Everything,* 178.
37. Honneth, "Reification," 99.
38. Bergelson, *The End of Everything,* 114, 118, 135.
39. Bergelson, *The End of Everything,* 131–32/234–35.
40. Bergelson, *The End of Everything,* 133/236.
41. James, *The Spoils of Poynton,* 26.
42. Bergelson, *The End of Everything,* 139/242.
43. According to Krutikov, this scene's ironic allusion to Peretz's "Between Two Mountains" is "meant to undermine the contemporary neoromantic Jewish myth" (*Yiddish Fiction and the Crisis of Modernity,* 197).
44. Miron, "Literary Image of the Shtetl."
45. Bergelson, *The End of Everything,* 262.
46. Willa Cather, "The Novel Démeublé," *New Republic,* April 12, 1922, 5–6, here 6.
47. Irving Howe, "Life Never Let Up: *Call It Sleep,*" *New York Times Book Review,* October 25, 1964.

48. See Steven G. Kelman, *Redemption: The Life of Henry Roth* (New York: Norton, 2005) for a detailed account of the author's life before and after *Call It Sleep*.
49. See the extensive discussion in Hana Wirth-Nesher, *Call It English: The Languages of Jewish American Literature* (Princeton: Princeton University Press, 2006).
50. Specifically, for Freud, in relation to the mother's sexuality and the boy's belief regarding her genitalia. See "Fetishism" (1927), in *The Complete Psychological Works of Sigmund Freud*, vol. 21, trans. J. Strachey (Hogarth and the Institute of Psychoanalysis, 1927), 147–57. Claude Lévi-Strauss, *The Savage Mind*, trans. George Weidenfield & Nicholson (Chicago: University of Chicago Press, 1966 [1962]), accessed July 6, 2021, http://web.mit.edu/allanmc/www/levistrauss.pdf.
51. Lévi-Strauss, *The Savage Mind*, 11. Jacques Derrida's reading of Lévi-Strauss cautions that *all* discourse is in fact intertextual bricolage, and that the engineer's intellectual prowess and "originality" is a myth. See his "Structure, Sign, and Play in the Discourse of the Human Sciences," in *Writing and Difference*, trans. Alan Bass (New York: Routledge, 1978), 278–94. For my reading of Roth's novel, and specifically the discursive universe in which David comes of age—the hands-on method of the tinkerer resembles that of the new immigrant, who encounters linguistic difference with verve and ingenuity.
52. Lévi-Strauss, *The Savage Mind*, 12.
53. Roth, *Call It Sleep* (New York: Farrar, Straus, Giroux, 1991), 35–36.
54. Lévi-Strauss, *The Savage Mind*, 12.
55. Roth, *Call It Sleep*, 22–23.
56. Sherry Turkle, ed., *Evocative Objects: Things We Think With* (Cambridge, MA: MIT Press, 2007), 9.
57. Roth, *Call It Sleep*, 327.
58. Roth, *Call It Sleep*, 327.
59. Roth, *Call It Sleep*, 172.
60. Roth, *Call It Sleep*, 297.
61. Roth, *Call It Sleep*, 298.
62. Roth, *Call It Sleep*, 400, 402.
63. The scene's melodramatic staging recalls the surreal confrontation between George and his father in Franz Kafka's story "The Judgment." David's evolving search for meaning and solace also resembles a key passage in James Joyce's *A Portrait of the Artist*: "The soul . . . has a slow and dark birth, more mysterious than the birth of the body. When the soul of a man is born in this country there are nets flung at it to hold it back from flight. You talk to me of nationality, language, religion. I shall try to fly by those nets." Joyce, *A Portrait of the Artist as a Young Man* (New York: Penguin Books, 2003 [1916]), 220.
64. Roth, *Call It Sleep*, 406–7.
65. Roth, *Call It Sleep*, 408, 413.
66. Roth, *Call It Sleep*, 419.
67. Roth, *Call It Sleep*, 434.
68. Roth, *Call It Sleep*, 441.
69. Jahan Ramazani, *A Transnational Poetics* (Chicago: University of Chicago Press, 1994), 99.

70. Yonatan Sagiv, *Indebted: Capitalism and Religion in the Writings of S. Y. Agnon* (Cincinnati: Hebrew Union College/University of Pittsburgh Press, 2016), 12.

71. Balak has piqued, challenged, and intrigued readers and scholars of Agnon's work for decades, and the dog has served as the frame for a number of allegorical readings. For a synthetic critical engagement with these views, see Boaz Arpaly, *Ravroman* [Hebrew; Masternovel] (Tel Aviv: Hakibbutz Hameuchad, 1998); and Michal Arbel, *Written on the Skin of a Dog* [Hebrew] (Jerusalem: Keter, 2006). For a reading of Balak in relation to language, see Todd Hasak-Lowy, "A Mad Dog's Attack on Secularized Hebrew: Rethinking Agnon's *Tmol shilshom,*" *Prooftexts* 24 (2004): 167–98. For an artistic interpretation of Balak, see the illustrations by Avigdor Arikha, from S. Y. Agnon, *Kelev Ḥutsot: Parasha ketana shel Tmol Shilshom* (Jerusalem: Sifrei Tarshish, 1960).

72. Ian Hodder, *Entanglement: An Archaeology of the Relationships between Humans and Things* (Malden, MA: Wiley-Blackwell, 2012).

73. Bruno Latour, *We Have Never Been Modern,* trans. Catherine Porter (Cambridge, MA: Harvard University Press, 1993), 3.

74. Bruno Latour, "The Berlin Key; or, How to Do Words with Things," in *Matter, Materiality and Modern Culture,* ed. P. M. Graves-Brown (New York: Routledge, 2000), 10–21.

75. Bill Brown, "Thing Theory," in *Things,* ed. Bill Brown (Chicago: University of Chicago Press, 2004), 4.

76. Dov Sadan and Gideon Ofrat have suggested that Bloykoff is based on the painter Samuel Hirszenberg, who died in Jerusalem after living there for less than a year. See Shmuel Werses, "Agnon in the World of Bezalel: Between Imagination and Reality" [Hebrew], in *Shai Agnon kepshuto* (Jerusalem: Mosad Bialik, 2000), 264–90, here 279.

77. S. Y. Agnon, *Tmol Shilshom* (New York: Schocken, 1945), 241; *Only Yesterday,* trans. Barbara Harshav (Princeton: Princeton University Press, 2000), 250. For longer quotations, the page number of the Hebrew edition follows the page number of the translation.

78. Dalia Manor, "Orientalism and Jewish National Art: The Case of Bezalel," in *Orientalism and the Jews,* ed. Ivan Davidson Kalmar and Derek Penslar (Waltham, MA: Brandeis University Press, 2005), 142–61, here 144.

79. According to Manor, "Orientalism and Jewish National Art," by the 1870s, there were already about one hundred Jews making olive wood souvenirs in Jerusalem. See also Gideon Ofrat, "The Beginnings of the Jewish and Christian Olive-wood Industry in Jerusalem" [Hebrew], accessed May 25, 2016, www.gideonofratwordpress.com/2015/12/13/100.

80. Otto Warburg, "Bezalel: The Palestine Polytechnic," *Jewish Chronicle,* June 7, 1907, 18, quoted in Manor, "Orientalism and Jewish National Art," 150.

81. See Sarah Chinski, "The Female Lace-workers of Bezalel" [Hebrew] *Teoria ve-bikoret* 11 (Fall 1997): 177–204.

82. Ivan Davidson Kalmar and Derek Penslar, "Orientalism and the Jews: An Introduction," in Kalmar and Penslar, *Orientalism and the Jews,* xxxvi.

83. For Agnon's ironic view of Bezalel, see Werses, "Agnon in the World of Bezalel." On Agnon's critique of Bezalel, and its founder Boris Shatz in particular, see Gideon Ofrat, "Agnon and Israeli Art" [Hebrew], *Gideon Ofrat Blog,* June 1, 2011.

84. Arjun Appadurai, ed., *The Social Life of Things: Commodities in Cultural Perspective* (Cambridge: Cambridge University Press, 1986), 26.
85. For example, see the discussion of the Asian porcelain trade in relation to Daniel Defoe's novel in Lydia Liu, "Robinson Crusoe's Earthenware Pot," *Critical Inquiry* 25:4 (Summer 1999): 728–57.
86. Agnon, *Only Yesterday*, 217/209.
87. Agnon, *Only Yesterday*, 241–42/234.
88. See Meron Benvenisti, "The Hebrew Map," *Sacred Landscapes: The Buried History of the Holy Land since 1948* (Berkeley: University of California Press, 2002).
89. See Rachel Poliquin, *The Breathless Zoo: Taxidermy and the Cultures of Longing* (University Park: Penn State University Press, 2012).
90. Sundhya Walther, "The Nation's Taxidermist: Ungovernable Bodies in R. K. Narayan's *The Man-Eater of Malgudi*," *University of Toronto Quarterly* 84:4 (Fall 2015): 74–89, here 74.
91. Agnon, *Only Yesterday*, 458/434.
92. Poliquin, *The Breathless Zoo*, 5.
93. The image and biographical details about Aharoni may be found online at https://upload.wikimedia.org/wikipedia/commons/9/9c/Israel_Aharoni_during_a_lecture.jpg (accessed July 6, 2021).
94. See Matthew Calarco, "Identity, Difference, Indistinction," *NR: The New Centennial Review* 11:2 (2012): 41–60, for a summary of how adherence to the animal-human divide effaces the potential diversity contained within each term.
95. In the words of Bruce Holsinger, "Practically all medieval writing survives on animal skin. So what?" In Bruce Holsinger, "Of Pigs and Parchment: Medieval Studies and the Coming of the Animal," *PMLA* 124:2 (2009): 616–23, here 619.
96. In his catalogue essay on Avigdor Aricha's Balak sketches, Mordechai Omer quotes an exchange between Agnon and one of the era's most formidable critics, Baruch Kurtzweil, shortly after the novel was published. Agnon maintains that he anticipated Balak would be a challenge for readers: "As much as I tried to erase the Balak episode from the story, it became even more necessary than at the start. . . . You know that I don't love allegory, and I didn't intend any kind of allegory in the world with Balak; I simply wanted to give expression through a beast and animal to what I couldn't do with a human being." Like Lévi-Strauss, Agnon seems to have found animals "good to think with." Mordechai Omer, *"Kelev chutsot" by S. Y. Agnon and Drawings by Avigdor Aricha* (Jerusalem: Agnon House, 2010), 15.
97. Barbara M. Benedict, "The Paradox of the Anthology: Collecting and *Différence* in Eighteenth Century Britain," in "Theorizing Genres I," special issue, *New Literary History* 34:2 (Spring 2003): 231–56, here 235.

CHAPTER 4. BETWEEN *SEFER* AND *BUKH*

1. See the essential introduction and selection of translated texts in Jonathan Boyarin and Jack Kugelmass, *From a Ruined Garden: The Memorial Books of Polish Jewry*, 2nd, expanded ed. (Bloomington: Indiana University Press/United States Holocaust Museum, 1998), with a geographical index and bibliography by Zachary M. Baker. Rosemary

Horowitz provides a valuable introduction and overview of the memorial books, including their production and reception, in her edited volume *Memorial Books of European Jewry: Essays on the History and Meanings of Yizker Volumes* (Jefferson, NC: McFarland, 2011). For other recent evaluations of *yizker* books, see Jeffrey Veidlinger, "'. . . even Beyond Pinsk': Yizker Bikher [Memorial Books] and Jewish Cultural Life in the Shtetl," in *The Jews of Eastern Europe,* ed. L. J. Greenspoon, R. A. Simkins, and B. J. Horowitz (Omaha: Creighton University Press, 2005), 175–89; and Michlean J. Amir and Rosemary Horowitz, "Yizkor Books in the Twenty-First Century: A History and Guide to the Genre," *Judaica Librarianship* 14 (2008): 39–56.

2. Estimates of the amount of memorial books range widely, and their catalogue definition varies in different institutions, archives, and libraries. Books produced by *landsmanshaft* (mutual aid society) volumes alone number seven hundred to eight hundred. According to Horowitz, Yad Vashem lists over one thousand books, perhaps due to a more expansive definition of the genre. For detail and context, I am indebted to Zachary Baker's indispensable appendix of memorial books in Boyarin and Kugelmass, *From a Ruined Garden.*
3. *Yizker* books resemble materials produced by other diasporic communities shaped by trauma and violent displacement. In her work on Palestinian memorial books, Susan Slymovics notes that "the presence of maps and photographs in memorial book texts asserts a Palestinian tradition of collective memory that is structured in ways similar to the Jewish, Armenian, and Bosnian historical interpretations found in their respective memorial books." Susan Slymovics, *The Object of Memory: Arab and Jew Narrate the Palestinian Village* (Philadelphia: University of Pennsylvania Press, 1998), 9. For a different perspective, see Rochelle Davis, *Palestinian Village Histories: Geographies of the Displaced* (Stanford: Stanford University Press, 2010). Davis expressly addresses the question of genre and embeds her reading of what she calls "village books" within a tradition of Arabic and Islamic histories of localities and towns.
4. On these earlier forms, see Israel Bartal, "The *Pinkas:* Communal Archive to Total History," *POLIN: Studies in Polish Jewry* 29 (2017): 21–40. Yosef Yerushalmi's classic discussion of Jewish memory and historiography elegantly demonstrates how premodern examples of local destruction were embedded within the longer history of Jewish catastrophe. See Yosef Hayim Yerushalmi, *Zakhor: Jewish History and Jewish Memory* (New York: Schocken, 1989).
5. These details are from Cecile Kuznitz's vivid account, "'From the Folk, for the Folk, with the Folk': Academic Work, 1925–1932," in her *YIVO and the Making of Modern Jewish Culture: Scholarship for the Yiddish Nation* (New York: Cambridge University Press, 2014), 71–111. See also Laura Jockusch, "*Khurbn-Forshung:* History Writing as Response to Jewish Catastrophe," in *Collect and Record! Jewish Holocaust Documentation in Early Postwar Europe* (New York: Oxford University Press, 2012), 26–27.
6. The term *Oyneg Shabes,* literally "Sabbath joy," refers to the celebratory gathering typically held on Friday evenings, featuring food, socializing, learning, and singing.
7. Samuel D. Kassow, *Who Will Write Our History? Rediscovering a Hidden Archive from the Warsaw Ghetto* (New York: Vintage Books, 2009 [2007]), 10.
8. However, Kassow notes important distinctions between the *Oyneg Shabes* and the memorial books: the former were written during the war itself and did not shy away from

depicting differences of opinion and divergent ideas about life in the Ghetto, while the memorial books were frequently either nostalgic or elegiac, glossing over behavior that might reflect unfavorably on the Jewish community (*Who Will Write Our History?* 270–72). Also regarding postwar writing, Jockush notes that "the organizers and activists of the postwar historical commissions and documentation centers for the most part appear to have been familiar with the documentation projects that emerged as a response to earlier incidents of anti-Jewish mass violence and the individual researchers that had brought them to life" (Jockush, *Collect and Record!* 37).

9. Susan Stewart, *On Longing: Narratives of the Miniature, the Gigantic, the Souvenir, the Collection* (Durham: Duke University Press, 1993), 136.

10. "Whereas the souvenir lends authenticity to the past, the past lends authenticity to the collection" (Stewart, *On Longing,* 151).

11. See Lisa Leff, *The Archive Thief: The Man Who Salvaged French Jewish History in the Wake of the Holocaust* (New York: Oxford University Press, 2015) for an absorbing and informative narrative about the vicissitudes of historical documents and their afterlives in the postwar period.

12. The phrase is from the title of what preoccupied S. Y. Agnon over the last fifteen years of his life, a literary memorial to his hometown of Buczacz. See Alan Mintz, *Ancestral Tales: Reading the Buczacz Stories of S. Y. Agnon* (Stanford: Stanford University Press, 2017).

13. Boyarin and Kugelmass, *From a Ruined Garden,* 24. See also Jack Kugelmass and Jonathan Boyarin, "*Yizker Bikher* and the Problem of Historical Veracity: An Anthropological Approach," in *The Jews of Poland between the Two World Wars,* ed. Yisrael Gutman and David E. Fishman (Hanover, NH: University Press of New England, 1989).

14. Yankev Shatzky, "Yizker bikher," *YIVO Bleter* 37 (1953): 264–82, trans. Herman Taube in Horowitz, *Memorial Books of European Jewry,* 54–67, here 63–64.

15. Yankev Shatzky, "Yizker bikher," *YIVO Bleter* 39 (1955): 339–55, trans. David Trachtenberg, in Horowitz, *Memorial Books of European Jewry,* 68–80, here 75.

16. Shatzky's second review, in Horowitz, *Memorial Books of European Jewry,* 76. Shatzky's suspicion of these texts may be related to a reluctance to historicize recent events, an issue that also shaped the production of Jewish ethnographic research in Vilna's YIVO in the 1920s. What was the appropriate interval before recent events could be understood in a critical fashion? See Kuznitz, "'From the Folk, for the Folk, with the Folk,'" 85–86. As Kunitz observes, "Shatzky managed to disagree with everyone" (87).

17. From Shatzky's 1955 review, in Horowitz, *Memorial Books of European Jewry,* 77. Also cited in Boyarin and Kugelmass, *From a Ruined Garden,* 25.

18. From *Yizker-bukh Pulaw* (1964), cited in Boyarin and Kugelmass, *From a Ruined Garden,* 38.

19. Nathan Blumenthal, "A New Literary Genre—the *Yizker* Book" [part 1], *Lebns Fragn,* January 1, 1960, 7.

20. Horowitz, "A History of Yizker Books," in *Memorial Books of European Jewry,* xx.

21. Blumenthal, "A New Literary Genre."

22. A. Sh. Stein, ed., *Pinkas Bendin* [Pinkas Beldin: A Memorial to the Jewish Community of Beldin] (Tel Aviv: Association of Former Residents of Bedzin in Israel, 1959), 7.

23. For example, *Księga Żydów Ostrołeckich* (Ostrołęka/Tel Awiw: Society of Friends of Ostrołęka, 2002), the first *yizker* book translated into Polish, which I viewed at the Jewish Historical Institute in Warsaw. See the discussion of Ostrołęka in Monica Adamczyk-Garbowska, "Reception of Memorial Books in Poland," in Horowitz, *Memorial Books of European Jewry,* which notes that the project (financed by Zalman Drezner, a native of the town) was meant to "educate young generations of Poles, to bring Poles and Jews together, and to teach tolerance and respect for the common past and warn against dangers" (109).
24. On the importance of material biographies for a new understanding of Jewish history, I am indebted to the work of Laura Leibman, especially her *The Art of the Jewish Family: A History of Women in Early New York in Five Objects* (Chicago: University of Chicago, 2020). On the idea of "material biographies" within anthropological discourse, see Janet Hoskins, "Agency, Biography and Objects," in *Handbook of Material Culture,* ed. Christoper Tilley (Thousand Oaks, CA: SAGE, 2006), 74–84. See also Leora Auslander's plea for historians to widen their sense of what constitutes a text to include visual and material culture in her "Beyond Words," *American Historical Review* 110:4 (October 2005): 1015–45.
25. Barbara M. Benedict, "The Paradox of the Anthology: Collecting and *Différence* in Eighteenth-Century Britain," in "Theorizing Genres I," special issue, *New Literary History* 34:2 (Spring 2003): 231–56, here 233.
26. Leora Auslander, "Material Culture and Materiality," in *Travelling Concepts for the Study of Culture,* ed. Birgit Neuman and Ansgar Nünning (Boston: De Gruyter, 2012), 353–69, here 354.
27. Facing the sheer number of volumes, scholars have to choose. Boyarin and Kugelmass state their rationale and preference thus: "personal selection based on a perusal of the Polish-Jewish memorial book literature in Yiddish" (*From a Ruined Garden,* 5).
28. The work of Malena Chinski is a notable exception; see Malena Chinski, "Ilustrar la memoria: Las imágenes de tapa de la colección *Dos poylishe yidntum* (El judaísmo polaco), Buenos Aires, 1946–1955," *E.I.A.L.* 23:1 (2012): 11–33. I am grateful to Samuel Spinner for bringing Chinski's essay to my attention. The dismissal of the visual dimension is connected, in my view, to other lacuna in Jewish studies. See Alexandra Nocke on the textual bias of Jewish scholarship, at the expense of space, in her *Jewish Topographies: Visions of Space, Traditions of Place* (Hampshire, UK: Ashgate, 2012); Catherine Soussloff on the Jewish resistance to art historical scholarship in *Jewish Identity in Modern Art History,* ed. Soussloff (Berkeley: University of California, 1999); and Auslander, "Beyond Words."
29. Abraham Wein, "Memorial Books as a Source for Research," in Horowitz, *Memorial Books of Eastern European Jewry,* 89–104, here 99.
30. See Daniel Magilow, "*Yizker* Books and Photographic Form" in Horowitz, *Memorial Books of Eastern European Jewry,* 200–221. Magilow's essay focuses on a single volume, *The Kalish Book* (Tel Aviv, 1967).
31. See *Ciechanowiec, mehoz Bialystok, sefer edut ve-zikaron* [Ciechanowiec-Bialystok District, Memorial, and Record], ed. E. Leoni (Tel Aviv: Ciechanovitzer Immigrant Association in Israel and the USA, 1964); and Y. T. Lewinski, ed., *Sefer zikaron le-kehilat Lomza* [Lomza, in Memory of the Jewish Community] (Tel Aviv: Former Residents of

Lomza in Israel, 1952). This preponderance of photographs led Wein to observe, somewhat churlishly: "It is regrettable that in more than a few cases the editors reproduce photographs of individuals or families who contributed financially to the book's publication. This transforms the memorial book, or part of it, into some kind of album." Wein, "Memorial Books as a Source for Research," 99.

32. Nathan Blumenthal, "A New Literary Genre—the *Yizker* Book" [part 2], *Lebns Fragns,* February 1, 1960, 8.

33. On the influence and importance of photographs for the documentation of prewar Jewish life, see the classic Lucjan Dobroszycki and Barbara Kirshenblatt-Gimblett, eds., *Image before My Eyes: A Photographic History of Jewish Life in Poland, 1864–1939* (New York: Schocken, 1977).

34. Y. Perlow and Alfred Lipson, eds., *Sefer Radom* [The Book of Radom: The Story of the Jewish Community in Poland Destroyed by the Nazis] (Tel Aviv: Former Residents of Radom in Israel and the USA, 1961), 505. A fifteen-page list of names and photos is followed by another twenty-four pages of names submitted by Radomers from all over the world, a catalogue whose ostensible comprehensiveness is both mind-boggling and heartbreaking.

35. Susan Sontag, "In Plato's Cave," in *On Photography* (New York: Farrar, Straus & Giroux, 1989 [1977]), 4.

36. On the role of the "private, 'internal' photography of east European Jewry" within public commemoration of the Holocaust, see Jeffrey Shandler, "'The Time of Vishniac': Photographs of Pre-war East European Jewry in Post-war Contexts," *POLIN* 16 (2003): 313–33.

37. See Paul Lowe, "The Forensic Turn: Bearing Witness and the 'Thingness' of the Photograph," in *The Violence of the Image: International Conflict and Photography,* ed. Liam Kennedy and Caitlin Patrick (London: Routledge/Taylor & Francis, 2020), 211–35.

38. For a moving example of how these photographs exist both individually and as part of a more monumental series, see the collection of images, letters, and interviews in *And I Still See Their Faces: Image of Polish Jews* (Warsaw: American-Polish-Israeli Shalom Foundation, 1996).

39. *Sefer zikaron le-kehilat Zborow* [Memorial Book of the Community of Zborow], ed. Eliyahu (Adik) Zilberman (Haifa: Zborow Society, 1975); *Rowne: Sefer zikaron* [Rowno: A Memorial to the Jewish Community of Rowno], ed. A. Avitachi (Tel Aviv: Former Residents of Rowno in Israel, 1956); *Pinkas Kolomey* [Memorial Book of Kolomey], ed. Sh. Bickel (New York: n.p., 1957); *Sefer Deblin-Modryzc* [Deblin-Modryzc], ed. D. Shotkfish (Tel Aviv: Association of Former Residents of Deblin-Modryzc, 1969).

40. *Khurban Proskurov* [The Destruction of Proskurov, in Memory of the Sacred Souls Who Perished during the Terrible Slaughter of the Haidamaks] (New York: Levant, 1924); *Felshtin: Zamlbukh lekoved tsum ondenk fun di Felshtiner kdoyshim* [Felshtin: Collection in Memory of the Martyrs of Felshtin] (New York: First Felshtiner Progressive Benevolent Association, 1937).

41. Loeb (1889–1968) was born in Poland and immigrated to the United States as a teenager; he worked as a commercial artist and illustrator for Jewish daily newspapers in New York and the Jewish National Fund, producing poster art with a variety of political themes, from socialism and Zionism to support for the Spanish Civil War. Loeb, an

active presence in socialist and labor groups in New York from the 1930s, was an associate of Eugene V. Debs, the labor organizer and activist.

42. *Yizker: Tsum ondenken di gefalene vekhter un arbeyter in Erets Yisroel* (New York: Po'ale Tsiyon Palestine Committee/Labor Zionist Organization of America, 1916). For the Hebrew edition, see A. Z. Rabinovitz,ed., *Yizker—Matsevet zikaron le-halele ha-poalim ha-ivryim be-eretz yisrael* (Jaffa: A. Ateen, 1911). This book also appeared in two more editions in 1918, in Lodz (Yiddish) and in Berlin (German). On the production and historical significance of the Hebrew volume, see Jonathan Frankel, "The 'Yizker' Book of 1911: A Note on National Myths in the Second Aliya," in *Crisis, Revolution and Russian Jews* (New York: Cambridge University Press, 2009), 183–215.

43. See Frankel, "'Yizker' Book," 211. Shabtai Tevet offers a detailed description of the publication of the Yiddish version in New York in *Kinat David: Ben-Gurion Ha-tsair* (Jerusalem: Schocken, 1966), 338–58.

44. Though published by different presses, the shared images and similar size suggest that New York's Yiddish edition of *Yizker* of 1916 and *Khurban Proskurov* of 1924 may have had a printer or editor in common. Gideon Ofrat goes so far as to draft Michael/Mitchell Loeb into the pantheon of "Zionist artists." "Who Are You, Michael Loeb?" *Gideon Ofrat Blog*, August 18, 2015, https://gideonofrat.wordpress.com/2015/08/18/. The images and papers in NYU's Tamiment Library and Robert F. Wagner Labor Archives suggest that Loeb's own political leanings appeared to evolve in a different direction. See the Mitchell Loeb Papers, TAM 627.

45. On *Felshtin*'s illustrations, see the sections in David Roskies, *The Jewish Search for a Usable Past* (Bloomington: Indiana University Press, 1999), reprinted also for the Felshtin Society, http://felshtin.org/the-shtetl-as-covenantal-landscape/.

46. Koslowsky's map bears an uncanny resemblance to contemporaneous drawings of Tel Aviv by Nachum Gutman. Gutman was also an illustrator of children's literature and these sketches were first published in A. Druyanov's *Sefer Tel Aviv* (1936), a *pinkas*-style historical account that subsequently contributed to the mythology of the city's "childhood."

47. See A. Trus and J. Cohen, *Braynsk, sefer hazikaron* [Brainsk, Book of Memories] (New York: Brainsker Relief Committee of New York, 1948); and *Tshenstokhover yidn* [The Jews of Czetochowa], ed. R. Mahler. (New York: United Czestochower Relief Committee and Ladies Auxiliary, 1947).

48. An annotated bibliography in the Noah Cotsen Library of Yiddish Children's Literature in the collections of the YIVO Institute and the National Yiddish Book Center contains fifteen separate headings for Koslowzky's work in this genre.

49. For what might be understood as a kind of "third narrative" of midcentury Jewish art, informed by attention to geographic and cultural negotiations, see Carol Zemel, *Looking Jewish: Visual Culture and Modern Diaspora* (Bloomington: Indiana University Press, 2012).

50. On the offensive potential of the image, see my discussion in chapter 5 of Neil Gaiman. Comics have historically been censored more often for visual content than for narrative: it is the immediacy of the image—once glimpsed—that most potentially offends.

51. In at least one instance, Torah scroll parchment was repurposed for the painting of a portrait. An exhibit about this discovery was held in 2012 at the Galicia Jewish Museum

in Krakow. See Jason Francisco, "The Other Side of the Torah," *Times of Israel,* September 3, 2012, https://blogs.timesofisrael.com/the-other-side-of-the-torah/.

52. "Rebellious Tombstones," in *Es shtarbt a shtetl: Megiles Skalat* (Munich: Central Historical Commission of the Central Committee of Liberated Jews in the U.S. Zone of Germany, 1948), 91–92. The work was published in an edition of five thousand copies; the photo appears on p. 89. English translation at https://www.jewishgen.org/yizkor/Skalat1/ska040.html (accessed July 13, 2021).

53. The image appears in both E. Leoni, ed., *Korets: Sefer zikaron le-kehilatenu she-ala aleha ha-koret* (Tel Aviv: Former Residents of Korets in Israel, 1959), 20, and G. Kressel and L. Oliczky, eds., *Sefer Kosow-Galicia ha-mizrahit* (Tel Aviv: Former Residents of Kosow and Vicinity in Israel, 1964), 2. The original print *El mole rachmim,* 1956, watercolor, appears in the Bronislaw Linke catalogue and introduction in Polish and English. Zbigniew Juzma, ed., *Kamienie krzyczą* [The Shrieking Stones], trans. Agnieska Glinczanka (Warsaw: Wydawnictwo Artystyczno-Graficzne RSW, 1959), n.p.

54. I use male pronouns here because women did not typically wear phylacteries in this time period.

55. Maria Dabrowska, introductory essay in Juzma, *Kamienie krzyczą,* n.p.

56. Dabrowska, introductory essay.

57. I have not been able to trace any specific evidence of the movement of this image between Warsaw and Tel Aviv. The image is mentioned in Michael Meng, "Muranow as Ruin: Layered Memories in Postwar Warsaw," in *Jewish Space in Contemporary Poland,* ed. Michael Meng and Erica Lehr (Bloomington: Indiana University Press, 2015), 74.

58. See Barbie Zelizer, "Gender and Atrocity: Women in Holocaust Photographs," and Marianne Hirsch, "Surviving Images: Holocaust Photographs and the Work of Postmemory," both in *Visual Culture and the Holocaust,* ed. Barbie Zelizer (New Brunswick: Rutgers University Press, 2001).

59. An exemplary instance of how Holocaust artifacts and photographs are continuously recontextualized may be found in Robert Jan van Pelt et al., eds., *The Evidence Room* (Toronto: New Jewish Press, 2016). On how museums may themselves become reliquaries, see Oren Steir, "Torah and Taboo: Containing Jewish Relics and Jewish Identity at the United States Holocaust Memorial Museum," *Numen* 57:3–4 (2010): 505–36.

60. For "architecture of memory," see Boyarin and Kugelmass, *From a Ruined Garden,* 12.

61. *Mayne shtetel Berezne* [My Town Berezne], ed. G. Bigil. (Tel Aviv: Berezner Society in Israel, 1954); *Bzehzhin yizker-bukh* [Brzeziny Memorial Book], ed. A. Alperin and N. Summer (New York: Brezeziner Book Committee, 1951); *Sefer zikaron le-keholot Rembertow, Okuniew, Milosna* [Memorial Book in Memory of Rembertov, Okuniev, Milosna], ed. Sh. Kanc (Tel Aviv: Rembertow, Okuniew and Milosna Societies in Israel, 1974); *Belchatow yizker-bukh* [Belchatow Memorial Book] (Buenos Aires: Association of Polish Jews in Argentina, 1951); Alex Sofer, *Krinik in khurban: Memuarn* [Krinik in Ruins] (Montevido: Los Comités de Ayuda a los Residentes de Krinki de Montevideio y Buenos Aires, 1948).

62. Dr. Shtokfish, ed., *Sefer yizker Dokszyce-Parafianow* (Tel Aviv: Association of Former Residents of Dokszyce-Parafianow, 1970).

63. See the influential view of J. B. Harley, "Maps, Knowledge and Power," in *The Iconography of Landscape: Essays on the Symbolic Representation, Design and Use of Past Land-*

scapes, ed. Denis Cosgrove and Stephen Daniels (New York: Cambridge University Press, 1988).

64. Auslander, "Beyond Words," 1035–44.

65. Sh. Kanc, ed., *Sefer zikaron Voislavitse* (Tel Aviv: Former Residents of Voislavize, 1970).

66. David Roskies, "Forging the Link: The Iconography of the Felshtin Yizker Book" (remarks presented to the Felshtin Society, February 7, 1999, New York), http://felshtin.org/forging-the-link-the-iconography-of-the-felshtin-yizker-book/.

67. Dan Miron, "The Literary Image of the Shtetl," *Jewish Social Studies* 1:3 (Spring 1995), 1–43, here 3.

68. A. S. Stein, ed., *Pinkas Krzemienca, sefer zikaron* (Tel Aviv: Former Residents of Krzemieniec in Israel, 1954); Sh. Kanc, *Sefer Rypin* (Tel Aviv: Former Residents of Ripin in Israel and in the Diaspora, 1962).

69. See B. Orenstein, ed., *Khurbn Otvotsk, Falenitz, Kartshev* (Bamberg: Former Residents of Otvotsk, Fanlenitz and Kartshev in the American Zone in Germany, 1948).

70. Denis Wood, *The Power of Maps* (New York: Guilford, 2002), 95.

71. "The beholder approaches the material legacy of the Holocaust in order to read its metonymic configurations and, in so doing, to pose questions about its graspable meaning," Bożena Shallcross, *The Holocaust Object in Polish and Polish-Jewish Culture* (Bloomington: Indiana University Press, 2012), 2.

72. A 2016 exhibit called *State of Exception/Estado de excepción* at the Parsons School of Design in New York included an enormous wall of backpacks and other debris left behind by migrants crossing the border from Mexico into the United States.

73. "The seizure of Jewish property cannot be viewed as the decisive motive for the German killings. Nevertheless, the seizure of all Jewish property was demanded by the internal logic of the same ideology that led to the physical destruction of the Jews." Martin Dean, *Robbing the Jews: The Confiscation of Jewish Property in the Holocaust, 1933–1945* (New York: Cambridge University Press, 2008), 209. For an extensive examination of this phenomenon, see Götz Aly, *Hitler's Beneficiaries: Plunder, Racial War, and the Nazi Welfare State* (New York: Picador, 2008). See also Sarah Gensburger, *Witnessing the Robbing of the Jews: A Photographic Album, Paris, 1940–1945* (Bloomington: Indiana University Press, 2015) for an account of the Mobel Aktion.

74. Dean, *Robbing the Jews,* 283. This excerpt suggests that children were also part of this network of theft and redistribution; indeed, "the widespread auctions of household items reveal the extent to which the general population shared this indifference to the fate of their Jewish neighbors" (248).

75. Dean, *Robbing the Jews,* 384.

76. See van Pelt et al., *The Evidence Room;* and Eyal Weizman, "Introduction: Forensis," in *Forensis: The Architecture of Public Truth* (Berlin: Sternberg, 2014).

77. On poetry composed in the ghettos, see David G. Roskies, "Scribes of the Ghetto" in his *Against the Apocalypse: Responses to Catastrophe in Modern Jewish Culture* (Cambridge, MA: Harvard University Press, 1984), 196–224; and Frieda W. Aaron, *Bearing the Unbearable: Yiddish and Polish Poetry in the Ghettos and Concentration Camps* (Albany: SUNY, 1990).

78. For a discussion of Szlengel's work, see Shallcross, *The Holocaust Object,* 17–35; and Kassow, *Who Will Write Our History?* 316–24. On Sutzkever, see Roskies, "The Burden of

Memory," in *Against the Apocalypse,* 225–57. For a reading of these two poems, see Aaron, *Bearing the Unbearable,* 39–58.

79. See David E. Fishman, *The Book Smugglers: Partisans, Poets, and the Race to Save Jewish Treasures from the Nazis* (Lebanon, NH: University Press of New England/For Edge, 2017).

80. The poem is dated January 7, 1943. *A vogn shikh* [A Cartload of Shoes], in *Lider fun yam hamoves* (Tel Aviv: Bergen Belsen Memorial Press, 1968), 41. This translation, slightly modified, is from Aaron, *Bearing the Unbearable,* 55–56.

81. The violence described in Markish's poem is part of same discursive memorial pattern observed in *Khurban Proskurov* (1924). See also Roy Greenwald, "Pogrom and Avant-Garde: Perets Markish's *Di Kupe,*" *Jewish Social Studies* 16:3 (Spring/Summer 2010): 65–84.

82. Jennifer Bonnell and Roger I. Simon, "'Difficult' Exhibitions and Intimate Encounters," *Museum and Society* 5:2 (July 2007): 65–66, here 65.

83. Robert Jan van Pelt with Luis Ferreiro and Miriam Greenbaum, eds., *Auschwitz: Not Long Ago. Not Far Away.* (New York: Abbeville, 2019), 26, 100, 152.

84. See discussion in Kassow, *Who Will Write Our History?* 316–24; and also note 86 below.

85. Władysław Szlengel, "Things," trans. John Carpenter and Bogdana Carpenter, *Chicago Review* 52:2–4 (Autumn 2006): 283–86.

86. There are various typed manuscripts of Szlengel's poems in Warsaw's Emanuel Ringelblum Jewish Historical Institute archives (ZIH, RH #226/Collection of literary works, 1939–1960); some poems were recovered after the war as part of the *Oyneg Shabes* archives, while others were discovered hidden inside a wooden table. The sheaf of manuscripts I examined includes two versions of *Rzecy* (Things): one using a distinctive layout with stanza breaks and indentations, the other in a single uninterrupted column. Neither draft is dated, and therefore it is unclear which was composed first. Does the pair of drafts record a dissolution of stability, or an attempt to instill order in the face of chaos as the ghetto collapsed? Bożena Shallcross suggests that perhaps the poet appreciated the visual dynamic between the two drafts—the one more expressly "list-like," the other possessing something resembling poetic form. Email communication with the author, April 25, 2017.

87. Judyata Pawlak and Przemysław Kaniecki, eds. *I Bring a Thing, I Bring a Story: Interviews with Donors* [Polish] (Warsaw: Muzeum Historii Zydów Polskich, 2016), 287.

88. According to David Roskies, the poem's date was attributed retrospectively; the first known draft is from 1944. Roskies, *Against the Apocalypse,* 250. According to David Fishman, it was the Germans who seized and melted down the Romm Press lead plates; the poem was based on an operation carried out by Jewish partisans, in which Kiddush cups, Torah pointers, and other ritualistic objects were melted down for gold and silver, which were then used to purchase arms. See Fishman, *The Book Smugglers,* 99–100.

89. Translation by Neal Kozodoy in Irving Howe et al., eds. *Penguin Book of Yiddish Verse* (New York: Penguin Books, 1988), 678–79.

90. See "A Daughter's Afterword," in Mayer Kirshenblatt and Barbara Kirshenblatt-Gimblett, *They Called Me Mayer July: Painted Memories of a Jewish Childhood in Poland Before the Holocaust* (Berkeley: University of California Press, 2007), esp. 376–77.

91. For Stella's work, see *Catalogue of the Exhibition "Frank Stella and Synagogues of Historic Poland,"* accessed July 7, 2021, https://www.polin.pl/en/news/2016/02/16/catalogue-of-the-exhibition-frank-stella-and-synagogues-of.
92. Mark Godfrey, *Abstraction and the Holocaust* (New Haven: Yale University Press, 2007), 102.
93. Godfrey, *Abstraction and the Holocaust,* 104.
94. Godfrey, *Abstraction and the Holocaust,* 102.
95. https://www.jewishgen.org/Yizkor/.

CHAPTER 5. FROM *MAUS* TO *THE RABBI'S CAT*

1. Comics scholarship is lively and contentious and the terminology is continually evolving, especially in relation to the idea of comics as a language, medium, or genre. *Graphic novels* is a widely used term that nonetheless is not universally beloved, especially by comics practitioners (as opposed to scholars). The term *graphic narratives* is perhaps both more capacious and more specific. See Hillary L. Chute and Marianne DeKoven, "Introduction: Graphic Narrative," *MFS: Modern Fiction Studies* 52:4 (Winter 2006): 767–82. I use "graphic novel" to describe this group of long-form, bound-book narratives that were conceived and published as such.
2. Like the artist's book as well as the little magazine, comics were often made and consumed "elsewhere": historically, comics were produced and circulated outside the publishing world's normative institutions, whether in the collaborative workshops of early issues of DC and Marvel, or later counterculture incubators such as *Raw* or *Mad.*
3. Podcast interview with Neil Gaiman, "Comics: Unrepentantly in the Gutter?" December 12, 2014, http://podacademy.org/podcasts/gaiman/. Scott McCloud's expansive definition has helped popularize the appreciation and teaching of graphic novels, but has also irritated both practitioners and scholars: for McCloud, comics are "juxtaposed pictorial and other images in deliberate sequence, intended to convey information and/or produce an aesthetic response in the viewer." Note that McCloud subsumes text within the category of "other images"—that is, text is appreciated first for its iconic features and only secondarily for its narrative content. Also, this definition seems to preclude both older, single-panel examples that might actually contain sequence or narrativity and more contemporary avant-garde comics that eschew the grid entirely. See Scott McCloud, *Understanding Comics* (New York: HarperPerennial, 1993), 9.
4. Thierry Groensteen, "The Impossible Definition," in *A Comics Studies Reader,* ed. Jeet Heer and Kent Worcester (Jackson: University Press of Mississippi, 2009), 126, 128.
5. According to Robert Harvey, "The verbal and the visual blend to achieve a meaning that neither is capable of alone without the other." "How Comics Came to Be," in Heer and Worcester, *A Comics Studies Reader,* 38.
6. According to Thierry Groensteen, "The plasticity of comics, which allows them to put in place messages of every order and narrations other than fictional, demonstrates that before being an art, comics are well and truly a language." "The Impossible Definition," 129.
7. This generalized definition of graphic narratives is also elucidated in Chute and DeKoven, "Introduction: Graphic Narrative."

8. Art Spiegelman, "Eye Ball, Rego Park, nyc. ca. 1960," in *Breakdowns: Portrait of the Artist as a Young %@*!* (New York: Pantheon Books, 2008), n.p.
9. Tubby Tompkins was a character created by Marjorie Henderson Buell in the 1930s as a male companion to her Little Lulu. From the cover image, we can see it's actually a specific issue, "Tubby" #15, drawn by John Stanley, January 1956, https://comicspriceguide.com/titles/marges-tubby/15/rbypm.
10. Harvey, "How Comics Came to Be," 39.
11. Joseph Witek attributes the idea of "reader discipline" to Will Eisner in Witek, "The Arrow and the Grid," Heer and Worcester, *A Comics Studies Reader,* 155.
12. Witek, "The Arrow and the Grid," 149.
13. Nearly an entire issue of the *Comics Journal* (no. 211, April 1999) is devoted to engaging with, and intermittently trashing, Scott McCloud's popular *Understanding Comics.*
14. In place of an analysis that juggles between image and text, Mitchell introduces a third term, meant to indicate their inextricable nature—*imagetext.* Language enters "the pictorial field itself, a field understood as a complex medium that is always already mixed and heterogeneous, situated within institutions, histories, and discourses: the image understood, in short, as an imagetext." From "Beyond Comparison," in Heer and Worcester, *A Comics Studies Reader,* 120.
15. See Ian Hague, *Comics and the Senses: A Multisensory Approach to Comics and Graphic Novels* (New York: Routledge, 2014).
16. For useful taxonomies describing the various relations between text and image, see McCloud, *Understanding Comics,* 153–55; and Benoit Peeters, "Four Conceptions of the Page," in Heer and Worcester, *A Comics Studies Reader.*
17. Charles Hatfield, "An Art of Tensions: The Otherness of Comics Reading," in *Alternative Comics* (Jackson: University Press of Mississippi, 2005), 37.
18. Art Spiegelman, *Metamaus* (New York: Pantheon Books, 2011), 165.
19. This is especially true of graphic novels that engage some kind of Jewish thematic, but the claims hold for the graphic novel as a genre more broadly.
20. See Pascale Lefevre, "The Construction of Space in Comics," in Heer and Worcester, *A Comics Studies Reader,* 157–62. I am less interested in this particular method, but appreciate Lefevre's broader project concerning the materiality (he uses the term *sensuality*) of comics.
21. Quoted in Hillary L. Chute, "History and Graphic Representation in *Maus,*" in Heer and Worcester, *A Comics Studies Reader,* 342.
22. See especially Hillary Chute, *Disaster Drawn: Visual Witness, Comics and Documentary Form* (Cambridge, MA: Harvard University Press, 2016).
23. Art Spiegelman, *Maus I: A Survivor's Tale: My Father Bleeds History* (New York: Pantheon, 1986), 12.
24. The idea of tabular versus linear as modes for reading the comics page originates with Pierre Fresnault-Deruelle, "Du linéare au tabulaire," *Communications* 24 (Paris: Éditions du Seuil, 1976), 17–23.
25. For Hatfield, a single panel may be both "a 'moment' in an imagined sequence of events, and . . . a graphic element in an atemporal design" (Hatfield, "An Art of Tensions," 48).
26. Hatfield, "An Art of Tensions," 58.

27. Spiegelman, *Breakdowns,* n.p., this strip from 1977. This publication contains the beginnings of *Maus* (dated 1972).
28. Spiegelman, *Maus,* 74.
29. See Kevin Haworth, "Actus Tragicus and the Making of an Israeli Comics Scene," in his *The Comics of Rutu Modan: War, Love and Secrets* (Jackson: University Press of Mississippi, 2019), 32–56.
30. "Rutu Modan Interview with Joe Sacco," in Modan, *Exit Wounds* (Montreal: Drawn & Quarterly, 2007), 178.
31. In his discussion of Modan's book in relation to other graphic novels about the Shoah published at around the same time, Kevin Haworth remarks: "Kubert and Kichka are older than Modan, and her approach in *The Property* may reflect a generational and even a geographic difference in how one speaks of the Holocaust" (Haworth, *The Comics of Rutu Modan,* 141). See also Victoria Aarons, *Holocaust Graphic Narratives: Generation, Trauma & Memory* (New Brunswick: Rutgers University Press, 2020).
32. Rutu Modan, *The Property* (New York: Drawn & Quarterly, 2013), 34.
33. Ariel Kahn, "Saving Fictions: An Appreciation of Rutu Modan," in *Drawn and Quarterly: Twenty-Five Years of Contemporary Cartooning, Comics, and Graphic Novels,* ed. Tom Devlin et al. (Montreal: Drawn & Quarterly, 2015), 362.
34. This common observation about Modan's style (an influence she herself refers to in early interviews) is productively explored in Haworth, *The Comics of Rutu Modan,* 85–90; and Michael A. Johnson, "How Clear Is the Clear Line in Rutu Modan's *The Property?*" *The Hooded Utilitarian,* July 24, 2014, https://www.hoodedutilitarian.com/2014/07/how-clear-is-the-clear-line-in-rutu-modans-the-property/.
35. Modan, *The Property,* 88–89.
36. "Rutu Modan Interview with Joe Sacco," 183.
37. "The Rutu Modan Interview," *Comics Journal,* May 29, 2013, http://www.tcj.com/rutu-modan/2/.
38. Kahn, "Saving Fictions," 362.
39. Modan, *The Property,* 203.
40. Joannn Sfar, *The Rabbi's Cat* (New York: Pantheon Books, 2005).
41. Leah Hochman, "The Ineffability of Form: Speaking and Seeing the Sacred in *Tina's Mouth* and *The Rabbi's Cat,*" in *Comics and Sacred Texts: Reimagining Religion & Graphic Narratives,* ed. Assaf Gamzou and Ken Koltun-Fromm (Jackson: University Press of Mississippi, 2018), 48–49.
42. Marla Harris, "Borderlands: Places, Spaces and Jewish Identity in Joann Sfar's *The Rabbi's Cat* and *Klezmer,*" in *The Jewish Graphic Novel: Critical Approaches,* ed. Samantha Baskind and Ranen Omer-Sherman (New Brunswick: Rutgers University Press, 2008), 181–97.
43. See Jill Lepore, *The Secret History of Wonder Woman* (New York: Knopf, 2014).
44. Tahneer Oksman, "'Not a Word for Little Girls': Knowledge, Word, and Image in Leela Corman's *Unterzakhn,*" in *Visualizing Jewish Narrative: Jewish Comics and Graphic Novels,* ed. Derek Royal (New York: Bloomsbury Academic, 2016), 29–40, here 33.
45. See Oksman's virtuoso exploration of these arguments in her *"How Come Boys Get to Keep Their Noses?" Women and Jewish American Identity in Contemporary Graphic Memoirs* (New York: Columbia University Press, 2016).

46. See Laurence Roth, "Contemporary American Jewish Comic Books," in Baskind and Omer-Sherman, *The Jewish Graphic Novel,* 3–21.
47. Spiegelman, *Metamaus,* 73. Among the voluminous research on how memory shapes our understanding of the Shoah, see especially Marianne Hirsch, "The Generation of Postmemory," in *The Generation of Postmemory: Writing and Visual Culture After the Holocaust* (New York: Columbia University Press, 2012), 29–54.
48. Victoria Aarons, "Found Objects: The Legacy of Third-Generation Holocaust Memory," in *Translated Memories,* ed. Bettina Hoffman and Ursula Reuter (New York: Lexington Books, 2020), 233.
49. Neither Spiegelman nor Sfar have shied away from the question of free expression and censorship: Spiegelman produced a series of broadsides in the wake of 9/11, and Sfar is associated with the French satirical journal *Charlie Hebdo.*
50. Gaiman, "Comics: Unrepentantly in the Gutter?" We can note the general principle of differing cultural attitudes toward the visual without essentializing, or reducing the work to any single position. On Gaiman's Jewishness, see Cyril Camus, "The 'Outsider': Neil Gamin and the Old Testament," *Shofar: An Interdisciplinary Journal of Jewish Studies* 29:2 (Winter 2011): 77–99.
51. The cover of R. Crumb's *The Book of Genesis Illustrated* contains this warning: "The first book of the bible graphically depicted! Nothing left out!" appears in capital letters on a scroll beneath a full-color image of a robed, voluminously bearded godlike figure pointing past a tearfully fleeing Adam and Eve, whose bodies are barely covered in leaflike cloths. Just below the title, the phrase "Adult supervision recommended for minors" is contained in an oval shape resembling a sticker placed on the cover to warn parents. Crumb's Genesis is a mash-up of two translations, the King James and Robert Alter's contemporary version, and the illustrations themselves—elaborately rendered in the artist's unique hand—are relatively tame, even with some partial nudity, especially compared with both Crumb's other work and *Old Testament Tales.* R. Crumb, *The Book of Genesis Illustrated* (New York: Norton, 2009), n.p.
52. Gamzou and Koltun-Fromm, introduction to *Comics and Sacred Texts,* xii–xiii.
53. See Ori Soltes, "Images and the Book of Esther: From Manuscript Illumination to Midrash," in *The Book of Esther in Modern Research,* ed. Leonard Greenspoon and Sidnie White Crawford (New York: T&T Clark International, 2003), 137–75.
54. See Jan Baetens and Hugo Frey, *The Graphic Novel: An Introduction* (New York: Cambridge University Press, 2015).
55. Susan Vick with Marc Michael Epstein, "Illuminating the Present: Contemporary Jewish Illumination," in *Skies of Parchment, Seas of Ink: Jewish Illuminated Manuscripts,* ed. Marc Michael Epstein (Princeton: Princeton University Press, 2015), 241. While now highly prized by contemporary archives and collectors, illuminated manuscripts were not originally considered sacred, and were in fact often commissioned for personal and home use.
56. These scrolls also reference the "banderole," a device from medieval manuscripts that indicates speech as text emerging from the hand in the form of a scroll. They are also called phylactery, which happens to be the term used to describe the traditional leather bindings (*tefillin*) that observant Jews wear during prayer. The terms are from the Latin and Greek, respectively, for "amulet." Readers may be amused by this idea of

the *tefillin* as a kind of speech bubble, a scroll of text emerging from the head, a spoken prayer.

57. For a discussion of singularity, commodification and the sacred, see Igor Kopytoff, "The Cultural Biography of Things: Commoditization as Process," in *The Social Life of Things: Commodities in Cultural Perspective,* ed. Arjun Appadurai (New York: Cambridge University Press, 1986), 66–68.

CHAPTER 6. ON THE SEAM

1. Robert Darnton, "What Is the History of Books?" (1990), in *The Broadview Reader in Book History,* ed. Michelle Levy and Tom Mole (Peterborough, Ontario: Broadview, 2015), 231–50.
2. Roger Chartier, "Communities of Readers" (1994), in Levy and Mole, *Broadview Reader,* 251–66, here 256. Chartier borrows here from Stanley Fish's notion of "interpretative communities," which locates the work of critical inquiry within a broad dynamic frame.
3. Edmond Jabès, "At the Threshold of the Book," in *From the Book to the Book: An Edmond Jabès Reader,* trans. Rosmarie Waldrop (Hanover, NH: University Press of New England, 1991), 32.
4. Rosmarie Waldrop, "When Silence Speaks," in Jabès, *From the Book to the Book,* xxvi.
5. Jabès, "At the Threshold of the Book," 34.
6. Jacques Derrida, "Edmond Jabès and the Question of the Book," in *Writing and Difference,* ed. and trans. Alan Bass (Chicago: University of Chicago Press, 1978 [1967]), 65.
7. From *The Book of Resemblances* (1976) in Jabès, *From the Book to the Book,* 156.
8. From *The Book of Questions* in Jabès, *From the Book to the Book,* 46.
9. Quoted in Waldrop, "When Silence Speaks," xxv.
10. Jabès, "At the Threshold of the Book," 58.
11. "Letter from Sarah to Yukel," in Jabès, *From the Book to the Book,* 209.
12. I am indebted here, and throughout this chapter, to Johanna Drucker's field-defining scholarship and bookmaking practice. For Drucker, "The book as a form is already a received idea, loaded with cultural and historical values and resonances. But it is a form which permits invention and innovation." Johanna Drucker, *A Century of Artists Books* (New York: Granary Books, 2004), 108–9.
13. For example, *Invisible Cities* (1991) and *The Silent Question* (2005). An extensive portfolio of Beube's work is viewable on the artist's website: https://dougbeube.com/home.html (accessed July 9, 2021).
14. See the artist's commentary at https://dougbeube.com/section/485957-Fallen-Borders.html (accessed July 9, 2021).
15. Richard Kostelanetz, "Book Art," in *Artists' Books: A Critical Anthology and Sourcebook,* ed. Joan Lyons (New York: Visual Studies Workshop, 1985), 29.
16. Drucker, *A Century of Artists Books,* 11, 14. The structure of Drucker's influential study honors her own devotion to the broadness of the term, creating a series of chapters that demonstrate the inner diversity of the genre; the categories sometimes contradict one another, though they do not cancel each other out. See also Ellen H. Johnson, *Modern Art and the Object: A Century of Changing Attitudes,* rev. ed. (New York: HarperCollins, 1995).

17. Ulises Carrión, "The New Art of Making Books," in Lyons, *Artists' Books,* 42.
18. Drucker, *A Century of Artists Books,* 93.
19. See Marian Cohn, ed., *Doug Beube: Breaking the Codex: Bodywork, Collage and Mixed-Media* (Brooklyn: Etc., Etc., the Iconoclastic Museum Press, 2011).
20. Ann Brener, ed., *Hebrew and Yiddish Artist's Books at the Library of Congress: An Illustrated Finding Aid from the Collections* (Washington, DC: Library of Congress, 2015).
21. Other books by Avadenka with Jewish themes include *Grandpa Isadore* (1997, fifty copies), an etching with a piece of short fiction by Amos Oz, in Hebrew and English, that approaches a *yizker* book in its feel for memory; and *I Am Sitting Here Now* (1994, twenty-five copies), a short poem by Yehuda Amichai, with etchings.
22. Avadenka, *By a Thread* (Huntington Woods, MI: Land Marks, 2006).
23. See also Nick Sousanis interview with the artist, "'Language Will Save Us': Lynne Avadenka's *By a Thread* and the Power of Words," 2009, http://www.vampandtramp.com/finepress/l/landmarkspress-interview.html.
24. Johanna Drucker, "Intimate Authority: Women, Books, and the Public-Private Paradox," in *The Book as Art: Artists' Books from the National Museum of Women in the Arts,* ed. Krystyana Wasserman (New York: Princeton Architectural Press, 2011), 16.
25. Drucker, "Intimate Authority," 16.
26. Judith A. Hoffberg, *Women of the Book: Jewish Artists, Jewish Themes* (Florida Atlantic University Press, 2001), 4–5.
27. Tatana Kellner, *B11226: Fifty Years of Silence, Eugene Kellner's Story* (Rosendale, NY: Women's Studio Workshop, 1992), n.p. The mother's story is told in a companion volume, *71125: Fifty Years of Silence* (Rosendale, NY: Women's Studio Workshop, 1992). For background on the production and a reading of Kellner's book in relation to Holocaust art, see Marianne Hirsch and Susan Rubin Suleiman, "Material Memory: Holocaust Testimony in Post-Holocaust Art," in *Shaping Losses: Cultural Memory and the Holocaust,* ed. Julia Epstein and Lori Hope Lefkowitz (Chicago: University of Illinois Press, 2001), 87–104.
28. From the first full page of text in Kellner, *B11226: Fifty Years of Silence.* See also the commentary by Kellner in Hoffberg, *Women of the Book,* 45.
29. Drucker, *A Century of Artists Books,* 111.
30. Artists—Vaclav Bostik (1913–2005) and Jiri John (1923–72).
31. N. Katherine Hayles, *Writing Machines* (Cambridge, MA: Mediawork/MIT Press, 2002), 75, 33.
32. Musrara was built under Ottoman rule in the late nineteenth century and became one of the first areas of modern settlement outside the walls of Jerusalem's Old City. Its Christian and Muslim Arab residents were displaced—they either fled or were forcibly evicted—in 1948. After the war, Israel confiscated these structures and the neighborhood became home to newly arrived North African immigrants; this population suffered decades of physical danger, living on the armistice line—next to the "no-man's-land" of the Jordanian border—as well as institutional and socioeconomic discrimination. In the early 1970s, following the war and Jerusalem's "reunification," the neighborhood became well known as the birthplace of the Israeli Black Panthers, a group that modeled itself on the American organization of the same name. They agitated on behalf of better living conditions for the neighborhood's population and civil rights for Mizra-

him across Israeli society. Some brief details about the house's provenance may be found in David Kroyanker, *The Street of Prophets, the Ethiopian and Musrara Quarters: The Story of a Place—A Portrait of a City, 1850–2000* [Hebrew] (Jerusalem: Yad Yitzhak Ben Tsvi/Keter, 2000), 60–61. About the neighborhood see also Adina Hoffman, *House of Windows: Portraits from a Jerusalem Neighborhood* (New York: Broadway Books, 2002).

33. Thomas Abowd, "The Politics and Poetics of Place: The Baramki House," *Jerusalem Quarterly* 21 (August 2004), http://www.palestine-family.net/index.php?nav=6–24&cid=11&did=3985.

34. See Rochelle Davis, "Ottoman Jerusalem: The Growth of the City outside the Walls," in *Jerusalem 1948: The Arab Neighborhoods and Their Fate in the War,* ed. Salim Tamari (Jerusalem: Institute of Jerusalem Studies, Bethlehem and Badil, 1999), 10–29.

35. Arik Kilemnik, curator, *The Print and Poem: An Artists Book Exhibition,* catalogue 26 (Jerusalem: Jerusalem Print Workshop, Summer 2000).

36. Irena Gordon, "The Artist's Book: Between Tradition and Revolution," in *Artists Books: Jerusalem Print Workshop,* catalogue 44 (Jerusalem: Jerusalem Print Workshop, 2011), 9.

37. Gideon Ofrat, "The Work of Art in the Age of Aura-Endowed Reproduction," in *Artists Books: Jerusalem Print Workshop,* 12.

38. Edna Moshenson, curator, *Moshe Gershuni: Thirteen Etchings for Poems by H. N. Bialik* (Jerusalem: Tel Aviv Museum of Art, Dvir Publishing House, Jerusalem Print Workshop, 1987), n.p.

39. See Alec Mishory, *Joseph Budko and H. N. Bialik's Complete Works, Edition of 1923: Modern Hebrew Poetry and Art in Harmony* [Hebrew] (Tel Aviv: Am Oved, 2006).

40. Moshenson, *Moshe Gershuni.* This miniature facsimile edition of Gershuni's book adds to the cascading chain of reproductions, further underlining the centrality of the Bialik-Budko edition as a landmark in Jewish visual print culture.

41. For Gershuni, the number 8 is a cyclical symbol related to circumcision, a covenantal ritual performed on the eighth day of a Jewish male infant's life. See "Udo Kittleman on Moshe Gershuni: Excerpts from a Conversation with Ory Dessau," in *Moshe Gershuni: No Father, No Mother* (Berlin: Nationalgalerie, Staatliche Museen zu Berlin, 2014), n.p. Yigal Zalmona also refers to the coded quality of Gershuni's work, a "secret cipher" that spoke to an intimate, even elite, coterie of friends and fellow artists. Zalmona, *A Century of Israeli Art* (Farnham, UK: Lund Humphries, 2013), 327.

42. For Hebrew and Yiddish versions of the poem and recorded versions of it set to music, see *Zemereshet: Early Hebrew Song,* accessed July 8, 2021, https://www.zemereshet.co.il/song.asp?id=2404.

43. Doreet LeVitte Harten, in describing the historical context of "why Jewish themes should be considered taboo within Israeli art," concludes: "Artists were defined as Jewish artists or modern artists, but they could not be both." "Through a Glass Darkly," in *No Father, No Mother,* n.p.

44. See Mario-Rosario Jackson, Joaquín Herranz Jr., and Florence Kabawasa-Green, *Art and Culture in Communities: A Framework for Measurement,* (Washington, DC: Urban Institute, 2003), http://www.urban.org/sites/default/files/publication/59196/311008-Art-and-Culture-in-Communities-A-Framework-for-Measurement.PDF.

45. See two podcasts with Andi Arnovitz: OCCSP (Orange County Community Scholars Program)—Podcast Network, "Tear/Repair" and "People of the Book/Artist's Books,"

March 11, 2019, https://podcast.occsp.org/wp/2019/03/12/csp-arnovitz-tearrepair/ and https://podcast.occsp.org/wp/2019/03/12/csp-arnovitz-people-of-the-bookartists-books/; and David Sperber, "Garments of Reconciliation: The Relationship between Judaism and Islam in the Artworks of Andi Arnovitz," *Women in Judaism: A Multidisciplinary Journal* 13:1 (2016).

46. Sperber, "Garments of Reconciliation," 6.
47. Email communication with the artist, November 1, 2020.
48. Arnovitz, "Tear/Repair."
49. Email communication with the artist, November 1, 2020.
50. Shahar Bram, "Wandering around the Library: On the Joint Book of the Poet Harold Schimmel and Photographer Avigail Schimmel," *Hebrew Studies* 55 (2014); 305–27, here 312, 324.
51. Harold Schimmel, *The Library* (Ra'anana: Even Hoshen, 1999), 14.
52. Schimmel, *The Library,* 1.
53. Schimmel, interview with Charles Bernstein and Ariel Resnikoff, 2017, https://jacket2.org/commentary/harold-schimmel-close-listening.
54. Schimmel, *The Library,* 4, 9, 15.
55. Schimmel, *The Library,* 9.
56. Schimmel, *The Library,* 17.
57. "Unpacking My Library," 59.
58. See Drucker, *A Century of Artists Books*; Marcia Reed, "The Book in General: Some New Directions," in *Artists and Their Books, Books and Their Artists,* ed. Marcia Reed and Glenn Phillips (Los Angeles: Getty Research Institute, 2018), 1–14.
59. Leah Price, *How to Do Things with Books in Victorian Britain* (Princeton: Princeton University Press, 2013).

Credits

Charles Reznikoff, "Jerusalem the Golden," "A Fifth Group of Verse" and "Early History of a Writer" from *The Poems of Charles Reznikoff: 1918–1975*, edited by Seamus Cooney. Copyright © 2005 by The Estate of Charles Reznikoff. Reprinted with the permission of The Permissions Company, LLC on behalf of Black Sparrow / David R Godine, Publisher, Inc., www.godine.com.

"A Retrospect" by Ezra Pound, from LITERARY ESSAYS OF EZRA POUND, copyright © 1973 by the Estate of Ezra Pound. Reprinted by permission of New Directions Publishing Corp.

Copyright © 2006 Johns Hopkins University Press. "Visions of Jewish Modernism" first appeared in *Modernism/modernity*, Volume 13, Issue 4, November 2006, pages 673–699. Published with permission by Johns Hopkins University Press.

"Picturing the Poetry of Anna Margolin" was originally published in *Modern Language Quarterly*, Vol. 63:4, pp. 501–536. © 2002, University of Washington. All rights reserved. Republished by permission of the copyright holder, and the present publisher, Duke University Press. www.dukeupress.edu.

"Framing the Native: Esther Raab's Visual Poetics" was originally published in *Israel Studies* (Winter 1999): 234–257. Reprinted by permission of Indiana University Press.

"Language and Style" by David Fogel was originally published in *Prooftexts* 13:1 (January 1993): 15–20. Reprinted by permission of Indiana University Press.

Poetry by Avraham Shlonsky reprinted with permission. Copyright by Hakibbutz Hameuchad-Sifriat Poalim Publishing House and Avraham Shlonsky's heirs.

Poetry by Esther Raab courtesy of Ehud Ben-Ezer.

Excerpts from Dovid Bergelson, *The End of Everything,* courtesy of the Yiddish Book Center, Northampton, MA.

Excerpt from CALL IT SLEEP by Henry Roth. Copyright © 1934, renewed © 1962 by Henry Roth. Introduction copyright © 1991 by Alfred Kazin. Afterword copyright © 1990 by Johns Hopkins University Press. Reprinted by permission of Farrar, Straus & Giroux, LLC. All Rights Reserved.

Excerpts from the English translation of Władysław Szlengel, "Things" courtesy of The Chicago Review.

Excerpts from Yiddish poems by Abraham Sutzkever, "A Cartload of Shoes" and "The Lead Plates of the Romm Press," courtesy of Rina Sutzkever.

"A Cartload of Shoes" by Abraham Sutzkever. Translation from Frieda W. Aaron, *Bearing the Unbearable: Yiddish and Polish Poetry in the Ghettos and Concentration Camps,* courtesy of SUNY Press.

"The Lead Plates at the Rom Press" by Abraham Sutzkever, translated by Neal Kozodoy; from THE PENGUIN BOOK OF MODERN YIDDISH VERSE edited by Irving Howe, Ruth R. Wisse, and Khone Shmeruk, copyright © 1987 by Irving Howe, Ruth Wisse, and Chone Shmeruk. Used by permission of Viking Books, an imprint of Penguin Publishing Group, a division of Penguin Random House LLC. All rights reserved.

Two panels from MAUS by Art Spiegelman. Copyright © 1973, 1980, 1981, 1982, 1983, 1984, 1985, 1986 by Art Spiegelman, used by permission of The Wylie Agency L.L.C. Graphic Novel Excerpt from THE COMPLETE MAUS: A SURVIVOR'S TALE by Art Spiegelman, Maus, Volume I copyright © 1973, 1980, 1981, 1982, 1983, 1984, 1985, 1986 by Art Spiegelman; Maus, Volume II copyright © 1986, 1989, 1990, 1991 by Art Spiegelman. Used by permission of Pantheon Books, an imprint of the Knopf Doubleday Publishing Group, a division of Penguin Random House LLC. All rights reserved.

Panel from BREAKDOWNS by Art Spiegelman. Copyright © 1972, 1973, 1974, 1975, 1976, 1977, 2005, 2006, 2007, 2008 by Art Spiegelman, used by permission of The Wylie Agency L.L.C. Graphic Novel Excerpt from

BREAKDOWNS: PORTRAIT OF THE ARTIST AS A YOUNG %@&*! by Art Spiegelman, copyright © 1972, 1973, 1974, 1975, 1976, 1977, 2005, 2006, 2007 and 2008 by Art Spiegelman. Used by permission of Pantheon Books, an imprint of the Knopf Doubleday Publishing Group, a division of Penguin Random House LLC. All rights reserved.

Graphic Novel Excerpt from UNTERZAKHN by Leela Corman, copyright © 2012 by Leela Corman. Used by permission of Schocken Books, an imprint of the Knopf Doubleday Publishing Group, a division of Penguin Random House LLC. All rights reserved.

Graphic Novel Excerpt from THE RABBI'S CAT by Joann Sfar, translation copyright © 2005 by Penguin Random House LLC. Used by permission of Pantheon Books, an imprint of the Knopf Doubleday Publishing Group, a division of Penguin Random House LLC. All rights reserved.

Permission for *Le Chat du Rabbin 1—La Bar-Mitsva* and *Le Chat du Rabbin 2—Le Malka des Lions* © DARGAUD 2002, by Sfar, www.daurgaud.com. All Rights Reserved.

Poetry and images from *The Library* courtesy of Harold Schimmel.

Index

Page numbers in italics indicate figures.